From Labouring to Learning

Palgrave Studies in Gender and Education

Series Editor:

Yvette Taylor, London South Bank University, UK

Titles include:

Anne Harris and Emily Gray (*editors*)
QUEER TEACHERS, IDENTITY AND PERFORMATIVITY

Emily F. Henderson
GENDER PEDAGOGY

Paula Burkinshaw
HIGHER EDUCATION, LEADERSHIP AND WOMEN VICE CHANCELLORS

**Palgrave Studies in Gender and Education
Series Standing Order ISBN 978–1–137–45634–2 Hardback
978–1–137–45635–9 Paperback**
(*outside North America only*)

You can receive future titles in this series as they are published by placing a standing order. Please contact your bookseller or, in case of difficulty, write to us at the address below with your name and address, the title of the series and the ISBN quoted above.

Customer Services Department, Macmillan Distribution Ltd, Houndmills, Basingstoke, Hampshire RG21 6XS, England

From Labouring to Learning

Working-Class Masculinities, Education and De-Industrialization

Michael R.M. Ward
The Open University, UK

© Michael R.M. Ward 2015

All rights reserved. No reproduction, copy or transmission of this publication may be made without written permission.

No portion of this publication may be reproduced, copied or transmitted save with written permission or in accordance with the provisions of the Copyright, Designs and Patents Act 1988, or under the terms of any licence permitting limited copying issued by the Copyright Licensing Agency, Saffron House, 6–10 Kirby Street, London EC1N 8TS.

Any person who does any unauthorized act in relation to this publication may be liable to criminal prosecution and civil claims for damages.

The author has asserted his right to be identified as the author of this work in accordance with the Copyright, Designs and Patents Act 1988.

First published 2015 by
PALGRAVE MACMILLAN

Palgrave Macmillan in the UK is an imprint of Macmillan Publishers Limited, registered in England, company number 785998, of Houndmills, Basingstoke, Hampshire RG21 6XS.

Palgrave Macmillan in the US is a division of St Martin's Press LLC, 175 Fifth Avenue, New York, NY 10010.

Palgrave Macmillan is the global academic imprint of the above companies and has companies and representatives throughout the world.

Palgrave® and Macmillan® are registered trademarks in the United States, the United Kingdom, Europe and other countries.

ISBN 978–1–137–44174–4

This book is printed on paper suitable for recycling and made from fully managed and sustained forest sources. Logging, pulping and manufacturing processes are expected to conform to the environmental regulations of the country of origin.

A catalogue record for this book is available from the British Library.

Library of Congress Cataloging-in-Publication Data
Ward, Michael R.M.
   From labouring to learning : working-class masculinities, education and de-industrialization / Michael R.M. Ward.
     pages   cm. — (Palgrave studies in gender and education)
   Summary: "From Labouring to Learning: Working-Class Masculinities, Education and De-Industrialization explores how economic changes and the growing importance of educational qualifications in a shrinking labour market, particularly effects marginalized young men. It follows a group of young working-class men in a de-industrial community and challenges commonly held representations that often appear in the media and in policy discourses which portray them as feckless, out of control, educational failures and lacking aspiration. Ward argues that for a group of young men in a community of social and economic deprivation, expectations and transitions to adulthood are framed through the industrial legacy of geographically and historically shaped class and gender codes. These codes have an impact on what it means to be a man and what behaviour is deemed acceptable and what is not." — Provided by publisher.
   ISBN 978–1–137–44174–4 (hardback)
   1. Working class—Education—Wales, South.   2. Young men—Education—Wales, South.   3. Education—Social aspects—Wales, South.   4. Wales, South—Economic conditions.   I. Title.   II. Title: From laboring to learning.
   LC5056.G7W37 2015
   370.9429—dc23
                                           2015019742

To my Grandfathers who dug the coal and my Grandmothers who kept everything else going

Contents

List of Tables viii

Series Preface ix

Acknowledgements x

Prologue xii

1. Introduction 1
2. The Valleys: History, Modernity and Masculinities 21
3. The Valley Boiz: Re-Traditionalizing Masculinity 39
4. The Geeks: Studious Working-Class Masculinities 72
5. The Emos: Alternative Masculinities? 95
6. Working-Class Masculinities in Vocational Education and Training Courses 106
7. Jimmy the Chameleon: Multiple Performances of Self 129
8. Conclusion: Growing Up into Uncertain Futures 149

Epilogue 159

Appendix 1: 'Doing' Ethnography: Understanding, Researching and Representing Young Working-Class Masculinities 161

Appendix 2 175

Notes 178

References 182

Index 200

Tables

3.1	The Valley Boiz: Educational and future trajectories, family backgrounds and sporting interests	42
4.1	The Geeks: Educational and future trajectories, family backgrounds and sporting interests	76
A.1	Research phases	163
A.2	Young men enrolled at Cwm Dyffryn High School sixth form, year 13	175

Series Preface

This series aims to provide a comprehensive space for an increasingly diverse and complex area of interdisciplinary social science research: gender and education. As the field of women and gender studies is rapidly developing and becoming 'internationalised' – as with traditional social science disciplines of e.g. sociology, educational studies, social geography etc. – there is greater need for this dynamic, global series that plots emerging definitions and debates, and monitors critical complexities of gender and education. This series has an explicitly feminist approach and orientation, attending to key theoretical and methodological debates, and ensuring a continued conversation and relevance within the inter-disciplinary and long-standing 'gender and education' field.

The series is better able to combine renewed and revitalized feminist research methods and theories with emergent and salient public and policy issues. These include pre-compulsory and post-compulsory education, 'early years' and 'life long' education; educational (dis)engagements of pupils, students and staff; trajectories and intersectional inequalities including race, class, sexuality, age and disability; policy and practice across educational landscapes; diversity and difference, including institutional (schools, colleges, universities), locational and embodied (in 'teacher'-'learner' positions); varied global activism in and beyond the classroom and the 'public university'; educational technologies and transitions and the (ir)relevance of (in)formal educational settings; and emergent educational mainstreams and margins. In operating a critical approach to 'gender and education', the series recognizes the importance of probing beyond the boundaries of specific territorial-legislative domains in order to develop a more international, intersectional focus. In addressing varied conceptual and methodological questions, the series combines an intersectional focus on competing – and sometimes colliding – strands of educational provisioning, equality and 'diversity', as well as providing insightful reflections of the continuing critical shift of gender and feminism within (and beyond) the academy.

Yvette Taylor
London South Bank University, UK

Acknowledgements

The journey to this final book which is now in front of you has been a long and hard one, with the initial seeds sown at the University of the West of England at the beginning of the millennium. I would first and foremost like to thank Debbie Epstein and Emma Renold who have offered guidance, support and vital criticism through the long PhD process at Cardiff and upon which this book is based. I will be forever in your debt for the patience you showed me and the encouragement you gave me to keep going and to keep writing. I would never have been able to have completed this study without them. My thanks must also go to Andrew Parker, who examined my PhD and has been a source of support and encouragement ever since. I would also never have been able to have conducted this study without funding from the ESRC, and the study leave I was given by my employer, The Open University, to finish off the final edits, so I thank them also. I express my gratitude to Palgrave Macmillan for accepting to publish this book and to Andrew James and Eleanor Christie for sticking with me through the many emails we exchanged around this project.

Inside academia, I'd also like to acknowledge some friends and colleagues I've met along this journey who have supported me in various ways, both intellectually and emotionally. First, my fellow PhD students who I studied with at Cardiff for over four years, Alice Clayton, Anne Crowley, Cheryl Alsop, David Frayne, Dan Gordon, Joanne Coates, Michael Donnelly, Michael Thomas, Naomi Holford and Nick Lord. Without their companionship in the office, at conferences and drinking sessions late into the night, I might never have made it to this point. Second, colleagues who I have met and who have kept me thinking and writing about masculinities and Goffman, teaching me about how academia operates and keeping me in work over the past few years. Especially, I thank Anna Tarrant, Brigid Featherstone, Gareth Terry, Garth Stahl, Laura Bentley, Martin Robb, Nicola Ingram, Peter Somerville, Richard Waller, Sandy Ruxton, Sam Hillyard and Thomas Thurnell-Read. David Morgan also deserves a mention as when we discussed title ideas for the book at an event in Milton Keynes, he gave me the inspiration for the final version.

There are also many I want to thank outside academia. While my parents Colin and Gaynor and step-parents Islwyn and Lynne did not always know exactly what I was doing and seemed to wonder why I was spending so much time hanging out with groups of young men, they have always been there for me and I love them deeply – thank you for everything. I likewise give my thanks to my proofreader who ironed out many of my errors and Celia Johnston-Morgan for checking over my references. I would also like to thank some others who have had to put up with me whilst I wrote this book and over the years of work behind it; my brother Andrew, friends Dave and Molly who I moaned at about work on holidays to see them in Canada, and Mike, Cat and members of 'team strobl', who kept me sane by letting me blow off steam, the next drink is on me.

This book which you are about to read would also never have been possible without Mr Simpson, the head teacher of Cwm Dyffryn High School. If he hadn't agreed for me to come into his school and to let me roam free in the first place, the stories that follow would never have been told. From the bottom of my heart, I also thank the young men from Cwm Dyffryn who let me into their lives. You will never really know what you have done for me by letting me hang around or 'bother' with you in school and on the many nights out when you invited me. Finally, I have one more person to thank who was there for me at my darkest, most frustrated moments and whose music helped me when nothing else would, cheers to 'the boss', Bruce Springsteen.... 'I come from down in the Valley, where mister when you're young, they bring you up to do, like your daddy done'.

Prologue

It can be a truly beautiful drive through the eight miles of bending winding roads to the town of Cwm Dyffryn. Depending on the season, the mountainsides on either side of the U-shaped valley can change through a range of vibrant colours, transforming through different shades of green, to reddish brown to greys as the year goes on. Although rare, severe winter snowfalls can turn the area into something resembling a Swiss alpine resort and access to many of the communities can become difficult. Settlements in the area can be traced back to the Bronze Age through burial grounds and circular cairns. There are also Roman fort remains hidden behind trees on the mountainsides around some of the villages and towns en route. As one travels north to Cwm Dyffryn across the large valley floor, and its gentle sloping sides, other towns and villages that grew around the industrial developments of the region in the 19th century are strung out along the route. The seemingly endless rows and rows of closely packed terraced houses, which were built at precarious angles and once held coalminers and their families, make it difficult to determine where one village ends and another begins. At the centre of the valley floor, a river and a railway line meander their way south to Cardiff – the capital city of Wales – and the coast around 30 or so miles away.

On the outskirts are the town's secondary schools, a couple of supermarkets, a global fast food franchise, petrol stations, a hospital, industrial estates and a large leisure centre with a rugby union pitch, a skate park and other playing fields. Residential areas overlap and post-war social housing estates are interspersed with modern housing developments which surround Cwm Dyffryn on all sides. The older residential streets, with their closely interlinked terraced houses, corner shops, chapels and primary schools, lead into the town centre itself, which is stretched out over a few main pedestrian streets that have seen more prosperous times. Amongst the boarded up properties, there are a collection of banks, building societies, discount department stores, hairdressing salons, nail bars, some small clothes outlets and an abundance of charity shops, betting shops and pawnbrokers. Adjacent to one of the main streets, there is also an older indoor market, with a collection of stalls selling a wide range of traditional goods. Cafes, fast food outlets, half a dozen pubs, a few working men's clubs, a bingo hall and the solitary nightclub make up the remainder of the civic centre. A car park, numerous offices and public buildings – magistrate courts, county council services, library, job centre – and a large church complete the picture.

The church is very busy, and even though we have arrived half an hour early, I had to park a fair distance away and stand with Ruben, Bakers and Tomo against the wall on the lefthand side as all the pews are full. We are surrounded by hundreds of other mourners and I recognize some familiar faces, mostly below the age of 20, but also some belonging to older teachers from the local high school. The music that is playing over the loudspeakers suddenly stops and all the conversations come to an end as a coffin enters through the main entrance. This coffin containing Davies's body is carried on the shoulders of four men, all dressed in black suits. As they pass down the aisle, one of them, a boy called Clive, is familiar to me and I note how young he looks at this moment. I fight hard not to let myself completely give in to the emotions that are raging inside me. I do this partly because the young men who are standing and sitting around me might see this as strange, as in many ways, even after knowing them for such a long time, I am still an outsider.

When the coffin reaches the front of the church, it is placed on a stand in front of the altar, and the four young men, directed by the minister, take their seats that have been kept empty for them in the front pew. The service proceeds with an opening prayer from the minister, a short hymn and then readings from the Bible. The minister speaks again and this is then followed by eulogies from Davies's family members and then his girlfriend. When she stands in the pulpit, she talks about the life they were planning together and how devastated she is that he is gone. Her hands shake as she reads from a piece of paper, and tears begin to roll down my cheeks, and my shoulders shudder. It's not so much Davies I am crying for, as I didn't really know him as well as some of his friends, but it is for the tragic loss of a young life and everything this death symbolizes about the consequences and dangers of particular types of behaviours that young men are so often involved in. The service ends with The Lord's Prayer, with the whole church seemingly taking part, something which I can't bring myself to join in with. A final plea from Davies's parents is delivered through the minister to the congregation. 'To all of you who drive, please just slow down. We have lost enough young men to driving accidents, we don't want to lose anymore, we need to make sure this doesn't happen again'.

Davies was 19 and had just started an apprenticeship with an electrical company a few weeks before. Early one morning, whilst travelling to work, he had been involved in a car accident on a road nearby. Whilst driving at high speed (some reports suggested that he was late for work), he had overtaken another vehicle and then lost control, careered across his lane into oncoming traffic and hit a van. He was pronounced dead at a local hospital a few hours later.

This young death occurred six months after the fieldwork had ended and I was busy trying to write up the study. I heard about it via social media, and contacted some of the young men you will meet in the coming chapters to see how they were coping. As we talked over the next few days, I asked if I could attend the funeral with them. During the previous two and a half years, I had grown very close to some of the group and wanted to be there not only to pay my respects, but to also support them through it. So whilst *From Labouring to Learning* is about the challenges a group of young working-class men face in a de-industrial community, it is also written for them. I thank you for letting me into your world and I hope it represents your lives, for good and bad, accurately.

1
Introduction

This book describes the lives of a group of young working-class men in a de-industrialized community in the South Wales Valleys (UK). Using a longitudinal ethnographic approach, I focus on how young men's masculinities are performed across a variety of educational and leisure spaces and indicate how social, economic and cultural processes impact on the formation of identity. In detailing these processes, this study contributes to the literature on young masculinities by describing how place can impact on the formation of a masculine self and also how everyday experiences within specific places and spaces can shape the way education and schooling are viewed. Ideas and issues drawn from Erving Goffman's work on the performance of self and the formation of social identity are central to the theoretical basis of the book, and the research adds to symbolic interactionist tradition. When applied to masculinities (and femininities), this framework highlights how gender comes into being through socially constructed performances which are acceptable in a given situation, setting or community, not as innate biological accomplishments but as dramaturgical tasks (Goffman, 1977; West and Zimmerman, 1987; Schrock and Schwalbe, 2009). This study is the first to look at these issues within a Welsh context, and the findings suggest that young men can only be analysed within separate historical and geographical contexts and through the social construction of gender within specific places. This focus on the local enables the complexity of multiple identities and fluid relationships in certain areas to be explored and to illustrate how young marginalized men deal with social and economic changes in different ways. The chameleonisation of masculinity metaphor, which is outlined in this book, is put forward in an attempt to understand these processes further.

At the centre of the study are the key questions which guided the research. How are young working-class men living in the Valleys adapting to change in insecure times and making sense of their position as they make the transition to adulthood? When young men are left with the historical legacy of industrial labour, do they perform and articulate traditional forms of masculinity in particular ways and by different means? In educational contexts, how do academic and/or vocational subjects impact upon specific classed masculine subjectivities? What are the broader social and spatial networks within the community (e.g. family, sports, nightlife, fast cars, music, sex) that mediate the identities of these young men and how do space and place impact who they can be and become?

Over two and a half years, I attempted to answer these questions by conducting fieldwork and following the educational and social lives of a cohort of young men (born between September 1991 and August 1992) in one town I refer to as Cwm Dyffryn.[1] From their last few months of compulsory schooling in the spring of 2008, to the autumn of 2010, when some of these young men entered university, I explore how these young lives are played out. To develop the study from the perspectives of the young men, methods such as participant observation, semi-structured and unstructured interviews and ethnographic conversations with individuals and groups of boys, teachers, caretakers, receptionists, secretaries, bus drivers, parents and even (on one occasion) a baroness (who visited the central school site) were conducted (see Chapters 3–7). Areas of observation included taking part in different lessons, time in the common room, the library, the lunch hall and the playground, but also other educational arenas such Further Education (FE) college classrooms and vocational spaces, such as mechanical engineering workshops and stables used for equine studies courses. As Connell (1989) noted, research on schooling is usually confined to the school and has the potential to miss other factors and influences that impact on young men's gender identities. Therefore in keeping with other researchers who have looked at multiple spaces of gender production (Nayak, 2003a, b, 2006), my research was undertaken across other arenas in order to provide a rich 'thick description' (Geertz, 1973) of their lives. This importantly led to a more meaningful and intricate understanding of how they understood and represented their world. Other regions of interaction including general 'hanging out' in the cars they drove, the fast food places they ate in, the pubs and nightclubs they drank and danced in, university open days and places of work such as sports centres, bars and supermarkets. I was also invited to attend sports events, to go shopping or to the cinema and important social occasions such as 18th birthday parties and on one occasion a lap dancing club (see Chapter 4). Online social networking sites such as Facebook were further used to communicate with the young men when away from the field. Finally, as the prologue made painfully clear, this also included the funeral of one of the young men from the study who died in a car accident.

In the opening chapter, I discuss the background to the study by looking at the changing transitions from school to work that have overtly affected young working-class men since the late 1970s and the impact this has had on contemporary forms of masculinity. I then turn to focus on the perceived 'crisis' in masculinity or the 'war on boys' that has accompanied these changes and the role sociology has played in understanding and theorizing men and masculinities. To conclude the chapter, I consider the part my own biography has played in shaping this study, before describing the structure of the rest of the book.

Changing transitions from school to work

The end of compulsory schooling is a key period of transition, when young people make decisions about their futures and when social inequalities really begin to sediment. When the school-leaving age in the UK was raised to 16 in 1972, many young people, especially working-class men (Willis, 1977), left school at this age. But with de-industrialization and shifts in the mode of production to other countries, entry to the labour market at 16 has now become the exception rather than the norm. The majority of young people in the UK (and in other countries in the global North) now continue in education not only to gain qualifications which will supposedly make them more employable, but because there are few other options available to them.

Since the late 1970s, the education systems of countries within the Organisation for Economic Co-operation and Development (OECD) have undergone major reforms leading to education and training becoming key strategies within economic and social policy. McDowell (2003) emphasizes these differences in the UK, reporting that in 1979, 47% of adult men had no formal qualifications, compared to 61% of adult women. By the end of the millennium, things had altered with only 15% of adult men and 21% of adult women being without qualifications. In keeping with the trends of OECD countries, educational polices by the Welsh Government such as *The Learning Country* (Welsh Assembly Government [WAG], 2001), *Learning Country, Learning Pathways 14–19* (WAG, 2002) and *The Learning Country 2: Delivering the Promise* (WAG, 2006a) have been implemented with the intention of transforming the 14–19 curriculum. The Welsh Government sees this as a key area that will shape the country's economic and social future providing a highly skilled workforce. Alongside more young people 'choosing' to continue in post-16 education in the UK, there are also more young people entering university than ever before. However, middle-class young people have been the chief beneficiaries of such changes (Reay et al., 2005; Bradley and Ingram, 2012), and there are still more working-class young male school-leavers in the UK without qualifications or with the lowest levels of educational attainment than almost any other group (Gillborn and Mirza, 2000; Gillborn, 2009).

As de-industrialization has continued, working-class young men are no longer likely to be 'learning to labour' (Willis, 1977) but 'learning to serve' (McDowell, 2000) in different industries to those in the past. The performances of a masculine self which accompany these newer industries are highly contradictory to what came before (Kenway et al., 2006; Walkerdine, 2010; McDowell, 2012). The service sector has, to a certain extent, replaced many of the former industries that would have employed those who left school at the earliest opportunity, but these jobs require different skills and attributes from those they replaced. On the one hand, there is the low-paid, low-skilled and repetitively unrewarding work found in telephone call centres, fast food outlets, shops, restaurants, bars or as cleaners, whilst on the other hand there are the high-paid, highly qualified, high-tech service jobs that are said to typify the 'knowledge economy'. The first version of service jobs lack mobility, security and some would argue satisfaction and the majority of these do not require high levels of qualifications. Some are often 'outsourced' to low-wage economies in poorer countries in the global South, such as India or Bangladesh. The second version of service jobs are based on higher educational qualifications, smaller in number and financially secure. But in times of recession, even these could be seen as being at risk and there is no guarantee of a 'job for life' in any sector of the economy. Accompanying these changes, a new set of theoretical debates has emerged in sociological theory and in policy discourse over the last two decades. This literature has sought to explore how the transformation of the labour market has impacted upon both employment and personal identity highlighting the growing uncertainty, insecurity and risk many people face in post-modernity (Giddens, 1991; Bauman, 1998; Beck, 1999; Beck and Beck-Gernsheim, 2002). As access to education and employment opportunities become gradually more uncertain, the impact this has on the social construction of masculine identities, especially for marginalized young men, becomes increasingly important.

Crisis in masculinity?

The changes in status and forms of employment patterns have also been accompanied by a common assumption that appears to have developed in the media and public policy since the mid-1990s indicating that there is an apparent 'crisis' in contemporary forms of masculinity or a 'war on boys' across the globe (MacInnes, 1998; Clare, 2000; Hoff-Sommers, 2000, 2013). Men, it has been claimed, are now the new disadvantaged. In 2010, *The Times*[2] newspaper dedicated a 35-page special publication to this 'crisis', and the discourse reared its head again in public debate in the spring of 2013 after a speech by the then UK Labour shadow public health minister Diane Abbott (Syal, 2013; Roberts, 2014). She argued that 'Britain's Crisis of Masculinity' was a result of economic and social change, greatly affecting male identity and that as a result there was a great lack of respect from men towards women and overt homophobia in contemporary society.

A further persistent media discourse suggests that it is now girls who are achieving in schools and becoming the more advantaged group to the supposed disadvantage of boys (Weiner et al., 1997; Epstein et al., 1998; Martino and Meyenn, 2001; Segal, 2007; Francis et al., 2012). These arguments of 'crisis' are reportedly additionally manifested through uncertainties around social roles, sexuality, high rates of suicide, truancy levels, the use of violence by young men and a lack of male role models (Tarrant et al., 2015).[3] Yet, what some studies have shown is that the loss of well-paid, secure, industrial and manufacturing jobs which has deeply affected the towns and cities that relied on these industries overtly disadvantages some subgroups of men over others (see MacLeod, 1995; Anderson, 1999; Arnot, 2004; Kenway et al., 2006; Weis, 2006, 2008; Ward, 2014). A second body of literature would argue that not all men are suffering this 'crisis' equally. In regard to educational achievement, in particular, there has historically been an issue with working-class white and black boys who have tended to achieve less well than their more privileged counterparts (McDowell, 2007; Nayak, 2009; Skeggs, 2009; Ingram, 2011). Further, there seems to be an implicit blaming of girls, teachers and feminists for this 'crisis' (Weaver-Hightower, 2008; Lingard et al., 2009) and a neglect of the fact that a large number of working-class girls are also not achieving the top grades. Further work by Gillborn and Mirza (2000) and Gillborn (2009) show that the biggest differences in educational outcomes are more to do with class and ethnicity combined, rather than gender (see also Francis, 2000; Francis and Skelton, 2005; Skelton and Francis, 2009; Roberts, 2014).

Despite this recent 'moral panic', we must view these arguments with a degree of scepticism. First, this concept continues to suggest an overly simplistic view of gender which only portrays masculinity and femininity as 'natural' differences between men and women (Connell, 1995). These 'supposed' opposites are formed through biological differences, psychology, social functions and aspirations. Second, as men still tend to operate all the key positions of authority and control throughout society through church, finance, education, media, government and forms of world power (Connell, 2009), these issues may not really be linked to a 'crisis' of masculinity at all, but more to one of social class inequality. Furthermore as Morgan (2006) asks, what does the term 'crisis' actually infer? Does the term refer to individual men or is it linked to all men? Does it apply to certain forms of masculinity or only dominant forms of masculinity? As Beynon (2002) has suggested, this 'crisis' is also not a new phenomenon, it is just the latest expression of a long debate going back over the past few centuries; Beynon lists the Boy Scout movement as just one example of an institution that was organized to 'rescue men' and equip Britain with the right type of men, fit to build an empire around at the start of the 20th century. Connell (1995), in addition, offers a list of other challenges to masculinity which have gone back even further to the Renaissance period, the growth of commercial capitalism and the development of war in Europe.

If such a 'crisis' does exist, it has roots in a number of political, social and economic areas that do not affect all men equally. Connell's (1995) 'crisis of the gender order' could be a better term as the practices of patriarchy are certainly by no means under threat. What is clear is that the development of a 'crisis' discourse overtakes other issues of poverty, racism and structural inequalities that impact on wider society. Furthermore, alongside these issues, there appears to be a lack of understanding that the definition of masculinity is a continual changing process over history and within and between different times, cultures and places.

The sociology of masculinities

Sociologists have approached masculinity as a multiplicity of different gendered practices enacted by men, whose bodies are assumed to be biologically male.[4] Early in the 20th century, psychologists and psychoanalysts became increasingly concerned with distinguishing between men and women (Connell, 1995; Kimmel, 1996). As a result, a 'normal' adult came to be defined in terms of their adjustment to their own 'sex role' (Pleck, 1987). Sociologists such as the structural functionalist Talcott Parsons (1954) increasingly saw these 'sex roles' as fundamental to the ordering of families, the economy and wider society. These 'sex roles' created a strong distinction between men and women, and Parsons suggested that any deviation from the roles of women as primary caregivers and men as breadwinners would create 'role strain' and ultimately weaken society. However, there were also other scholars writing at the same time, who although they did not address the issues of masculinity or gender directly, did indicate that there were differences within, as well as between, the sexes. As Goffman (1963: 128) states:

> In an important sense there is only one complete unblushing male in America: a young, married, white, urban, northern, heterosexual, Protestant, father, of college education, fully employed, of good complexion, weight, and height, and a recent record in sports... Any male who fails to qualify in any one of these ways is likely to view himself – during moments at least – as unworthy, incomplete, and inferior.

It is clear that some, like Goffman, were beginning to highlight that a more nuanced approach to gender was required. Although first wave feminists, such as Mary Wollstonecraft (1989), had begun to challenge 'sex roles' towards the end of the 18th century, and the suffragette movement in the UK continued to fight for gender equality in terms of voting rights for women in the 1910s and 1920s, it was not until the growth of the women's movement in the 1970s that feminist theorists really began to explore and challenge 'sex role' theory. Some feminists began analysing how power was embedded in these 'sex roles' and how relations between men and women were social, rather than natural, and therefore an identity formation ultimately created through patriarchal inequality (Hartman, 1976; Delphy, 1977; Kessler and McKenna, 1978). Pascoe (2007: 6) suggests that Dorothy Dinnerstein (1976) and Nancy Chodorow (1978), working within a psychoanalytic framework, argued that contemporary masculinity:

> is the result of a family system in which women mother. Identification with a mother as primary caregiver provides much more problematic for a boy than for a girl child, producing a self we understand as masculine characterised by defensive ego boundaries and repudiation of femininity.

Feminist psychoanalytic theorists associated masculinity with a search for independence and separation from a feminine 'other'.

The feminist movement directly influenced the growing literature on the sociology of masculinity (Tolson, 1977), and as Morgan (1992: 6) put it, 'feminism provided the context, the overall set of assumptions within which the current studies of men and masculinities' were conducted. As an area of study, research on masculinities did not really develop until feminists began to challenge taken-for-granted political and social traditions, thus offering radical implications for men (Brittan, 1989). Nonetheless, it was with the publication of 'Towards a New Sociology of Masculinity', the paper by Carrigan, Connell and Lee (1985), that a new model for understanding masculinities really began to emerge and illustrated how masculinity was linked to power relations amongst men, as well as over women. This paper highlighted the links between masculinity and heterosexuality, emphasizing that not all men were equal players in the patriarchal oppression of women. This enabled masculinity to be defined not as one single character trait (returning to a theme Goffman initially highlighted 20 years previously), but as a form of domination and as collective male practice.

Since the publication of Carrigan, Connell and Lee's (1985) and Connell's (1987) significant contribution, a growing body of sociological work has developed that has sought to understand patterns of masculinity and has changed understandings of gender throughout the social sciences and the humanities. Kimmel (1987) and Messner and Sabo's (1990) edited collections, alongside David Morgan's (1992) persuasive book, *Discovering Men*, underlined the continual importance of feminist scholarship for studies on men and masculinities. These texts further indicated that it was vital to begin to understand that there were a number of masculinities in existence and not one universal characteristic that defined manhood. Cornwall and Lindisfarne (1994) began this mapping with a collection of ethnographic explorations into the lives of men across the globe. This was closely followed by Connell's (1995) seminal text *Masculinities,* which provided a conceptual framework for theorizing the plurality of masculinities. Additional edited collections of papers by Mac an Ghaill (1996) and by Whitehead and Barrett (2001) further explored the multi-faceted nature of masculinity, and this developing sociology of masculinity became a 'critical study of men, their behaviours, practices, values and perspectives' (Whitehead and Barrett, 2001: 14).

The *Handbook of Men and Masculinities* edited by three of the most prolific writers in the field, Kimmel, Connell and Hearn (2005) was one of the more recent collections which surveyed much of this sociological work (see also Flood et al., 2007; Flood, 2008; Janssen, 2008; Roberts, 2014). What this collection of work on masculinities highlights is that in different cultures and over different time periods, there are multiple definitions of what constitutes manhood and there are diverse ways for men to operate within the wider gender order and across class, racial and sexual contexts. I now turn to look in more depth at how two different authors working within the field have gone about theorizing men and masculinities before moving on to address what can be learned from them and applied to this study and what can be discarded.

Theorization of masculinities

The ideas presented in the influential paper by Carrigan, Connell and Lee (1985) were further developed a few years later by Connell (1987) into a systematic sociological theory of gender and sexualities. Reviewing theories of gender from feminist, psycho-analysis, sex role theory and sociobiological perspectives, and drawing on both present-day and historical evidence from multiple sources, Connell (1987) outlined the multiple structures that influence gender relationships. These included theories of patriarchy and the related debates over the role of men in transforming patriarchy, the new left and women of colour. Elaborating on this earlier work, and drawing on Antonio Gramsci's (1971) analysis of class relations, which refer to the cultural and material dynamics through which different groups can assert and maintain a leading position in social life, Connell (1995) applied this to gender. Connell (1995) argued that in the social hierarchy, individual men embodied different forms of masculinity within the wider gender order, termed *hegemonic, complicit, subordinated* and *marginalized*. The most visible bearers of *hegemonic masculinity* are not always the most powerful and Connell stressed that hegemonic masculinity was not a fixed character type, always and everywhere the same, but that it was the 'culturally exalted form of masculinity' (Carrigan, Connell and Lee, 1985: 592). Connell (1995: 41) also emphasized that even though a very small number of men actually embody hegemonic masculinity, all men still benefit from the 'patriarchal dividend'. *Subordinated masculinity* is based on sexuality and refers to homosexual men's subordination by hegemonic heterosexual men. This occurs through a range of practices from political and cultural exclusion, to systematic abuse through religious doctrine, legal violence, street violence and economic discrimination.

Complicit masculinity refers to men who benefit from patriarchal oppression, but do not enact hegemonic masculinity: 'A great many men who draw the patriarchal dividend also respect their wives and mothers, are never violent towards women, do their accustomed share of the housework, bring home the family wage, and can easily convince themselves that feminists must be bra-burning extremists' (Connell, 1995: 80). While men that fall into this category do not receive the same benefits and privileges as those who are seen as purely hegemonic, they do still support patriarchy and are controlled by it, and the practices which constitute it are used to judge the conduct of other men. Connell's final form of masculinity is termed *marginalized masculinity* which describes those men who benefit from a powerful gender position, but not in terms of class or race. What Connell further highlighted was that these forms of masculinity were not everywhere the same and were open to change.

Connell's model of multiple masculinities led to the concept of hegemonic masculinity being highly important in developing the field of masculinities research. As a concept, it has been utilized in countless studies, reports and books and across a wide range of social institutions.[5] However, this body of research has not escaped opposition. Critics have argued that the application of the concept tends to promote and reproduce static categories or fixed typologies that are difficult to use analytically without reproducing simplistic accounts of masculinity (Clatterbaugh, 1997; Demetriou, 2001; Anderson, 2009). There has also been some criticism of who, if anyone, actually embodies hegemonic masculinity (see Donaldson, 1993; Martin, 1998; Wetherell and Edley, 1999; Beynon, 2002). For example, how can working-class men (who may hold the hegemonic position within a working-class community) maintain this hegemonic position whilst dominated by the overarching social structural inequalities of the class system? In response to these criticisms, Connell and Messerschmidt (2005) provided a reworking of the concept. They argued that in any given setting a form of masculinity exists which is associated with authority and power. Therefore, hegemonic masculinity can be found in different forms at the local, national and global levels through different 'configurations of practice' (Connell and Messerschmidt, 2005: 847) rather than a set of prescribed traits to ensure that it is not conceived in an essentialist way. These forms of masculinity do not have to be based on types of violence or superiority of numbers, but the existence of a dominant version of masculinity continues to privilege the position of men over women. Nonetheless, because hegemonic masculinity has often been used to describe negative male behaviour which subordinates other men and women, the term has become something which is associated with the worst excesses of masculinity and, in particular, with young men synonymous with macho, 'hard' or 'laddish' identities. What is also apparent is that these negative attributes are more likely to be applied to certain groups of working-class men than any other group (see McDowell, 2012; Ward, 2014).

The emergence of a 'softer' masculinity?

Other recent work which is increasingly becoming a source of debate on young masculinities has argued that different educational institutions act as spaces for questioning the meaning of contemporary understandings of masculinity. Anderson (2009) and McCormack (2012) have suggested that contemporary masculinities are much more fluid, flexible and open especially around aspects of sexuality, than previously noted. Eric Anderson (2009) terms this 'inclusive masculinity'. Drawing on a number of ethnographic studies with gay and bisexual young men (often white, middle-class university students living in urban or metropolitan communities), Anderson suggests that decreased levels of overt homophobia and more open, fluid forms of homosocial relations have challenged hegemonic patterns of masculinity and that this 'archaic archetype of masculinity' (Anderson, 2009: 4) is now on the decline.[6] Further ethnographic research conducted by McCormack (2012), which applied Anderson's inclusive masculinity theory, looked at the lives of a group of young, white, mainly middle-class students, at sixth-form colleges in the South West of England. McCormack (2012) found that his male participants were much more comfortable with being physically affectionate with one another than has been noted in previous studies with young men. In addition, he deduced that these participants were more likely to have pro-gay attitudes, have friendships with students who were openly gay and engaged in activities such as face stroking and resting heads in each other's laps. McCormack concludes that from his research findings that homophobia has reduced in schools.

While Anderson and McCormack show that for some young men there appears to be a decline in homophobia, and something which should be celebrated, nonetheless it must be remembered that the privileged position that the majority of these young men hold as white, educated men is perhaps exactly what enables them to engage in behaviours that were once seen as sexually deviant or unacceptable, without the accompanying risks. Furthermore, the behaviours and practices of masculinity described by these authors are very different from other contemporary research findings on masculinity and homophobia (Stonewall, 2007; ILGA, 2014; Simpson, 2014), and in this section of their work at least, both fail to address issues of social class or the impact of locality of life chances. McCormack's (2014) more recent paper does begin to tentatively apply a class analysis to these issues, and this step should be noted, as their work has attracted growing criticism for it's reluctant to address social class issues. It would also appear that this approach to theorizing masculinities is fast becoming something that masculinities scholars feel they need to engage with and often oppose Ironically, this critical engagement and opposition has led to the theory's growing visibility and drawn attention away from the many issues men and women still face through growing social and economic inequalities (for a further discussion and debate of these theoretical developments, see De Boise (2014), Roberts (2014) and O'Neill (2015)). In addition to these other comments, I argue that neither author takes into account that multiple forms of masculinity have co-existed with each other throughout history, that sexuality is only one aspect of masculinity (see Kimmel, 1987; Cohen, 1998; Segal, 2007) and that these findings cannot be applied in a global context (see Connell, 2007; ILGA, 2014).

Although the concepts and issues raised by Connell and Anderson are undoubtedly useful for considering the complexity of gender relations, I suggest they both fail to adequately address the everyday processes through which working-class masculinities operate and are deployed, contested and refined, and they fail to acknowledge the different positions individual men can occupy in different situations. What is also problematic when looking at masculinity is the categorization of masculinity under consideration (e.g. working-class masculinity, black, Latino, gay, bisexual) as this implies that all individual men in each category are similar and perform masculinity in the same ways. So while they are a useful starting point, such a strategy has a tendency to obscure in-group variations, so I suggest we need to explore these categories in more depth.

Despite the difficulties with hegemonic masculinity that I have outlined above, I continue with Connell's concept. However, I also explore whether 'softer' forms of working-class masculinity, which I characterize as being less aggressive, macho and boisterous, can still exist for individuals alongside hegemonic versions of working-class masculinity at the local level, rather than being totally dismissed by the young men, as Anderson and McCormack claim. Is it possible for working-class young men in a de-industrialized community to display open, 'softer' tendencies expressed through being diligent and compliant in school, talking about emotions, anxieties, thoughts and feelings and speaking positively about relationships with girls, as well as engaging in performing those characteristics associated with more traditional forms of masculinity in different situations?

Working within social constructionist traditions, Schrock and Schwalbe (2009) suggest that the common theme between men is not the individual body, but the type of act which signifies a masculine self. If men are to remain in a dominant gender position, these authors suggest that men must signify possession of a masculine self. This comes through the ways an individual male is viewed by others during different interactions, behaviours and appearances.

Recognizing that masculinizing practices and processes extend beyond individual male bodies as displays, in the next section I turn in particular to the work of Erving Goffman, which enables the various ways young masculinities are performed, deployed and refined through interaction to be analysed in greater depth. I suggest that this facilitates a greater insight into how young working-class men recognize structural understandings of masculinity, and how they display agency in interpreting, conforming to or subverting masculine norms.

Goffman's legacy

The symbolic interactionist perspective sees gender as representing a range of dramaturgical performances that individuals display through a number of face-to-face interactions within different settings and situations (Goffman, 1959, 1977; West and Zimmerman, 1987; Brickell, 2005; Grazian, 2007; Schrock and Schwalbe, 2009). As West and Zimmerman (1987: 137) propose, 'doing gender means creating differences between girls and boys and women and men, differences that are not natural, essential or biological'. This perspective argues that femininities and masculinities are not instinctive or innate biological accomplishments, but are undertakings of human behaviour which appear 'natural' because individuals gain knowledge of (and adhere) to strict social codes and signifying practices learned through the interaction order (Goffman, 1983). These expressions are then performed through a number of acts, or displays which convey to others how we regard them and indicate how individuals interact with others during a range of social situations.

In Goffman's most renowned work *The Presentation of Self in Everyday Life* ([1956] 1959), he lays out a dramaturgical framework to represent the conduct of an individual's interactions using the stage metaphors of front (made up of setting, appearance and manner) and back regions to illustrate how the self is a social product of performances that individuals or 'teams' of individuals (Grazian, 2007; Hughey, 2011) display in different situations. Goffman argues that the front-stage or front region is the part of the individual or team performance that functions 'to define the situation for those who observe the performance' (1959: 32). Front is the 'expressive equipment of a standard kind intentionally or unwittingly employed by the individual during his performance' (Goffman, 1959: 32). Goffman suggests that there are three different parts to this front performance. First, there is the *setting* which provides the location for human interaction to take place and which is then played out inside, before or upon it. A *setting* is geographically fixed. So, for example, performances within a vocational educational institution (see Chapter 6) cannot begin until performers bring themselves into that particular place. Secondly, alongside the *setting*, there are other parts of front that are termed 'personal front' which convey the additional items that are identified with the performer, which Goffman refers to as *appearance* and *manner* which are the scenic parts of the performance. *Appearance* is the stimulus which tells us about the performer's social status and their temporary or ritual status at a given time or situation within the life-cycle. *Manner* is the stimulus which tells us what interaction role the performer will potentially play in a given situation.

A large number of acts can occur behind a social front performance and different routines can be presented behind the same front. This means that there is not always a perfect fit between the character of a performance and the socialized guise. As I show in Chapters 3–7, young men can display different performances of masculinity in a variety of settings. These performances are then overtly validated and a sense of front self develops. Goffman also uses the term 'team' to refer to sets of individuals who 'co-operate in staging a single routine' (1959: 85). These co-operations then help to express meaning within different social relations and the overall team impression can be seen as a performance alongside the individual acts, through forms of impression management. Away from the front, things can be adjusted and changed. In Chapters 3 and 4, I show how two of my respondent groups 'The Valley Boiz' and 'The Geeks' do this in different ways. Some aspects of an activity in a given situation can be accentuated to portray the identity the young men want to project. However, other actions, which might spoil or ruin the performance and the overall impression, are suppressed. For Goffman, these performances of self (and therefore gender) occur not only within social interactions between individuals, but also within the wider culture of a given social setting. Goffman (1974: 10–11) argues that frames organize social experience and help create 'definitions of the situation [that] are built up in accordance with principles of organization which govern events...and our subjective involvement in them'. It is also these frames which govern how we talk (Goffman, 1981) and the arrangement between the sexes (Goffman, 1976, 1977), allowing us to see how we 'do gender' (West and Zimmerman, 1987) through social interaction and how this social interaction is framed through specific contexts and within wider social, economic and cultural histories. Frames contain various levels of reality, and organize actor's experiences and events. These experiences are governed by rules and norms and we learn to present behaviour in accordance within the frame of interaction. In Chapter 6, I show how these frames become particularly apparent when studying vocational courses.

Rehabilitating interactionism

Jackson and Scott (2010) suggest that there is a need to rehabilitate the insights of the interactionist tradition that I outlined in the previous section, in order to highlight and re-establish its continued relevance to sociology and feminist analysis of sexuality and gender identity. It was this tradition, they argue, that first developed a sociological theory of sexuality and began to understand gender relations in the 1970s (Gagnon and Simon, 1973) by challenging biological determinism. While interactionism is still popular with gender and masculinities scholars in North America (Thorne, 1993; West, 1996; Pawluch, Shaffir and Miall, 2005; Schrock and Schwalbe, 2009), only a few have continued to utilize this form of sociological enquiry in the UK when addressing issues of gender (see Plummer, 2007). Indeed, interactionism has suffered what Jackson and Scott (2010: 812) call 'theoretical amnesia' among feminists and sociologists of gender within recent years (see also Maines, 2001; Atkinson and Housley, 2003). This perspective has been eclipsed by the rise of Foucauldian, post-structuralist and queer theory (Foucault, 1978, 1980; Butler, 1990; Davies, 1994; Jagose, 1996). While much of the latter work has been influential in theorizing the ways in which gender, performativity and the subversion of gender norms are connected, Jackson and Scott argue that much has been lost by forgetting the insights of interactionism. What is missing from much post-structuralist work is attention to the practices, embedded in everyday social life and the local social relationships and meanings that shape gender identities, rather than the analysis of discursive practices.

In keeping with Jackson and Scott's reappraisal of interactionism and, taking into account some of the difficulties within the theorization of masculinities I have outlined above, I believe that there is a need to return to an approach inspired by the interactionist tradition to address contemporary aspects of young working-class masculinities. By combing this with an analysis of place when looking at masculinity (see Chapter 2), a real insight into the ways young men's lives are played out can be gained.

Auto/biographical beginnings

As Miller (1995) argues through her concept of the 'autobiography of the question', it is important to note the part that a researcher's biography plays in the development of research and writing (see also Van Maanen, 1988; Coffey, 1999; Denzin and Lincoln, 2005). Epstein and Johnson (1998: 7) suggest that biography is inextricably linked to research and state that:

> Books are written from particular standpoints...it is important for readers to understand where we are coming from, in terms of who we are as much as in terms of what we think.

My interest in working-class masculinity has grown out of my own educational journey and the development of my own sociological imagination (Mills, 1959). It was the autumn of 1999 and I was in the final year of my A-levels in a comprehensive school in the South Wales Valleys similar to the one attended by the young men in this study. I was searching for an interesting university course as I knew I did not want to continue studying what I was doing at the time (English literature, history and geography). Neither of my parents or my step-parents had been to university, leaving school at 16 with few qualifications and working in the public sector and the retail industry at jobs which they disliked. I was left to make my own mind up about the type of course I wanted to study and which university I applied to.

I literally stumbled upon sociology one day in the tiny sixth-form library of our school. There was a course which appeared to be about how and why people behaved in certain ways and how they were shaped by the time and place in which they lived. Autobiographically, it seemed the right fit. Both my grandfathers had been coal miners and trade unionists and their great-grandparents had moved to South Wales because of the coal industry in the late 19th century and left school at the age of 14 to join their fathers in the collieries. Politics and current events were always talked about around the dinner table with my parents. Sociology seemed very much about the underdog and it looked like it fitted in with many of the conversations from my working-class upbringing. After gaining the grades I needed, I arrived at the University of the West of England in September 2001. I was unaware of it at the time, but it was here that my outlook on the world would begin to change and where I was to be able to make sense of the social and cultural experiences I had experienced whilst growing up. However, I was no overnight sociologist, failing my first essay, but I kept reading and writing, and after three years I graduated. After my degree, sociology slipped under the radar for a few years, but I returned to university, first to do a PGCE (teaching qualification) to teach A-level sociology, and then a PhD at Cardiff University.

As I taught young people and adults in an FE college in a community similar to Cwm Dyffryn, I increasingly wondered why I had chosen to continue in education. Many of my peers, some of whom achieved far higher GCSE (General Certificate in Secondary Education) grades than I did, had left school at the earliest opportunity. Looking back on the time I grew up in the Valleys, I was never quite sure what friendship group I belonged to either and how this reflected on my own performance of masculinity. I was interested in sports and like a lot of young men in the area played rugby but, in addition, I liked to read and write and held ambitions to escape the area by travelling and going to university. These desires alienated me from some of my former classmates when I progressed to the Sixth Form (Years 12 and 13). I also found going out and drinking in local pubs and partying in nightclubs to the early hours much more interesting than studying for my A-levels. I wanted to know what the young people, and in particular young men, thought about these issues and if any of them experienced the same thoughts and feelings I did. These ideas then became my doctoral study.

Although I have written and talked about young masculinities over the past few years in different contexts, ranging from international academic conferences, to local radio and outreach events, when I began the PhD I struggled with the academic environment and felt I didn't quite fit in (maybe I still don't!), but I also feel I never quite fitted in back in my own community (see also Hobbs, 1993). As Wakeling (2010: 41) puts it: 'There is no going back to working-class origins because university education and upward mobility change the individual psychologically and set them apart in the eyes of those left behind.' This is something that seems quite a common trend among academics who have written about their working-class upbringings (Dews and Law, 1995; Halsey, 1996; Winlow, 2001; Childers, 2002; Hey, 2003; Wakeling, 2010) but one which is needed to highlight the influences upon one's own position when conducting research. Clearly, I have learned to code-shift (Anderson, 1999) to a certain extent or I would not have continued to do a PhD and ultimately write this book. However, like Halsey (1996) I can never quite shake the feeling that research and academia is not 'really work'. I have provided this autobiographical narrative in order to enable the reader to 'place' the remainder of the book into the context from which it stems and to also illustrate that even though my education had provided me with a little distance, I too was a young man from the same culture I describe in the coming pages.

Structure of the book

In the chapter that directly follows this introduction, I describe the research locale in more depth and highlight the significance of place to understanding young men's masculinities. I outline the industrial development of the region and the consequences of the demise of the coal industry. I specifically focus on the construction of a particular type of stoic masculinity that was connected to this form of industry and the challenges that economic, social and culture changes have made to what it means to be a man in the area. This chapter also addresses the role of ethnography as a tool for the generation of data and its role in analysing masculinities.

Chapters 3–7 turn to the analysis of the lives of the young men that were at the centre of the study. These empirical chapters present the young men's lives through what Ball et al. (2000: 17) term 'analytic sets'. This device is adopted to present, analyse and introduce the complex lives that were studied and that I was a part of. Through these analytic sets, which draw on ethnographic field notes, individual interviews and biographical histories, the research questions are explored and addressed. Each can be read as a standalone chapter, as different literature is drawn upon to support the empirical work, but they will make more sense and hopefully be more enjoyable to the reader if read in order.

Chapter 3 concentrates on The Valley Boiz, a group of young men who came from families that would not have traditionally continued into post-compulsory education and who performed a specific version of hegemonic masculinity influenced by the industrial past of the area. I show how the historical legacy of a former era was re-traditionalized in different ways both within and beyond the school. I suggest that these practices formed the 'front stage' display of these masculinities. However, behind the archetypal macho masculine front, other performances were also evident which provided some contradictions to the front displays.

Following on from the previous chapter, in Chapter 4 I show how The Geeks, another set of working-class young men from the same community, displayed a more studious working-class masculinity, characterized by academic achievement in school and being interested in comic books, technology and reading. These 'softer' performances brought with them risks and bullying sometimes occurred. But like The Valley Boiz contradictions in their performance of masculinity were also apparent and cracks in their more studious front occurred. I also illustrate in this chapter the difficulties which these young men experienced in trying to escape the locale and progress to university as working-class academic achievers.

Chapters 5 focuses on The Emos, who were a very distinctive friendship groups who like The Geeks displayed a non-normative performance of masculinity that attracted victimization, bullying and intimidation. Yet whilst these young men displayed 'alternative' masculinities through being involved in a subcultural scene, they still evidenced many traditional discourses of masculinity. Moving away from the school, Chapter 6 looks at the lives of Bakers, Frankie and Ian and explores the performance of masculinity in three different vocational educational courses in three different FE colleges. Two traditionally 'masculine' courses (motor mechanics and engineering) are compared with a more 'feminized' subject (equine studies) to see whether these vocational spaces can frame and validate traditional working-class forms of masculinity, and also provide a space to enable subversive forms of masculinity to be performed. I further look outside the vocational spaces where these performances are displayed and examine the role of car culture, which was important in these young men's lives.

One of my central arguments is that young men are not locked into one particular version of masculinity. A repertoire of masculinities would seem evident, performed in different ways with different audiences and within different settings. In Chapter 7, I draw specifically on the case study of Jimmy to foreground the immense struggles he experienced while undergoing educational, social, cultural and spatial transition. I show in detail the problems that occur when a locality's specific historical legacy collides with contemporary masculine practices and the demands Jimmy was under to negotiate multiple performances of self, or as I put it, to 'chameleonise' his masculinity.

In this final chapter, I draw together the central arguments of the book and provide some implications for policy and the field of study. First, I reiterate the argument that there are diverse ways to be a young man within a working-class community. Second, I suggest that masculinities must always be understood in time and place and that while new times demand new ways of being, not all young men find transition easy. Third, I advocate that the ability to hold together the contradictions of multiple performances rests upon some complex familial, social, cultural and historic dynamics. Finally, I suggest that being a young 'man' cannot be read off entirely from educational pursuits as it might have been from previous industrial employment practices.

2
The Valleys: History, Modernity and Masculinities

Introduction

In this chapter, I focus on the town of Cwm Dyffryn and the surrounding area to enable what follows in subsequent chapters to be considered in the economic, social and political context of this formerly industrial place. Most, if not all, of the young men featured in this study (and their parents and grandparents) were born and brought up in this one locale, although as will become clear, their lives were far from restricted to this specific place. As the young men were able to move between spaces, this study moved with them and I followed them to different educational institutions around the locale and to the different towns and cities in South Wales. However, Cwm Dyffryn was their main base and was therefore the main location for the study. Since industrial change and the performance of masculinity is central to the book, and as few people reading this will have visited places like Cwm Dyffryn[1] or be aware of the history of the area beyond generalizations or stereotypical imagery,[2] I offer this chapter as a way of letting the reader 'place' the narratives and descriptions of my participants into a given, yet still constructed, context.

This chapter begins with a brief historical account of the development of the South Wales Valleys before moving on to focus on Cwm Dyffryn in the post-millennium era. I then look at the consequences of the collapse of the coal mining industry in the area and the impact that the economic, social and cultural changes have had on notions of masculinity. The impact of place on masculinity making, is also discussed.

A brief history of the South Wales Valleys

Industrial heritage

The Valleys area of South Wales is a region measuring around 150 miles stretching from the coastal city of Swansea in the west to the town of Newport in the east. The communities of the South Wales Valleys are often presented as classic working-class communities forged out of heavy industry in the late 19th century (Smith, 1984; Adamson and Jones, 1996; Day, 2002). Similar to other regions across Britain that developed due to the expansion of the iron, steel and coal mining industries, the Valleys have traditionally demonstrated a specific composition of economic, political, social and cultural characteristics. These were produced through the development, growth and slow decline of what were once vital areas of the British economy.

Up until the beginning of the 18th century, agriculture was the principal occupation of the county of Glamorgan and the population was constrained to a collection of small hill farms. The Welsh language was the majority language spoken (Grant, 1991) and did not alter until the influx of immigrants as the century progressed. The development of the iron works in Merthyr Tydfil, for example, saw it develop into one of the largest towns in Britain during the industrial revolution and its population rose from 7,700 in 1801 to 49,794 by 1861 (Rees and Stroud, 2004). As the world economy expanded, the demand for steel grew with it, leading to a vast amount of coal being required. Having once just been an adjunct to the iron industry, the South Wales Valleys soon became a rich source for the 'black gold'. According to Day (2002: 30), an 'unspoilt rural landscape became densely inhabited and totally polluted'. This led to a massive population increase in South Wales, drawing first from the agricultural areas of the country and then from the border counties of England and other regions of Cornwall, the North and the Forest of Dean. Migrants from Ireland, Italy and parts of Eastern Europe also moved into the area to work (Jones, 1999; Williams, et al., 2003). Day (2002: 31) likens the growth of the area to the 'frontier towns of the wild west' with many similarities to the gold rush of 1849 in California with primitive working conditions and cramped hurriedly built communities. In the Rhondda Valley,[3] the arrival of immigrants altered the population so drastically that the number of inhabitants increased from 545 in 1801 to 113,735 in 1901 (John and Williams, 1980: 342). As Smith (1984: 23) put it, these radical, social and economic conditions changed the nation and 'an industrial people' emerged.

By the beginning of the 20th century, the coal industry of the region had become not only a major component of the British economy but also of global markets (Smith, 1984; Williams, 1985; Rees and Stroud, 2004). The peak of production came during the First World War when the South Wales coalfield employed up to a quarter of a million men and produced nearly 57 million tons of coal a year one-third of the world's coal exports (see Arnot, 1975; Egan, 1987; Cynon Valley History Society, 2001).

By 1914, coal from the region was being used by the world's major navies and merchant shipping companies and the area played a vital role in the war. However, even though employment levels were high, working conditions remained poor and pay was low. Strikes were common and tensions existed between mine owners and their workers with the government eventually taking control of the South Wales coal industry towards the end of the war (Cynon Valley History Society, 2001). This was a turning point for the South Wales coal industry. Despite an increase in workers, investment by mine owners in the industry was low and working conditions continued to deteriorate. The South Wales Miners Federation was formed to demand reduced working hours, increased wages and the nationalization of the industry and was highly influential during the General Strike of 1926 (Arnot, 1975; Francis and Smith, 1998; Cynon Valley History Society, 2001). However, as the 1920s progressed and the collieries of Western Europe recovered from war, foreign markets declined, unemployment rose and production fell so that by 1929 coal production in the area had drastically decreased from almost a third to only 3% of world output (Morgan, 1981; Egan, 1987; CIHS, 1997). The problems of 1920s were compounded by the collapse of the world economy in the 1930s, and the depression that followed greatly affected the area. The risks of economic dependence on a single industry were highlighted with unemployment reaching a peak of 140,000 in 1931 (CWM, 2002).

There was a brief revival to the industry during the Second World War, with an increase in production, and the nationalization of the industry in 1947 brought better wages and working conditions for miners. However, the slow decline continued and around 90 collieries closed during the 1940s and 1950s. These closures continued into the 1960s with another 75 collieries being shut down under wider UK industrial restructuring (CWM, 2002; Rees and Stroud, 2004). Despite these closures, Rees and Stroud (2004: 6) show that by the beginning of the 1970s there were still 'over 50 collieries employing some forty thousand men'.

By the late 1970s, the closure of these industries began to affect great swathes of the nation. The UK general election of 1979 and the victory of the Conservative Party was to be a major turning point in the social and economic history of the Valleys communities (Jones, 1999). Industrial subsidies were cut and substantial job losses were incurred. By the beginning of the 1980s, there were still around 35 collieries remaining with a workforce of around 25,000, but after the 1984–1985 miners' strike, the remaining collieries were shut down and, by the early 1990s, only one deep mine remained in South Wales[4] (Cynon Valley History Society, 2001; CWM, 2002). Jones (1999: 14) argues that between 1980 and 1985, 60,000–120,000 people became unemployed in South Wales and as a result a generation 'were consigned to the dole and the social consequences in many parts of Wales were profoundly destructive as unemployment led inevitably to poverty and all its associated evils'.

In recent times, this total has diminished further with only 7,000 jobs left in mining in Wales by 2005 (BBC Online, 2005). With the closure of Tower Colliery (the last deep mine in South Wales) in January 2008 (BBC Online, 2008), only a handful of smaller drift mines or open cast mines, remain employing far fewer than the 7,000 in 2005. Given the speed of the closures, the results were profoundly traumatic for those working in the industry at the time and for those who relied on it for other employment opportunities in the wider communities.

Cultural heritage

The development of the South Wales coalfield had an impact far beyond the industrialization of a region (Smith, 1984; Baldwin, 1986). As the population increased, distinct forms of terraced housing were built at precarious angles on the mountainsides for colliers and their families. Social institutions grew with them, and by the start of the First World War, chapels, trade unions, working-men's clubs and pubs, musical halls and theatres had come to be an integral part of the many small communities. The vibrant social scene in the Valleys during the 1920s and 1930s drew the stars of screen and stage to perform at theatres and music halls in the area. Paul Robeson, the black American civil rights activist and soul singer, appeared in concerts and films to support the miners, and others, such as the actress and comedienne Gracie Fields, regularly performed across the region (Baldwin and Rogers, 1994; Cameron, 2002). The Queen and other members of the royal family also visited the area to attend social events such as the Welsh eisteddfods and to open a collection of pithead baths. These were introduced after campaigns by miners' wives to ensure that all collieries provided miners with a place to wash, thus alleviating the pains of using tin baths in front of open coal fires when they returned from work (Baldwin, 1986; Cameron, 2002). There was also a large sporting scene with some professional football sides playing in the English leagues, many amateur Rugby Union teams and a prolific number of professional boxing champions (Davies and Jenkins, 2008). Education and health care provision (often funded through voluntary contributions from miners pay) also improved during the early part of the 20th century and a vibrant social and cultural environment developed. These relationships were important in shaping a collective working-class identity and were integral to the development of the South Wales coalfield. Francis and Smith (1998) suggest that the nationalization in 1947 of the coal industry was the climax of this collective solidarity.

Despite the growth of a collective identity, to describe the 'Valleys' as a homogeneous community today is rather misleading. First, the towns and villages that developed during the 19th century began as small isolated communities spread out over the valley floors and across the mountainsides. Due to the influx of people and developing infrastructure, only then did they become geographically connected to each other. In general, links between communities within each valley were strong, and remain so today, with ties through local newspapers and social institutions, such as school programmes, sporting events and other local organizations (see Baldwin, 1986; Baldwin and Rogers, 1994; Cameron, 2002). However, due to the geographical dimensions of the region, links between individual valleys have always been less strong, and although distances between towns in the wider area can seem small when viewed on a map, the infrastructure of the region has changed little. Over the past 20 years there have been major improvements in the road and railway networks surrounding the area, but the shortest route is still often up and over individual mountains on small, sometimes impassable, roads.

Second, there is great economic, health and educational diversity within the region. The recently defined Heads of the Valleys (WAG, 2006b) area for example (which is made up of constituencies from the Rhondda Valley, Cynon Valley, Merthyr Tydfil and Blaenau Gwent) consists of some of the poorest communities in Europe, which are in receipt of EU Objective 1 funding (WEFO, 2012). Those living in the lower boroughs nearer the M4 corridor are more likely to have better access to employment, healthcare and educational opportunities (Fevre and Thompson, 1999; Day, 2002; UCU, 2009).

Third, over the past century 'official' local authority recognition of towns and villages has altered (Smith, 1999), and as numerous districts, county councils and constituencies criss-cross the region, differing in population size and geographical scale, one 'catch all' definition seems problematic. Given these complexities, it is important to recognize that while the Valleys themselves may be seen as something of an 'imagined community' (Anderson, 1983), they do provide 'the contours of identity' (Fevre, 1999: 111) through a shared historical consciousness and as a site of public representation (Dicks, 2004). Despite these difficulties, I use the term 'Valleys' as a convenient way of referring to the area as a whole and as a way of anchoring lived experience to a given geographical place. Having described the historical background of the locale, I now concentrate on the main town where this study was conducted, before turning to the implications of these developments on masculinity, young people and education within the region.

Cwm Dyffryn in the post-millennium era

The population of Cwm Dyffryn stands at around 40,000 and the town is part of a larger local authority area of Rhondda Cynon Taf (RCT), which brings together the districts of the Rhondda Valley, the Cynon Valley and the Taf Vale region.[5] RCT is ranked high out of the 24 local authorities in Wales for rates of child poverty and for overall deprivation (Welsh Government, 2014). In 2010, 19.8% of people of working age were claiming benefits, compared to 15.4% for Wales and 12.2% for Great Britain (ONS, 2012). Unemployment in the region is high, and in 2014 this was especially so with younger people, as 9.6% of those aged between 16 and 24 were recorded as claiming Job Seekers Allowance and 21% classified at NEET – Not in Employment, Education or Training (RCT, 2014). For those who are in employment, workplace-based earnings are low, with those in full-time occupations averaging around £447 per week, which is lower than that of both Wales (£460) and Great Britain (£503) more widely (ONS, 2012). It should of course be remembered that these averages are based on full-time work, not part-time or flexible contracts, which make up a lot of the opportunities in these communities, so real wages are much lower. As we can see, labour market conditions in RCT are therefore fragile, with lower numbers of people in employment than the national rates. The recent recession has thus affected these indicators disproportionately.

In 2009, there were 5,125 businesses based in RCT, 89% of these employed fewer than 20 people, highlighting the importance of smaller companies to the area's economy (RCT, 2012). The service sector is by far the biggest employer with the largest number of businesses. As only around 10% of workers within RCT are in professional or managerial roles, compared with 14.5% of workers throughout Wales and Great Britain (RCT, 2006), the region is still predominantly working-class. The working-class nature of this former industrial community is further illustrated through qualification levels. In 2011, 16.6% of all adults aged between 16 and 64 were recorded as having no recognized qualifications, compared to 11% in the UK more widely (ONS, 2012). There are also a high numbers of children on free school meals (FSM) in the area with 27% of nursery and primary school pupils and 22% of secondary school pupils in receipt of them. By comparison, in neighbouring England, 15.9% of children in nursery and primary schools and 13.4% in secondary schools receive FSM. At the beginning of their school careers children in Wales are similar to others in the UK in terms of attainment levels, but as they get older a gap develops (Gorard et al., 2004). This continues with only 22.5% of people holding a NVQ level 4 (HND, degree or higher degree) qualification when compared to 31.3% of the UK (ONS, 2012) or 42.5% of those in Cardiff (UCU, 2009). Gorard et al. (2004: 142) suggest that these low scores are interlinked and that what these relationships identify is 'an underlying pattern of cause, termed variously "deprivation", "exclusion" and "disengagement"' with the latest of these being the 'poverty of aspiration' discourse (see Roberts and Atherton, 2011).

Cwm Dyffryn and the South Wales Valleys more broadly are examples of localities strongly rooted in the modern industrial era, which are experiencing difficulties in transforming economically, socially and culturally to cope with a de-industrial society. The economic, social and cultural conditions described above have also had a significant impact on how masculinity has been shaped and re-shaped within this environment.

Industrial masculinities in the South Wales Valleys

As discussed above, from the early 19th century, Cwm Dyffryn and the surrounding area relied almost entirely on coalmining as a form of employment (see Arnot, 1975; Smith, 1999). Although, as I have shown, periods of hardship, recession and unemployment occurred – especially between the two world wars – working-class men could usually find work somewhere within the South Wales coalfield or move to work in other coal mining areas within the UK. From 1843, when the Mine Regulation Act (which excluded women and children under the age of ten from working underground) was introduced, mining was an exclusively male occupation (Humphries, 1981; Cynon Valley History Society, 2001). Working hours were long, with 12-hour days common until the Coal Miners Regulation Act (also known as the Eight Hours Act[6]) in 1908 and then the Coal Mines Act (Seven Hours Act[7]) in 1919 reduced the hours that could be worked underground. As miners tended to work piecemeal, being paid for the amount of coal they produced, these Acts resulted in a reduction of wages and increased the pressure on miners to produce the same amount of coal in a shorter space of time. Much of the work was considered highly skilled with some trades receiving higher wages than others.

> To say that the job of a miner is unpleasant and dangerous is a statement against which few would seek to argue, except perhaps to say it is not as bad as it was in years gone by. The dangers affecting the miner at his workplace deep in the earth included the emission of gas from the coal, leading to explosions or suffocation, explosions of coal dust, inundations, accidental fires, injuries caused by machinery and haulage, the inhalation of dust and falls of roof... sometimes the pressure of gas would be so high as to burst out from the strata when it would be termed a blower.
> (Cynon Valley History Society, 2001: 147)

These conditions demanded (and helped produce) a specific form of industrial embodied masculinity based on considerable strength, stamina and skill. Men earned respect for working arduously and 'doing a hard job well and being known for it' (Willis, 1977: 52).

Winlow (2001: 36) suggests that 'young boys were keen to enter the world of work as soon as possible to establish their masculinity'. This rite of passage from the family home to the world of tough, physical labour would serve to separate the real 'men from the boys' (Winlow, 2001: 36). This process of distancing one's self from the weakness of childhood to gain the sense of belonging to a collective group of working adult men enabled young men to gain a confidence in their masculinity which was then proved through physical and dangerous work. It also enabled a positive male image through a certain sense of worth and accomplishment about their labour. Walkerdine and Jimenez (2012) further argue that physical forms of employment, such as coal mining or steel production, demanded this kind of masculinity in South Wales, which was then invested in, celebrated and reified as a way of coping with a dangerous and hard job, but it also enabled the communities these men lived in to survive. The importance of work then to the development of masculinity within the region cannot be over emphasized, and I would argue that such work demanded a tough, stoic 'masculinity'. The ability to provide for a family and remain in employment was also seen as integral to working-class men's responsibility and respectability (see Willis, 1977, 1979; Humphries, 1981; Rutherford, 1988). Periods of unemployment created depression and anxiety, and the failure to work meant the removal of one's identity (Lush, 1941; Morgan, 1992). In this context, men would have found it difficult to neglect the social, cultural and economic pressure to provide for their families by taking on the role of breadwinner. Kimmel (1996: 265) writing of the US, notes that this pressure to be a successful breadwinner was 'a source of strain and conflict not pride and motivation'.

The coalfield was also an environment in which intense male friendships were formed and one's sense of self developed. As Kimmel (1996: 7) notes, 'in large parts, it is other men who are important to men... men define their masculinity not as much in relation to women, but in relation to each other'. Nonetheless to develop their masculinity, they also demanded certain qualities and labour from women (e.g. having babies, staying home to cook and clean) which created gendered spatialities and societies. Whereas middle-class men can exert institutional power, Kimmel (1996) argues that their working-class counterparts utilize different forms of power through acts of aggression, fighting and playing contact sports. This is further accompanied by drinking large amounts of alcohol, machismo practices and displays of sexual competence acting as signifiers of a collective bravado (Willis, 1977; Corrigan, 1979; Collinson, 1988; Canaan, 1996; McDowell, 1997). Collinson (1992) and Collinson and Hearn (1996) further suggest that subcultural workplace processes also aid the reproduction of a specific form of working-class masculinity. Interaction at work resulted in masculinity being performed not just through the physical act of labour, but through a whole range of signs and signifiers, through in-jokes; coarse, often sexist language; the 'piss take' of one another; having a laugh; homophobic banter/jokes and the exclusion of the feminine.

Likewise, the workplace and the camaraderie underground (in the mines) took on an enormously important part in the construction of masculinity in the Valleys. But work itself was also influential in the construction of masculinities and shaping social relationships beyond the workplace. As Day (2002) suggests, because coal mining was among a selective band of extreme occupations that were so omnipresent in their impact, entire forms of life appeared to be dominated by them. Day goes on to argue that localism was therefore a key part of the mining community identity, where all those living there would shop, work, reside and marry in close proximity (see Sewell, 1975; Town, 1978). Weeks (2007) writes in detail about the omnipresent stifling environment of the Valleys and the impact on those who lived there. Reflecting on the area of the Valleys where he grew up, Weeks states that 'as the mainstay of its economy declined, [the Rhondda] built for itself a conservative, defensive culture; conservative in terms of its gender, family and sexual values' (Weeks, 2007: 33). For those who did not conform to and/or deviated from normal expectations of manhood, by rejecting physical labour, sports and hard drinking, 'a mocking sissyhood remained the only fate' (Weeks, 2007: 30).

As the traditional 'masculine' infrastructure in the area has declined, heavy industry has, in part, been replaced by an expanding service sector economy. Women now make up over half the labour force (ONS, 2012) in a region that was once associated with a physically hard, tough, and dangerous heavy industry.[8] In a de-industrial world workers are required to be mobile, flexible, with high levels of technical skill and large amounts of cultural and economic capital to thrive in a global market (Beck, 1999). Clinging to traditions of work, social class and locality are seen as a hindrance (McDowell, 2002, 2003). With the closure of the coalmines, ex-miners found they could not adapt as easily to new forms of labour. This 'feminization' of the labour market, as Massey (1995: 203) conceptualizes it, made Welsh ex-miners feel that they could not 'be expected to turn their attention to making marshmallows or underwear'. The uniqueness and the status of the masculine nature of work that the geographical dimensions of the locality created have not been equalled by the growth of newer service sector industries, part-time work or fixed-term contracts. Given these transforms, one of the key questions to ask is how are working-class young men adapting to these changes in insecure times?

Young masculinities 'at risk' in the South Wales Valleys in the post-millennium era

In this context of global restructuring, new ways of living-out working-class lives are formed inescapably around masculinity (Weis, 2004). Men establish new forms of working-class lives alongside the emergence of new gender patterns (Delamont, 2000; Walkerdine and Jimenez, 2012). Nonetheless, as Adkins (1999, 2002) and as Kenway and Kraack (2004) have noted, many of these processes actually re-traditionalize gender patterns instead of transforming them. In a study of marginalized masculinities in Australian communities that had once been built around mining, fishing or farming, Kenway et al. (2006) suggest that many young men find it difficult to 'unlearn' attitudes associated with manual employment and local forms of hegemonic working-class masculinity (Connell and Messerschmidt, 2005). While those working-class young men who successfully invest in mental labour may escape traditional patterns of masculinity, this does not mean that future life chances will automatically follow (Ball et al., 2000; Breen and Jonsson, 2005; Platt, 2007).

In these de-industrialized times, groups of working-class young people have striven to reinvent themselves through educational achievement, be it through traditional academic courses, vocational courses or new forms of work connected to the development of new technology and the media (Arnot, 2004; Ingram, 2009). Yet the former traditions of work and identity are still deeply connected to the communities of the South Wales Valleys. As Green and White (2007) highlight, it is important to recognize that these young men's attitudes towards education, training and work opportunities are also formed through their wider social networks and attachment to place. What is evident is that there are competing dichotomies occurring in the Valleys with the emphasis from educational policy on developing educational skills, versus the historical legacy of the locale where the body is valued over the mind. The situation has also been exacerbated as I showed in the previous chapter through a media and political discourse in Britain that has seen young men, especially young white working-class men, as problematic and deemed them in 'crisis' or at 'risk'.

A large number of scholars have highlighted how schools are located within wider processes of class, sexuality and race in the formation of identities since the 1960s (Jackson and Marsden, 1962; Willis, 1977; Brown, 1987; Connell, 1989; Mac an Ghaill, 1994; Sewell, 1997; Skeggs, 2004; Pascoe, 2007). A common strategy for presenting young men's subject positions within these studies has been through the use of friendship groups. In Kessler et al.'s (1985) study there was the 'bloods' and the 'cyrils'; Walker (1988) had the 'footballers', the 'competitors', the 'Greeks', the 'three friends' and the 'handballers'. Connell (1989) had the 'cool guys', 'swots' and 'wimps'; Parker (1996b) the 'hard boys', 'conformists' and 'victims'; Edley and Wetherell (1996) the 'hard lads' and the 'opposition group'; Warren (1997) the 'princes of the park' and the 'working-class kings'; Martino (1999) the 'cool guys', 'party animals', 'squids' and 'poofters'; Dalley-Trim (2007) the 'bad lads' and the 'roguish lads and larrikins'. Hollingworth and Williams (2009) also clearly highlight how different youth groups are defined by students themselves and in relation to each other as 'hippies', 'poshies', 'goths', 'emos', 'skaters', 'jitters', 'rockers', 'gangsters', 'townies' and 'chavers'.

Some writers, such as Francis (2000) and Swain (2006), have suggested that whilst friendship groups may correctly demonstrate that multiple versions of masculinity may exist in a singular setting, they often appear too static, simplistic and limit the portrayal of the multifaceted nature of 'real life' and have a tendency to produce typologies. The use of strict friendship groups also fail to show the ability of young men to move between groups or to change groups altogether as they grow older.

Whilst I recognize these difficulties, the chapters in this book presenting the young lives studied take the friendship group as a starting point for a number of reasons. First, I argue that while young men perform multiple performances of self and can move in and out of friendship groups, many of these performances still occur as Goffman (1959) put it within 'teams' of individuals, so it is important to recognize the power of the friendship group. Second, the friendship group enables the front and back performances of masculinity within these 'teams' to be examined. Third, I suggest that this tactic also enables comparisons with other studies and acts as a cross-referencing point throughout the field of masculinities research. Nonetheless, as I spent more time with the young men both inside and outside the school, I also came to recognize the difficulties with this approach. In acknowledgment of this, in Chapter 7, I highlight some of the problems and complexities that some young men, who did not fit easily into straightforward categories, encountered when trying to move beyond and between groups.

Nonetheless what is still missing in much of this work is how home life, individual neighbourhoods, regions and nations shape the performance of young men's masculine identity and the way they view education and schooling. Place and space is therefore important in gaining a deeper understanding of not only the performance of young masculinities in schools and why some embrace education and others do not, but, more importantly, about the particular influences on these performances. Massey (1984) gives a clear definition of the social and the spatial on which I draw to provide a more place-specific analysis of young masculinities. Massey (1984: 5) suggests that:

> [The] term space includes a whole range of aspects of the social world. It includes distance, and differences in measurement connotations and appreciation of distance. It includes movement... geographical

differentiation, the notion of place and specificity and of differences between places.

Massey (1994, 1995) has argued that because places can be conceptualized as social spaces bringing together different forms of social interaction, place should also be seen as a process which is experienced in different ways by different people. This then also leads to differences within as well as between genders. Despite Massey's insights, Urry (2000) has argued that sociology as a discipline has traditionally failed to look at the geographical intersections of regions and place alongside class, gender and ethnicity, and instead focused on occupation, income, education and social mobility. It was the work of Jackson (1991, 1994), in the early 1990s, that marked the start of a geographical interest in the social and cultural construction of masculinity and questioned aspatial accounts of men's lives. Interdisciplinary studies began linking the notion of place and space to employment (Massey, 1995; McDowell, 1997), and further work across a range of studies explored the complex relationship between masculinities in different spaces. For example, Bell (2000) explored the different gay cultures outside urban areas in the UK and Brandth and Hauggen (2000) analysed changing masculinities in forested areas of Norway. However, it was not until a few years later that a sustained analysis (using Connell's concept of multiple masculinities) began to be applied within the field of social geography (Berg and Longhurst, 2003). A collection of papers by van Hoven and Horschelmann (2005) called *Spaces of Masculinity* was a key text in this developing body of work on the impact of spaces and places in the formation of male identities. This literature explored the changes to gender identities and relationships to specific places and spaces and the place/space variations in the construction and reconstruction of masculine identities. This work, as Massey (1994: 178) put it, states why 'what it means to be masculine in the Fens is not the same as what it means in Lancashire'.

Kenway et al. (2006) support this body of work further with an in-depth study of masculinities in de-industrialized areas of Australia which used to have large mining, fishing, and logging industries. They investigate how the different spatial regions of these locales impacted on formation of a masculine self and argue that place and space exists in a mutually beneficial relationship. Drawing on the work of Latour (1987), Nespor (2000: 40) suggests that 'topologies of masculinity' exist and that different kinds of spaces can produce different interspatial modes of masculinity. He terms these 'bounded clusters' which are associated with hegemonic forms of masculinity, 'leaky spaces' with ambiguous masculinities and 'distributed networks' which transport ideas of masculinity across the globe through the different forms of media. Masculinity then becomes a network, rather than a form of embodiment.

In keeping with this literature, I suggest that young working-class masculinities are not just shaped by place, but masculine identities shape and influence the specific character of places themselves. In a direct link between the interactionist tradition and spatial theorizing, Lefebvre ([1974] 2001: 162) suggests that it is 'by means of the body that space is perceived, lived and produced'. The identity of place comes not simply from its historical developments but also from the day-to-day reality and specificity of its 'interaction with the outside' (Massey, 1994: 169). Place therefore is both a heuristic device for positioning oneself and others, and also, as Scourfield et al. (2006: 15) argue, a 'social construct arising out of our interactions'. Therefore, there are multiple ways of experiencing the same place.

Scourfield and Drakeford (1999), in a rare paper to focus on masculinities in Wales, argue that to understand Wales, there is a need to understand its inhabitants, both those with and without power. They argue that, by analysing Welsh men, it is possible to critically explore the 'social process of the construction, production and reproduction of masculinities' (Scourfield and Drakeford, 1999: 4) within the nation. However, given the diversity of the country, in terms of those who speak the Welsh language, social class dynamics and the north/south/urban/rural divide, I suggest that Welsh men must be analysed within separate historical and geographical contexts and within the social construction of gender within a specific area of Wales (Mannay, 2014). This then enables 'the messiness of layered subjectivities and multi-dimensional relations in particular localities' (Hopkins and Noble, 2009: 815) to come through.

Hopkins and Noble (2009) have pointed out that it is only in the situated, empirically grounded analysis of actual men in actual places, that we can understand power relationships and masculinities better. It is here that masculinities can really be understood as performances played out through specific practices and processes (West and Zimmerman, 1987; Schrock and Schwalbe, 2009). It is place, then, that shapes the character of institutions like schools, colleges and the identities that are performed within them. Masculinities can therefore been seen as socially and culturally constructed, but also through social interactions that change between spaces and over time. I suggest that there needs to be a greater understanding of place and context when conducting studies with young men. It is not enough to recognize that gender intersects with other forms of identity, such as class and ethnicity, but also that there exists a range of dimensions of masculinity within these wider identities. What then are the broader social and spatial networks within a community (e.g. family, sports, nightlife, fast cars, music, sex) that influence the identities of these young men and how does space and place impact upon who they can be and become?

Ethnography: Getting to know a culture

Ethnography played a vital role in early UK, US and Australian studies that sought to explore young male subcultural identity in schools (Hargreaves, 1967; Lacey, 1970; Cusick, 1973; Everhart, 1977; Willis, 1977; Bullivant, 1978; Larkin, 1979; Ball, 1981). More recently ethnography has also been utilized in a range of critical masculinity studies exploring the lives of young men both within and increasingly beyond educational institutions (see, for example, Connell, 1989; Mac an Ghaill, 1994; Haywood and Mac an Ghaill, 1996; Martino, 1999; Swain, 2000; Messner, 2001; Winlow, 2001; Nayak, 2003a; Renold, 2004; Kenway et al., 2006; Pascoe, 2007; Anderson, 2009). Indeed, Connell (2000) has suggested that it is one of two core research methods (the other being life history interviews) specifically used to explore the social construction of masculinities and examine how subjective experience is affected by class, ethnicity, sexuality, cultural locations and within specific times and places. The 'ethnographic moment', as Connell (2000: 9) puts it, from the 1980s to the turn of the millennium, helped bring attention to how multiple versions of masculinity exist. This 'moment' also provided a way of exploring different aspects of the same life in much more complex and nuanced ways than might be possible through other forms of social science research.

Although there are various criticisms of specific elements of ethnographic research, such as ethical concerns, issues of objectivity, 'representative' samples and the dangers of 'going native' (see Appendix 1 for full details of the research process), the method can break down a number of research conventions. For example, Nayak (2003a: 30) suggests that ethnography can 'implode established dichotomies between structure/agency, public/private, theory/practice, talk/action, fact/fiction and even researcher/researched'. Also, unlike interview-based studies, where participants only offer glimpses into their often complex lives retold to an interviewer, I participated in many of the same activities as my respondents. Aside from experiencing the conditions of others, Goffman (1989: 125) suggests that ethnography is also a way of 'subjecting yourself, your body and your own personality and your own social situation, to the set of contingencies that play upon a set of individuals so that you can physically and ecologically penetrate their circle'. My interpretations and understandings were therefore formed through personal knowledge and deep relationships with the young men, and this account is as much about my journey, as theirs.

The multilayered dimensions of ethnography means it remains an invaluable research tool through which to highlight sociological concepts and provide empirical examples of how young lives are lived at the margins of society. Within spatial accounts of young men's lives, ethnography is also a useful method to highlight the lived experience of place. By bringing together geographical theories of space and place with ethnographic traditions a more nuanced picture can be gained. The methodology allows for a more intensive analysis and for fine-grained detail to emerge by providing a connection between the social and geographical world people inhabit.

Conclusion: Rethinking young masculinities, class, place and identity

The South Wales Valleys constitute a geographically, economically and culturally distinct region, historically associated with an intensive extractive and manufacturing history through 200 years of coal mining and iron and steel production (Smith, 1984; Day, 2002; Hall et al., 2009). However, the economy has changed and Britain's landscape has altered. There is no longer an industrial nation or an industrial people in Wales (Smith, 1999); de-industrialization has left places like the South Wales Valleys with severe economic and material problems. Its heavy industrial past is now only visible through heritage museums (Dicks, 2004). Economic transformations which are still being felt in the advanced industrial West have undoubtedly altered gender relations. Some authors have observed this as a positive move that has assisted in the decline of patriarchy (MacInnes and Perez, 2009), whilst others would argue that rather than declining, patriarchy has taken on new forms and increased on a global scale (Connell, 2009).

It is clear that research around masculine identity in recent years has gone beyond the essentialist ideas of masculine identity. A critical relational approach to analysing the multiple versions of masculinity has begun to be developed, a move which Berg and Longhurst (2003) have suggested is long overdue. In building upon this literature, this book weaves together insights into place and space with an interactionist perspective. In keeping with others who have sought to rehabilitate interactionism (Jackson and Scott, 2010), I return to an interactionist analysis of gender and therefore masculinities, as I believe that this can provide a better understanding of what young working-class men do, both individually and as a group in a specific locale. This will enable the practices and processes at the local level to come through more succinctly.

Drawing on the work of Goffman, I explore within a specific research context, how place and space mediates front and back performances of young working-class men's masculinity. How do young men deploy and negotiate multiple performances of self within a de-industrialized space? Are front performances of masculinity always displayed through dominant, aggressive, macho behaviours similar to those noted by Connell and others? Are there alternative front performances that come closer to Anderson's more 'inclusive' masculinity? Does the back-stage offer respite from maintaining the front-stage? Can the back-stage be an area where the impregnable dominant expectations of a masculine self –such as the ability to be seen as strong, aggressive, sexually promiscuous, competitive and emotionally distant – be resisted and challenged (see Walker and Kushner, 1997; Reay, 2002; Fisher, 2009 for notable examples)? Or, can the back-stage also be a place for shared private communication between individuals where the front of the performance is fostered and refined?

The presentation of self, and therefore a masculine self, comes through the ways an individual male is viewed by others during different interactions, behaviours and appearances. It is not psychological or biological, but conveyed by signs, face-to-face and virtual interaction. Masculinities can be multiple, contested, changeable and variable within wider gendered spaces. This, then, make the processes and spaces of identity productions important in the construction of young working-class masculinities and the ways of understanding them in relation to life chances. These are some of the issues I take up in the forthcoming chapters by looking within and beyond educational contexts.

It is also important here to offer a brief explanation (and clarify for the reader) regarding one key decision before moving on. Throughout this book, I refer to my participants as both young men and boys interchangeably for two reasons. First, it reflects the ambiguities and the complexities within the masculinities literature during the teenage years (see Frosh et al., 2002 for a wider discussion); second, and more importantly, because in many South Wales communities men present themselves (and are presented by others) in an eternally youthful way, being commonly referred to as 'boys' when they are very much men (Holland and Scourfield, 1998); for example, the phrase 'going out with the boys' is often used well into old age when referring to socializing with male friends.

3
The Valley Boiz: Re-Traditionalizing Masculinity

Introduction

In the opening chapters of this book, I outlined how the South Wales Valleys were once major contributors to the British coal industry, but due to economic restructuring in the 1980s, there has been a drastic transformation in the relationship between employment and masculinity. Men once earned respect for working arduously, and these roles were often seen as heroic, with punishing physical labour that involved different degrees of manual skill and bodily toughness, creating a strong, stoic masculinity. Male camaraderie, which was established through physicality and close working conditions underground or at steel furnaces, also developed through joking around, storytelling, sexist language and banter at the work site. One's life often depended on friendships in these dangerous industries. These relationships were further supported through organizations such as miners' institutes, trade unions, chapels, pubs, working men's clubs and sports. Rugby Union in particular (and to a lesser extent boxing and football) still maintains a powerful positions in the culture of the locale and the Welsh nation as a whole, influencing those who play it, those who watch it, those who reject it and those who are deemed unfit for it (Holland and Scourfield, 1998; Howe, 2001; Harris, 2007). A strong division of labour accompanied these communities, and the ability to maintain a distance from anything 'feminine' was essential for a strong masculinity that would enable the communities to survive (Walkerdine, 2010). Yet despite the changes that have taken place over the past quarter century, the attitudes to work and identity are still intrinsically connected to the area.

In this chapter, I concentrate on a group of young men who performed a specific variety of white working-class masculinity influenced by the industrial heritage of the region. Considering the total absence of opportunities for young men to now enter industrial labour, which would have originally produced a form of stoic working-class masculinity, I explore how the legacy of the past and the cultural milieu of the locale, were re-traditionalized through other acts across different educational and leisure spaces. These acts included studying BTEC or vocational school-based qualifications, alongside sporting interests notably Rugby Union and football, which served to marginalize other ways of 'doing boy' in the area. These sporting interests were accompanied by practices such as drinking large amounts of alcohol, going out in search of young women for sexual conquests ('on the pull') and engaging in 'risky' leisure pursuits, including fighting, driving cars very fast and experimenting with recreational drugs. Nonetheless, while these practices enabled The Valley Boiz to display an archetypal masculinity through re-traditionalizing practices, it also became clear over time that they operated and illustrated just one region of these boys' performances of masculinity. I argue that, on occasions, this archetypal masculinity could be replaced by a less 'hyper' (Beynon, 2002) performance of masculinity characterized by different attributes such as sensitivity, caring and rejecting machismo.

In the first two sections, I look at the front region of these performances in more detail. I begin by introducing the friendship group or, in Goffman's (1959) terms, 'the team', before moving on to examine the school site and the subjects that The Valley Boiz studied. I then turn to their lives beyond the school gates looking at some of the social and leisure activities they participated in. These descriptions of social spaces also set the scene for the other young men who use them throughout the book. In the final section of the chapter, I then switch to the backstage of these performances, which provide some interesting contradictions to the front displays and allows for a deeper insight into their lives to emerge and a more complex understanding of their performance of masculinity.

Family biographies and industrial heritage

The Valley Boiz were a group of about a dozen white, working-class, young men who were all born and brought up in Cwm Dyffryn. Their behaviours and attitudes to education were similar to those documented in other ethnographic studies of working-class young men both in the UK and USA of a similar age since the end of the 1970s (for example, see Willis' (1977) 'Lads', Mac an Ghaill's (1994) 'Macho Lads', MacLeod's

(1995) 'Hallway Hangers' and Nayak's (2003b) 'Real Geordies'). However, there were a number of differences between these young men and The Valley Boiz. First, The Valley Boiz persevered with the profoundly contradictory process of 'staying on' in education post-16 (which clashed with the traditions of the community and their general anti-school behaviour) due to the limited employment options available to them in the locale. Second, returning to school not only enabled the group to delay uncertain futures for a further year or two, but it was also a safe and familiar space for them. Third, it was a way to collect a small amount of money in the form of the Educational Maintenance Allowance (EMA).[1] Depending on the household income (less than £23,000 per annum) up to £30 per week could be gained as an incentive to stay in education post-16. Finally, for a minority it was also seen as a viable route to getting into a local university.

The table below introduces these young men and highlights their post-16 educational and future trajectories, family backgrounds and leisure interests (Table 3.1).

Although The Valley Boiz were a large friendship group, other young men who were loosely affiliated joined them for nights out in the town, drinking or driving around in their cars as they grew older. Table 3.1 illustrates the core members of the group, which comprised of Dai, Birdy, Jonesy, Shaggy, Clive, Hughesy, Davies, Brad, Cresco, Tomo and Bunk.[2] The group dynamics were quite fluid, and others such as Jimmy, Frankie, Bakers and Ian (whose lives we will come across in future chapters) also joined the group on occasion. As the young men progressed through the sixth form, their friendships changed and some broke up due to arguments, fights, developing deeper relationships with girlfriends or moving to different educational institutions or the armed forces. Shenkin, for example, who was originally interviewed with the others in Year 11, joined the British army after his GCSE exams and subsequently left the group (and is not included in the table) and was rarely seen after this.

The legacy of the region's industrial past was evident in their family backgrounds, with the young men speaking of grandfathers and great uncles who had worked in the coal industry or occupations that had been linked to it, such as working in coal cleaning plants or driving lorries delivering coal around the area. Their fathers, who had grown up when the industry had been on the decline, had continued the tradition of working-class occupations by entering various other male-dominated jobs. These included working in the building (construction) trade, or being employed as scaffolders or wall and floor tilers, plumbers, or as

Table 3.1 The Valley Boiz: Educational and future trajectories, family backgrounds and sporting interests

Name	Subjects studied, post 16	Parents' occupations	Parents with higher education degrees	Siblings	In receipt of EMA	Team sports	Final exam results year 13	Immediate post-school destination
Dai	BTEC National Diploma in Sport, BTEC Applied Science	F: ? M: ?	None	1 older sister	Yes	Rugby	Pass, Pass	Unemployed
Birdy	A Level English A Level Business Studies A Level Geography	F and M: Small business owners (Post Office)	None	Only child	No	Rugby (also judo)	B, C, C	Swansea University, BA, Geography
Jonesy	A Level Physics A Level IT A Level Business Studies	F: 'Works in big office somewhere in Cardiff?' M: Absent lives in France	None	?	Yes	None	Failed to finish, left school in the spring of Year 13	Unemployed
Shaggy	BTEC National Diploma in Sport BTEC National Diploma Public Services	F: Scaffolder M: Housewife	None	1 younger sister	Yes	Football	Pass, Pass	University of Glamorgan, HND, Public and Emergency Services
Clive	BTEC National Diploma in Sport, BTEC National Diploma Applied Science	F: Electrical fitter M: Officer administrator	None	1 older brother	Yes	Football	Distinction Pass	University of Glamorgan, BA, Nutrition, Physical Activity and Community Health

Name	Qualifications	Parents	Siblings' qualifications	Siblings	?	Sport	Results	Current status
Hughesy	A Level English; A Level Applied ICT; BTEC National Diploma in Applied Science	F: Bus driver; M: Supermarket assistant	None	1 younger brother	Yes	Rugby	C, C, Pass	University of Glamorgan, BA, Criminology
Davies	A Level Electronics; A Level Applied ICT; BTEC National Diploma in Sport	F: Builder; M: Housewife	None	2 older brothers	Yes	Football	Failed to finish, left school at Christmas of final year	Employed with father, General labourer
Brad	A Level English; BTEC National Diploma in Sports; BTEC National Diploma in Applied Science	F: Wall and floor tiler; M: Course assessor at local college	None (Father, dropped out in first year of IT degree)	1 younger sister	No	Football	C, Pass, Pass	Employed with father, Wall and floor tiling
Cresco	BTEC National Diploma in Sports; BTEC National Diploma Public Services	F: Retired bus and lorry driver; M: Cleaner	None	3 older brothers	Yes	Football	Pass, (failed to finish public services qualification)	Employed at a local refuse and recycling centre
Tomo	A Level Physics; A Level Electronics; A-Level Applied I.C.T	F: Small business owner (electrical factory); M: House wife	None	Only child	No	None	B, D, D	Apprenticeship, Tara Steel Europe
Bunk	A Level Physics; A Level Electronics; A Level Maths	F: Plumber; M: Admin assistant, local council	None	1 older sister	Yes	None	B, C, E	Unemployed

electrical fitters. Some, like Hughesy and Cresco, had fathers who were employed as bus or lorry (truck) drivers. A small portion of the group had families who owned their own businesses such as Birdy's family who ran a local Post Office and Tomo's father who, along with six other men, owned an electrical factory employing 23 people. Others, like Dai and Jonesy, were somewhat unsure as to what their parents did or were reluctant to admit to it. All Jonesy could tell me, for example, was that his father *worked in a big office somewhere in Cardiff*, which, as far as he was concerned, was enough and not terribly important in defining his father to him.

The circumstances of the young men's female family members was slightly more varied, with mothers being described as 'housewives', cleaners, secretaries or clerical workers and retail assistants. Some, like Dai, had older sisters in higher education. Brad was a little unsure of his mother's exact job title, but he said that she worked as an 'assessor' in the local college. Brad was perhaps indicating here that she was involved in some form of teaching or training role. None of the groups' parents concerned had any experience of higher education, apart from Brad's father who had briefly attended university in his late twenties before dropping out. While a contradictory class position was evident for a few of the young men, due to their parent's slight upward mobility (as small business owners), as a group these boys came from traditional white working-class families. In this sense, their relatively stable family backgrounds (only Jonesy had parents who had divorced) and employment histories indicate that these boys were quite distinctive from those of their counterparts who had completely disengaged from schooling at the age of 16 and who were not involved in education, employment or training (NEETs).

Post-16 choices

During a group interview conducted at the beginning of the study, I enquire about what their plans were after their looming General Certificate in Secondary Education (GCSE) exams. Some of these aspirations seemed clear whilst other less so:

Bunk: Apprenticeship.
MW: OK, you want to tell me a bit about that?
Bunk: I've applied for one with Ford and Quick Fit...
MW: So that's work as well as college or...
Bunk: Yeah...
Tomo: That be good that is, be paid to do an apprenticeship!

Bunk: I think Quick Fit was like £280 a week...
MW: OK sounds good...
Hughesy: ...stay on and see about something.
Brad: I'm going to go to the sixth form till Christmas, so I can go skiing again and err then I'll go and work with my old man then...
MW: Shaggy what about you then...
Shaggy: Whatever happens...
MW: OK whatever happens...
Birdy: I want to go to uni cos of the girls...
[*Group Interview*]

In this excerpt, we can see that Bunk had already looked into a Modern Apprenticeship and reports that he had applied for two different schemes with national motor vehicle companies. Tomo seems impressed with this and illustrates that he has already some background knowledge about the Modern Apprenticeship because he realizes it is accompanied by a paid wage. The validation for Bunk's choice comes through the ability to earn whilst studying in an 'acceptable' (male-dominated) industry and therefore reproducing an idealized form of masculinity. Those who are not sure what they want to do, but have decided to continue in education, like Hughesy, Brad and Birdy, validate their choices in different ways. Hughesy expresses nonchalance without committing to anything, whilst Brad justifies his decision to return to the sixth form purely because he can go skiing again[3] and will then go to work with his father in an 'acceptable' manual occupation as a floor tiler. Birdy was the only one of the group to look beyond the immediate future by suggesting he wanted to go to university. Nonetheless, he justifies this quickly by saying *because of the girls*. His educational aspirations are covered up by emphasizing (hetero) sexual motives, rather than any academic or occupational ones and he continues to collude with the masculine front of the overall 'team' performance.

'Staying on': The performance of an acceptable front

Despite some uncertainty, after their GCSEs, all of The Valley Boiz returned to the school's Sixth Form and enrolled on a mixture of two-year science, maths or technological-based traditional A levels (Birdy, Jonesy, Bunk, Tomo); vocational or applied BTEC National Diploma courses, where assessment was based solely on projects and coursework (Dai, Clive, Cresco, Shaggy); or a mixture of both (Davies, Hughesy,

Brad). Interestingly, Hughesy, Birdy and Brad were also persuaded by the head of Sixth Form to take a joint A level in English literature and language alongside their other qualifications, after gaining high grades at GSCE in this subject area. The contradiction of this for their re-traditionalized macho front is something I return to later in the chapter.

As with the *Real Geordies* in Nayak's study (2003c) of the North East of England, The Valley Boiz families' manual occupational biographies were reflected in their post-16 educational choices via the prioritization of vocational or 'acceptable' subjects. The BTEC National Diploma qualifications in science (a general course covering physics, chemistry and biology), sports studies and the A level in applied IT, were particularly favoured because they did not contain written examinations. When talking about their post-16 educational choices, Clive and Cresco told me that they had opted for the BTEC National Diploma in Sport because they '*had always wanted to do something with sports*' (Cresco) or because that they were '*interested in sports*' (Clive). They were sceptical about other academic courses and, in many ways, seemed to have chosen these options not only to fit in with their interests, but to maintain an acceptable front performance of masculinity which was based on the re-traditionalization of acceptable skills from the industrial era through the development of a sporting body (Messner and Sabo, 1990; Gorely et al., 2003). But during an individual interview it became clear that these choices had, to a certain extent, been influenced by teachers at the school. Clive had been two months late returning after his GCSEs (he had had an unsuccessful time at a local college) and was told that the AS and subsequent A Level in PE and the separate sciences, would have been too difficult for him. This was despite achieving A*–C grades for his GCSEs in English, Science and Maths. Similarly, Cresco who admitted to being *in the special needs class* prior to the Sixth Form was told he could only take *specific stuff* and was enrolled on a public services course alongside his sports course without his consent. It would seem then that some teachers were influential in the choices made by these young men and also contributed to the formation of a socially acceptable form of masculinity in the school and the wider community.

Uniform

The status of The Valley Boiz as sporting students enabled them to occupy a valued position in the school, as a different uniform was sanctioned for those who were taking the BTEC National Diploma in sports qualification. The normal school uniform of black trousers, black jumper, white shirt, red tie and black shoes was replaced by a colourful sporting tracksuit emblazoned with the school crest and accompanied by a polo shirt and trainers. This uniform was only supposed to be worn during days when the subject was studied, but this rule was not fully enforced and it was disregarded totally in the sixth form. These artefacts then operate as forms of what Goffman (1959: 32) refers to as 'expressive equipment' of personal front. This enabled The Valley Boiz to perform their own recognizable identity and constituted a way of affirming and honouring a hegemonic version of masculinity, based on physical sporting prowess.

This hegemonic position was also supported through influential roles within the school which, like the sports uniform, added to the front of the performance. Dai, Hughesy and Brad had been selected by the head of Sixth Form to work as paid dinner-hall monitors. This meant keeping order in the dinner hall and providing the Free School Meal (FSM) tickets to younger pupils. With 23% of those at the school being entitled to a FSM, this amounted to a considerable number. These positions not only supported their already recognizable status within the school, but they also had the added benefit of having been personally chosen by a member of the school's senior staff, which therefore validated their position further. Any sporting success (however small) was celebrated by the school and various photographs were evident throughout its halls celebrating these achievements. In contrast, even though Sam from The Geeks friendship group (see Chapter Four) had been selected as the schools head boy in Year 13, he was not regarded as having the same status. This position of authority held no influence with other pupils and Sam was more of a symbolic figure, to be rolled out to give speeches at prize nights or to attend civil ceremonies. Through these practices, an official status (school sanctioned and created) and an unofficial status (influenced by the peer group and wider culture) were created amongst the young men.

Power relations

Inside the confines of the school The Valley Boiz were able to further achieve a dominant position through their loud and disruptive practices in class and their behaviour out on the playing fields and other spaces around the school buildings. In Year 11, they tended to dominate the classroom discussions and shouted out answers to questions that the teacher asked, without raising their hands as the school rules indicated they should and not necessarily because they had the right response to the teacher's comments. In one particular mathematics lesson some of this disturbance is recorded in my field notes below:

48 *From Labouring to Learning*

> The boys near the back of the classroom were constantly talking and laughing. Davies put his headphones in and turned to look in case I could see. Another boy looked to be texting on his mobile phone held under the table, just out of view of the teacher who was trying to guide the class through an equation on the white board.
> [*Fieldnotes*]

This texting on mobile phones and listening to MP3 players whilst in class led to a repeated battle with the teacher who had to continually ask for these devices to be put away and turned off. The boys were also boisterous, messed or joked around, misbehaved, and generally ignored the lesson. These practices therefore enabled the continuation of a form of masculinity based on the working-class culture and traditions of a former era. In-group banter and joking around were key components once used for dealing with arduous working conditions underground and a tool employed when dealing with the overman (supervisor)at the colliery.[4]

When walking in corridors on the way to lessons or waiting outside classrooms for lessons to begin, this front performance was further achieved by the pushing and shoving of younger pupils who tried to walk past The Valley Boiz. The playground was another scene of dominance where games of rugby and football were played which took over the whole yard. This pressed younger members of the school and those in their year group who did not participate, to the margins of the social spaces available. On one occasion when I played football with The Valley Boiz, it was clear that their dominance caused conflict as younger boys were shouted at they dared to walk into the game. Such abuse was also followed by physical intimidation.

Hughesy: If you get in the fucking way again I'll have you!
Younger Boy: I was only walking across...
Hughesy: I don't give a shit, fuck off.
Dai: Yeah piss off butt!
[*Fieldnotes*]

Following this remark, Hughesy then kicked the ball towards the younger boy and hit him on the back, which caused great hilarity to those watching and the young boy to run to the edge of the yard to relative safety. The colloquial comment 'butt', which is used here by Dai in place of the term 'mate', to tell the younger pupil to more away from the game, was in common usage between the boys and is used right across Wales. Again, like the nicknames, they used when referring to each other, the term 'butt' linked back to an era of industrial work, where the term 'butty' was synonymous with coal miners working together underground (Penlington, 2010). As Kamoche and Maguire (2011: 727) explain further:

> The history and mythology of mining is a history of disasters and change, characterized by a variety of (often) conflictual employment and sub-contracting methods. An example was the butty system, in which the work was contracted to butty men who in turn sub-contracted to men to whom they supplied pick and shovel.

The term 'butty' or 'butt' (colleague/friend) is thus synonymous with the industrial work that had shaped their community and the contemporary Welsh nation and its association with a strong masculine tradition was still continued by The Valley Boiz.

Casual behaviour and sexual story telling

After passing their GCSEs and progressing to the Sixth Form, The Valley Boiz continued to turn up to school regularly, as attendance had to be proven to receive their EMA, but they did not always attend every lesson, and often opted instead to sit around the common room chatting about girls, plans for the weekend or making use of computers in the library to surf the Internet. When they did go to lessons, their classroom behaviour was not as disruptive as it had been when they were in Year 11, but it was still far from that of those middle-class pupils recorded in other studies (Edley and Wetherell, 1997, 1999; Heward, 1988; Kehily and Pattman, 2006; McCormack, 2012). During lessons, their interactions with teachers were casual and a lot of banter was exchanged about sporting results from the previous weekend. Mr Harper, who taught some of The Valley Boiz for part of the BTEC Applied Science course, was awarded the honour by Clive of being *'like one of the boys'*. When I asked Clive to elaborate further he told me: *'he talks to us normally so you respect him a bit more like, but some teachers abuse their authority and shout at you!'* Mr Harper was liked because he did not shout at them or pressure them into handing in work and because he talked to them 'normally'. Here, Clive is makes a distinction between a teacher who treats him and the others like young men, almost on an equal level, with similar cultural and social interests and other teachers who still see them as children in need of discipline.

In the excerpt from my field notes below, this banter is further illustrated:

I noticed that their interactions with the teacher were different to that of The Geeks in the A-level Chemistry or Biology classes. They uttered informal comments on parts of the lesson such as when Hughesy said in a surprised, sarcastic tone to the teacher, *'Organised today Sir,'* in regards to the worksheets and handouts he had printed out in advance of the class. The teaching styles also seemed to differ as well and the teacher talked with these boys instead of at them. Dai also hadn't brought a pen with him and therefore had to borrow one off the teacher. This is something I didn't think would happen with the A-level class.

[*Fieldnotes*]

When compared to the separate A-level science classes (Physics, Biology, and Chemistry), the BTEC lessons were not only more informal due to the interactions between the boys and the teacher, but amongst The Valley Boiz themselves. Even in the empty classrooms (there were only around half a dozen at most taking the BTEC courses), The Valley Boiz tended to sit at the back of the room as far away from the teacher as they could. In a throwback to their compulsory school days, they still exhibited an indifference to being close to the front of the classroom, which might have meant being seen by the others as over-investing in the lesson and therefore gaining a derogatory label as a swot or a geek. Sitting at the back of the class out of earshot of the teacher meant that a certain amount of banter, 'piss taking' and sexual storytelling could occur during lessons. During a group science experiment in another BTEC applied science class, Hughesy recounted such a tale from the weekend's activities

> The boys began 'taking the piss' out of Hughesy about an incident with a caravan. I asked to hear more about this and Hughesy told me eagerly. He'd been out on a Saturday night in the town and 'pulled' an older woman in a nightclub. After getting a kebab (which he'd dropped all over his black shirt), he'd gone home with her. But instead of her inviting him into her house, she took him into a touring caravan (trailer) that was parked outside it. When he awoke in the morning (with scratches all over his back he was happy to tell us) he had no idea where he was. Alongside the *'rough bird'* he had *'pulled'* there were a few Doberman dogs in the caravan which he said looked *'fucking scary!'* He called everyone on his phone to try and get a lift home and only Clive had answered and gone to collect him in his car, at 8:30am on the Sunday morning. Clive had commented that Hughesy had sounded *'well quiet'* and shy on the phone. As Hughesy

wasn't exactly sure where he was, it took Clive a while to find him by driving around the streets and villages of Cwm Dyffryn looking for the Caravan. Hughesy admitted not calling her again and lying to her about his age. He told her he was in university so that she would think he was older and would sleep with him.
[*Fieldnotes*]

Three things seem to be going on in the telling of this tale, which continues the front performance of masculinity. The Valley Boiz are engaging with a practical science task and whilst carrying it out are reproducing normative expectations of heterosexual prowess. By interacting around a practical task, a sanitized older world of industrial work is also being re-traditionalized in the classroom space. Second, through storytelling one of the 'team' members occupies an honoured position and reaffirms dominant myths about what constitutes a 'real man'. As Goffman (1959: 44) puts it, this impression of front is 'idealized in several different ways'. Hughesy is enjoying being the centre of attention and his desires are shared by the others as he portrays himself as something of a hero. He went through dangers (the Doberman dogs), incurred injuries (the scratches on his back) and needed to be rescued from the ordeal by his friend (who drives to find him) after the event. His story is also validated by this rescue as some of the tale (only the unnamed girl can fully authenticate the story) is commented on by Clive. Finally, the sexual objectification of the girl is complete when Hughesy states that he did not call her again and admits lying about his age in order to sleep with her. This incident strengthens the group identity and acts as a collective normalizing practice by reinforcing myths about the roles of traditional masculinities in the locality and through emphasizing a heterosexual prowess. Outside the classroom and school setting these practices continued and The Valley Boiz engaged in a number of 'risky' behaviours through which the re-traditionalization of white working-class masculinities continued to be displayed.

Beyond the school gates: 'Risky' behaviours

A drinking heritage

The drinking culture of the South Wales Valleys is intrinsically linked to the industrial heritage of the region with the majority of the pubs and working men's halls in the area being built during the industrial revolution. Working men's halls (along with general hospitals) in particular had been built through contributions from coal miners and the large buildings, many of which are now dilapidated, still dominate the main streets of the towns and villages across the Valleys. In Cwm Dyffryn, these industrial hallmarks live on in these numerous pub names, such as the Colliers Arms Tavern, The Blast Furnace Inn and The Pick and Shovel, whilst others such as the Marquis Inn, The Bute, The Cyfaertha, The Mackworth Arms, The Osborne Hotel and The Nixon's were named after the canal, mine or iron work owners. Others such as The Rock Inn, stem from the numerous breweries that provided the alcohol for these establishments that spread across the region in the 19th century and names like Temple Bar and The Hibernian Club, reveal the legacy of Irish immigration into South Wales. Occupying another important position in this drinking culture is the local Rugby Union team's clubhouse (Howe, 2001, 2003). Whilst being an official headquarters, the clubhouse also provides a gathering place to celebrate birthdays, engagements, weddings, christenings or to mourn after funerals. Alongside these functions, it further acts as a focal point for people to get together to watch the Welsh nation play international Rugby Union matches on wide-screen televisions, usually at the beginning of every year (February to April) when the Six Nations championship is played. Win, lose or draw, a party atmosphere occurs and a day of heavy drinking, is quite often followed by a bar room fight. During my research I found these drinking spaces act both as a form of resistance for young men and also as a way of reproducing local and national identity.

Despite the demise of the industrial base, the night-time economy of Cwm Dyffryn has changed little over the past half century until relatively recently. Most of the pubs belong to national brewing companies, but retain a local character, employing local owners and staff. Even though large chain pubs and clubs have generally stayed away, in the last few years a Wetherspoons chain pub[5] has opened in the centre of the town bringing with it a change in local drinking customs. This cheaper alcohol and food has had an effect on other pubs in the town and resulted in closures. This historic backdrop provides insight into the national and regional leisure practices, and drinking can therefore be seen as something of a 'cultural praxis' (Wilson, 2005: 12), helping to shape and define the region's identity and indicative of wider working-class culture.

The Valley Boiz had already started going out drinking alcohol whilst in Year 10, and by Year 11 (aged 15 and 16), this had become a regular weekend event in the park or in a local pub, which was known to 'turn a blind eye' and ignore drinking underage:

MW: OK... what about drinking then, do you drink?
Davies: Yeah, Friday, Saturday, regular.

Tomo: Have a few cans innit.
MW: So, where would you go then?
Tomo: We go to The Harp,[6] or just down the park.
MW: And where do you get the money to do it?
Davies: Milk Man, part time job like.
Birdy: Get it off my parents.
Hughesy: Yeah, my old man gives me some money like.
Shenkin: I do some gardening.
          (Group laughter)
Brad: ...(talks over him)...No you don't!
Shenkin: Yeah I do right, I do some for the people in my street, get paid for it as well like...
[*Group Interview*]

By the final year of compulsory schooling, going out to drink in the town's park was an important part of The Valley Boiz social lives and can be seen as another key signifier of a masculine front for these young men. The Valley Boiz, like their fathers and grandfathers would have done before them, were celebrating the end of a 'working' week, even though their week consisted of classroom bases activities instead of a workplace. Drinking in the park and the occasional foray into a pub, acted as a rite of passage and training ground before progressing to the adult environment of the pub or the nightclub full time (Blackshaw, 2003). This underage drinking was funded by a range of part-time jobs and ingenious money-making schemes, such as gardening for other people, and also supported and sanctioned through money from parents. Whilst the wider world may have moved on since Willis' (1977) 16-year-old 'lads', for The Valley Boiz, going out at night was still a way to connect to an older world of industrial work and the working-class culture of the locale at this young age.

During the Sixth Form some of The Valley Boiz secured other part-time work in the service economy to help fund their out-of-school activities. Tomo worked in a factory cleaning, before moving to the large chain Wetherspoon pub, after being made redundant, while Hughesy, Clive and Birdy worked in fast food outlets (McDonald's and KFC) situated on the outskirts of the town. By the final year of Sixth Form, Davies and Brad (now joined by Jonesy) were still helping the local milk man on his early morning deliveries, but because the milk round involved getting up at 4am, on some occasions Jonesy would turn up for school and fall asleep in the library or common room instead of going to his morning lessons. For others, like Shaggy and Cresco, money for going out was gained solely through their weekly EMA.

Out on the town

The Valley Boiz portrayed a collective drinking uniform and went out at night dressed in mainstream fashionable clothes (paid for by their part-time work) from high street shops. They wore tank tops, vests, checked or striped shirts, multi-coloured T-shirts with logos and jeans accompanied by leather jackets or hoodies. A local pub – The Harp – on the outskirts of the town was still their favoured meeting point as they grew older. On certain nights of the week they often went there for a *'quiet pint'* and to play pool and to use the jukebox. The pub acted as a social base for The Valley Boiz and they were able to joke and laugh with the landlord and other older men in the pub. It was also a place where they could belong to something, which they did not quite feel in school and which they seemed always in resistance to.

At the weekend, after a few initial drinks in The Harp, the young men would move into the town centre itself and to the Wetherspoons pub before ending up in Polka's the single nightclub. Once The Valley Boiz moved off from one pub to the next, text messages or Facebook status updates, would be used to convey to others where they were and direct friends to meet up with the group. Drinks were sometimes bought between two or three people to save going repeatedly to the bar. Having little money, this was also easier than running the risk of buying a large round of drinks for the whole group and not receiving a drink in return. Pints of lager or cider were favoured by The Valley Boiz, but on occasion Guinness, bottled beers (such as Budweiser or alcopops such as WKD Blue) were also consumed. To accompany these drinks, shots of neat spirits or vodka jellies (jelly made with vodka instead of water) were often 'knocked back' or 'downed'. During wilder nights out Jagerbombs (a shot of the dark Jagermeister spirit dropped into a glass of the energy drink Red Bull) or tequila slammers were also drunk. By going out in a big group and drinking large amounts of alcohol, the front performance of the 'team' which as we have seen was fostered inside the school through appropriate curricular subjects, aggressive and macho behaviours and relationships to teachers and their peers, was continued.

On some occasions when out at night, some of The Valley Boiz would encounter problems when drinking too much and would in turn result in them being barred from certain pubs for the evening.

> Bunk came over to our table and told us that Hughesy had been thrown out of the venue by the bouncer [doorman] because he had been caught *'chucking'* [throwing] a plastic pint glass which he had urinated in, against the roof of the toilets. This was now dripping

from the ceiling and as I had to return to the toilet again that night, I had the pleasure of confirming this.
[*Fieldnotes*]

These drunken antics had a dual function. Not only did they illustrate the continual performance of a working-class, localized form of masculinity, but also during the post-night-out discussions in school the next day, these events could then be dissected and laughed at. This also allowed for the collective process to be pooled and shared with others who might not have been present and stories to spread around the year group. One story of Tomo doing a series of press-ups in a local river on the way home after a night out (and one too many beers), was an often repeated story which I heard many times during my time in Cwm Dyffryn High School.

Out on the pull

Drinking alcohol for The Valley Boiz, was usual a male-only affair with few, if any, female friends present. Girlfriends were rarely invited to come along. This process acted as another continuation of older local traditions, where men would have often gone to the pub, leaving wives at home (see Howe, 2003). As more of the group reached the legal drinking age of 18, the problems of being denied a drink or entrance to a pub or club diminished. This meant that they began to leave the town for nights out, often arranging mini-buses with others from their year group to bigger clubs in the cities of Cardiff or Swansea. Only on nights out away from the town was it acceptable for girlfriends to be asked along (likewise mixing socially with other members of the year group) and ultimately the decision as to whether a girlfriend was invited, seemed to lie with the young men themselves. There was a general rule between The Valley Boiz that it was *bros before hoes*, indicating the group objectification of their girlfriends.[7] Nonetheless, this mantra was not without some flexibility and as Cresco explained to me when talking about his girlfriend, he tried to *spend one weekend up her house, next out, just to keep her happy innit*. It was unacceptable to spend too much time with a girlfriend over being with male friends. Also by having girls along, the chances of 'pulling'[8] were reduced.

For The Valley Boiz drinking and looking for (hetero) sexual conquests seemed to go hand-in-hand with a night out. The performance acted as a further strategic display of their masculinity. Grazian (2007: 221) argues that the ritual of going out 'girl hunting' (or on 'the pull' in the local vernacular) is a practice which:

Reinforce[s] dominant sexual myths and expectations of masculine behaviour, boost[s] confidence in one's performance of masculinity and heterosexual power and assist[s] in the performance of masculinity in the presence of women.

On nights out whilst drinking (without their girlfriends), this elaborate performance of masculinity was practiced on the dance floors of night clubs. The Valley Boiz would often move onto or 'attack' the dance floor as a group and whilst dancing would manoeuvre themselves into positions alongside groups or pairs of girls. An almost mating-like ritual would then follow, where individual boys would try to get noticed by dancing closer and closer to a girl, with subtle and not so subtle movements. Some of these techniques included dancing near a particular girl whilst looking across to her to make eye contact and simultaneously trying not to look as if one was interested by dancing with male friends. Other not so subtle movements included trying to physically take hold of girls and spinning them around while dancing, standing behind a girl and gyrating with her to the music or hi-fiveing a friend on the dance floor above the head of a girl. The friends often goaded each other into dancing with as many different girls as possible, and there seemed to be an enormous amount of pressure to comply with a heterosexual masculinity. On occasion, these tactics and strategies seemed to be reciprocated or even instigated by the girls themselves and resulted in couples passionately kissing or 'meeting' (as it was described in the local area) on the dance floor. On other occasions, this process did not go smoothly. In an individual interview, Clive and Cresco retold me of an incident where Clive's advances had been spurned:

Clive: Ah, I was dancing with her, but she wasn't having any of it.
Cresco: (Laughs)
Clive: And then she slapped me. There was another time when she didn't slap me, just rejected me.
MW: Ah right.
Clive: All the boys dancing around her, I thought I'd take it a step further, you know I'm seeing someone, well she doesn't know, but I just grabbed her and she turned around and went like that to me [waves finger in air, mouths the word '*No*'].
MW: No, right.
Clive: I thought you slag, I just want to dance with you.
Cresco: Dance innit, don't want to kiss you!

Clive: She was too minging [unattractive] to kiss anyway, I just wanted a dance and she wasn't having any of it like, and she was dancing dirty weren't she!
Cresco: She what?
Clive: Dirty dancing wasn't she, in Polka's [nightclub]!
Cresco: Ah filth.
Clive: Getting on tables and that and you're like asking all of us to get inside of you, be honest, and she was having none of it like, couldn't fucking believe it, bitch, shock of my life!
[*Individual Interview Year 13*]

Here the implications of the performance of a compulsory heterosexuality in this interview are laid bare. For Clive, his masculinity in this situation is not validated by the successful act of picking up or pulling a girl, but just in the endeavour of trying to engage in this practice amidst a male peer group. Both young men then re-tell the tale, this time during a recorded interview. The reason they give to me and to others as to why Clive was unsuccessful was not because the girl in question spurned his advances, but because she was too '*dirty*' to dance with him. If she had been '*dirty*' dancing with him, then this might have been a far more acceptable action and something Clive might not have been so quick to dismiss and to subsequently label her as too '*minging*' or unattractive to kiss. What is also clear here is that a compulsory heterosexual performance is engaged in by the young women as well as the young men in a night club, and this space becomes excessively sexualized.

As the nightclubs that these young men attended tended to be very busy, crowded places accompanied by loud music, conversation was not an easy task, but the ability to talk improved the chances of meeting girls and 'pulling'. One way of doing this was through 'chat-up' lines, which were often practiced in quieter venues before moving on to a nightclub:

I'm sitting with Clive, Cresco, Brad, Tomo and Birdy on high chairs around a tall table in the middle of a large Wetherspoons pub drinking bottles or pints of lager. The pub is very busy and I lean in closer to hear the conversation on the other side of the table, which is mainly about which girls in the room are '*fit*' or '*hot*'. Tomo suggests that Birdy should try out his chat-up line on a table of girls of a similar age who are sitting near them. After some encouragement from the others, he finished his pint and along with Clive, goes over to talk to them. When the two boys approach the table Birdy asks the group of unsuspecting girls a pre-planned question, '*How much does a polar bear weigh'?* One of the girls offers a hesitant response, *'Ah what....um I don't know'?* Confidently, Birdy replies by saying *'enough to break the ice'*. This is met with a chorus of groans and laughs from the girls, but it is enough for Birdy and Clive to start a conversation and they are allowed to join the girls at their table.

[*Fieldnotes*]

Here the experience of the chat-up line is not just an individual achievement but also a collective group experience. For these young men, the end result is important, but so too is looking good to their friends and to have 'a laugh' and some banter through the process. Even though the remainder of the group look on in passive support of Birdy and Clive's endeavour, they exhibit a form of what Connell (1995) has argued constitutes a 'complicit masculinity'. Those not involved add value to the archetypal masculine performance by validating the 'patriarchal dividend' and sanctioning the action. These boys inhabit a world in which masculinity is conducted in relation to other boys and men in the classrooms at school and in the pubs outside of it. Girls here are dehumanized and seen as sexual objects or as conquests. Alongside drinking, other influences and pressures to perform traditional masculine identities arrived from a variety of directions.

Drug taking

Alongside drinking, some of The Valley Boiz also admitted to taking recreational drugs and on occasion being offered illegal substance in pubs and clubs around the town. Whilst it would seem that The Valley Boiz were happy to participate in – and talk about – drinking alcohol a great deal, the issue of drug taking was an altogether different matter. As I have indicated, the cultural milieu of the region sanctioned many social and leisure activities, but, drug taking, which is, after all, an illegal activity, was not held in as much esteem as alcohol consumption. It must be acknowledged that these young men may have hidden their wider drug use from me or refrained from talking about such practices in front of me. Nonetheless, considering the amount of time I spent with them, I believe that if they had participated in illicit drug use, I would have been aware of it. It did occur, as the snippets from the following conversations I had below show, but it was conducted amongst close friends or acquaintances which they knew from their housing estates and small villages in which they lived, not as a collective group practice:

Cresco: To be honest with you I've done it twice.
MW: Smoked weed [cannabis] now?

Cresco: But the first time, I was curious, I took a drag, but the second time I was like chilled, I was in my brother's house, I was on my Playstation, and he went shall we try it? And I was like 'Ah whatever...'
[*Individual Interview Year 13*]

Brad: I have smoked a bit of weed before, and obviously if you go out in the town, people ask you, if you got anything, I've been asked if I got pills, if I got coke, or stuff like that.
[*Individual Interview Year 13*]

Clive: Boy come up to me at the bar in Polka's and went to me, '*I can get you any drugs you want*', I was like thinking fuck off, but I didn't say anything, he was massive, so I just went '*Na*' and he walked off.
[*Individual Interview*]

Going on a night out not only held the risks of drinking to excess, getting into fights and being thrown out of clubs, but also the risk of being asked if they wanted to buy drugs, or in the case of Brad, if they had any themselves to sell. Smoking cannabis was something that some had participated in, but this created problems that Tomo found difficult to deal with when some of his close friends began overindulging. He shed some more light on the drug 'scene' in Cwm Dyffryn during an individual interview. This was something which I was unaware of even after years of living in a similar community. It appeared that Tomo had a lot of older friends aside from The Valley Boiz, whom he had met whilst getting into DJing. He had his own mixing desk and played at different venues and entered DJing competitions in clubs, but he had found this an expensive hobby and had to stop doing it. It was here that he acquired his knowledge of this underground economy:

Tomo: There is a massive underlying drugs problem, loads of different crowds as well, people go out and drink and take loads of coke, then people who won't drink at all, but smoke weed, like Trevor and Jonsey that's all they do. Every time I see Trevor, he's stoned off his face, he's just no fun to talk to and the day after he's like a slouch. I just don't waste my time trying to talk to him, Trevor used to be my best friend, now I don't talk to him, me and him, cars bikes, but now...
[*Individual Interview*]

Here we can see the impact smoking cannabis had on Tomo's friendship with Trevor. It is unclear whether or not Tomo participated in smoking with Trevor, but I am inclined to think he did at one time or another, as his knowledge of the 'scene' was remarkable. Tomo is clearly angry at his former best friend and the distance the drug use has created between them. Drinking was a way of reaffirming an archetypical form of masculinity, but smoking cannabis and taking harder drugs was less likely to be participated in as a team activity and looked down on by others. In many ways, as I have shown throughout this chapter, The Valley Boiz front performances of masculinity were conducted through older traditions and practices some of which were potentially damaging. But, some of these boys do see alternative or different futures to other young men in the area. Tomo recognizes the waste that surrounds him and some of his friends and is keen to push past this, and expresses sadness that others cannot. Away from the pubs and clubs of the town, other spaces of masculine production were also part of their lives. I turn briefly now to the role of cars in their lives and the impact this had on confirming ideas about a certain form of masculinity.

Car culture and the continuation of front

Research on young men and the roles cars play in their lives has often centred around the risk of accidents and injuries (Walker, Butland and Connell, 2000; Granié, and Papafava, 2011), car theft (Mullins and Cherbonneau, 2011) or on the role car culture plays for young people as a networking tool and as a form of social space (Mellstrom, 2004; Kenway and Hickey-Moody, 2009). Accompanying youthful car cultures is the risk of tragic death. Whilst carrying out this study I personally witnessed hazardous driving, high-speed car chases and listened to stories about accidents and injuries to friends and vehicles. As I outlined in the prologue to this book, six months after the cessation of fieldwork the consequences of these practices became tragically clear as one of the young men featured in this chapter suffered a serious injury whilst driving at high speed and died a few weeks after his 19th birthday. My focus here (I return to discuss the role of car culture in more depth in Chapter 6) is to illustrate briefly how important cars were to the continuation of this archetypal front performance of masculinity.

Apart from Tomo and Davies, none of the group owned their own cars. The majority were insured as named drivers on their mothers' or occasionally their fathers' vehicles. As more of The Valley Boiz passed their driving tests, they began to drive to school. This often created arguments with their teachers, as there was a ban in place on students parking in the school grounds. This meant that anyone who drove to school had to park in the car park across the road from the school, something that was not always adhered to. One lunchtime during Year 13, a fight erupted between Birdy and Davies in the yard outside the main building of the school. Davies had taken a wheel trim off one of Birdy's car wheels as a joke. At lunchtime, when some of The Valley Boiz went out to their cars, Birdy found that one of his wheel trims was missing. A bystander in the crowd that has gathered around Birdy's car pointed out that Davies had done this and when Davies then drove past, he waved and beeped his horn. Birdy then chased after the car on foot and grabbed one of the door handles, which promptly came off in his hand. Davies then stopped his car and a fistfight ensued until it was broken up by some teachers who had come running out of a nearby school building. During a conversation a few days later whilst sitting in class registration, Tomo was telling others sitting around him about the incident. Davies had mentioned that even though Birdy had had him pinned down on the floor and had one hand around his genitals and the other around his throat chocking him, he had not attempted to punch him. The group then began to comment on how weak this was of Birdy for a boy so tall and with a black belt in Judo. Hughesy stated that Birdy could have '*battered him*' (beat him up) but because he did not throw a punch, referred to him as '*a bit of a knob*'. Here possessing the ability to fight but not doing so was met with confusion, and Birdy was criticized for his behaviour and for not punching Davies. The emphasis on masculine prowess was illustrated further through driving fast, doing circuits around the town and bringing cars into the school space to help endorse and validate the front of the macho performance. It was also a way to bring the outside world into the school, where driving gave them an equal footing with older men in the community. But, away from the front display of the overtly masculine performances of the 'team', both in school and beyond it, contradictions occurred. In the last section of this chapter I look more closely at some of these conflicting and multiple presentations of self.

Behind the mask of heritage

For The Valley Boiz, a background of skilled and semi-skilled traditional masculine occupations had a significant impact on how the boys viewed school, education and what they did in their leisure time. However, during social interaction it is the 'back region or backstage' (Goffman, 1959: 114) of a performance where contradictions make an appearance. Thus, the performances of masculinity that I have described so far in this chapter illustrate only one region of The Valley Boiz masculinities. When undertaking a performance, the discrepancies or effects which would undermine such a performance, can be hidden. Through a series of complex interactions at the peer group and individual level, an alternative side to members of The Valley Boiz emerges. I use these examples to argue that the industrial traditions of the region, which were being re-traditionalized in different ways by the group, were also being challenged and were open to subversion.

Brad, Birdy and Hughesy; Studying English Literature

As I highlighted above the school subjects chosen by some of The Valley Boiz were an important arena for the performance of a particular form of dominant working-class masculinity, along with macho swaggers and posturing, sexual comments, physical toughness and an 'anti-school' attitude which continued even when The Valley Boiz had progressed to the Sixth Form. Yet, three of these young men, Brad, Birdy and Hughesy, were also enrolled on the more traditionally 'feminine' A level English Literature and English Language course which, as Redman and Mac an Ghaill (1997) point out, is a supposedly 'soft subject' lacking in masculine rigour (see also Mac an Ghaill, 1994; Epstein et al., 1998; Renold, 2001; Stahl, 2015). The Joint Council for Qualifications *GCE A Level Results Report* would seem to support this argument further. The year these young men sat their final exams only 6.8% of male candidates who were enrolled on A2 level courses sat English (literature and language) exams, compared with 13.6% of female candidates.[9] Brad, Birdy and Hughesy were therefore combining both academic and vocational subjects and challenging the meaning of what it meant to be a 'real' boy (or young man) in this context.

The excerpt from my fieldnotes below is taken from part of an English Literature A level lesson. The archetypal macho performance is highly visible; but, some of the contradictions of this performance are also evident:

> Mr Berry opens the lesson with the music video for the song *Dakota* by the rock band Stereophonics, playing on the electronic whiteboard at the front of the classroom. He's using the YouTube website and the music is blaring out of the speakers. Some of the boys smile and comment on this as they enter the room in ones and twos for their first lesson of the day. When Hughesy walks in he's eating something which looks like a bacon roll and through his full mouth mumbles '*I've had no breakfast see Sir*' as some form of explanation as he finds

his seat. The students are split into two tables with some of The Geeks (Sam, Alan, Gavin, Sean and Nibbles) sitting on one, whilst the other is occupied by Brad, Birdy and Hughesy along with another guy Ed, who tends to be a bit of a loner in the year group and keeps himself to himself. The music is switched off and the class quietens a little. The lesson opens with the learning objectives for the session being given by the teacher, which centre on the book being studied, which is *Death of a Salesman* by Arthur Miller. Mr Berry questions each of the students in the class individually about their progress to date on coursework. Sam offers a really articulate answer when Mr Berry enquires about the piece of writing he's doing and what bit he's concentrating on at the moment. Whilst this is going on Hughesy stands up, walks the length of the classroom and noisily slams the packaging from his now finished bacon roll, into the bin. As he returns to his seat Alan and Gavin continue to update the teacher on their progress and describe in detail where they are with their writing. When it was Hughesy's turn to talk he doesn't articulate himself quite so well and seems a bit lost, indicating that he wasn't sure what he was doing. Birdy and Brad both answer nonchalantly and appear to be behind the others in their progress.

The lesson moves on and Mr Berry sets a very precise 11-minute task to read the opening part of a scene and compare it to a passage from the Shakespeare play *King Lear* that they had previously read and discuss it as a group. The Geeks begin to read the scene straight away, but the others seem to take a while to begin and are never really all quiet. Hughesy asks Mr Berry if he can borrow a pen and for another copy of the book as he hasn't brought his version with him. After a few minutes (in regards to a passage in the text the group are comparing), Hughsey asks an insightful question to Mr Berry about sympathising with characters like *King Lear*, who do not share the same value system as those who maybe reading it. Birdie nudges Brad who he is sitting alongside and sniggers as Hughsey asks this. Brad then laughs loudly and accuses Birdy of being rich, so to just be quiet. When Mr Berry responds to Hughesy's question, Hughsey just sits quietly and doesn't contribute anything further to the discussion and the group begin to talk about the previous weekend. Later Mr Berry gets different members of the class to read a passage from the book out loud. Whilst Sam reads and articulates his words well, Brad seems less confident and takes his time. Nonetheless despite this, when Mr Berry asks the class as a whole what type of sentence the author is using, Brad

very quickly gives the correct answer and competes with Hughesy to explain how this can be used to analyse the text.
[*Fieldnotes*]

This example of classroom interaction illustrates how different performances of masculinity are being displayed in one micro setting. Hughesy, Birdy and Brad can answer the questions that are delivered, but not in as much depth as some of the others in the class. Yet it is clear that they are aware of the answers. In this lesson, the ability to analyse and to think critically about the text, alongside the capacity to write about what is studied, would seem to indicate that a more studious or passive performance of masculinity is most valued and is illustrated by Sam, Alan and Gavin in their account of their writing to their teacher and their ability to complete the classwork. This type of middle-class performance of masculinity contrasts with how Hughesy, Birdy and Brad act, chastising each other for asking questions, talking over each other and shouting out answers. Yet there are occasions where something else is visible, and a more insightful, studious performance is evident, for example when Hughsey attempts to formulate an answer, but this is unsuccessful as he is laughed at by close friends, which acts as a reminder that the lad image has to be maintained alongside the more studious or passive one required in the English classroom or else attract criticism. The ability to attempt to adapt one's behaviour as a response to different situations is interesting and drawing further from fieldnotes taken from another English lesson, these contradictions again seemed to occur:

> Mr Berry started the lesson with some talk about the weekend football results and the new Cardiff City Football stadium which led into a discussion about discourse and hedging. He asked the class to remind him what this meant and Hughesy was quite eager to answer. He said '*it's something to do with a topic...I know it sounds stupid but... ah...I don't know...*' which caused Brad and Birdy to laugh out loud and even after further prompting from the teacher, Hughesy just mumbled something and sank lower into his chair. Later, when Mr Berry posed the question to the class about what literature actually was, Hughesy shouted out '*it's the expression of the mind*' nudged Birdy and laughing as he did so.
> [*Fieldnotes*]

Here, Hughesy highlights the complexity of the position he occupies as one of The Valley Boiz. He clearly has an awareness of and interest in the topic in question, but cannot be seen by his close friends or The Geeks to be over-investing in the subject. By showing too much interest, he draws laughter from Brad and Birdy and is quick to put himself down before anyone else can. I noticed that he, Birdy and, to a lesser extent, Brad all did this in different ways throughout the lesson. Given these contradictory performances, I wanted to know what the written work of The Valley Boiz was like, to see what their expected grades were so I stayed behind after the lesson had finished and asked Mr Berry. He informed me that Hughesy, Birdy and Brad had all achieved B grades in the AS modules at the end of the Year 12, and he was positive they would achieve a good result at the end of their final year. For The Valley Boiz studying English and achieving good grades resulted in a constant process of impression management. Laughing, messing around, banter and put-downs took place in the classroom so that the contradictions of studying a studious or passive subject like English, could be minimized.[10]

Sean, one of *The Geeks*, commented on these contradictions during an individual interview when I asked him about some of the Valley Boiz in his class:

MW: So is it weird then that Hughesy and Birdy are doing English...
Sean: Yeah! But they're really good at it as well (MW yeah?) but like they put on this big thing like. They go *'ahh go drinking like'* [impersonates harsh regional accent] and then when it comes to lessons and they are reading their creative writing out, it's really good like.
MW: Do you find that bizarre then?
Sean: Ah yeah it is, they are clearly putting on a front like don't do it, just be normal! Umm...I'm trying to think of an example ...but a couple of weeks ago I think Birdy, who hasn't been in for a while, so Hughesy been on his own and he's been really nice and tidy [meaning he is ok and friendly], talking to us and stuff, having a laugh bit of banter, Birdy then back in today now and then he's not knowing us, it's gone like! You can tell, keeping up appearances kind of thing like...but like it's weird cos like when you talk to them on their own like, say um I was talking to Birdy the other day, like you talk to um and you have a laugh with um, but they laugh at the things you're saying and you feel alright, ah this is tidy like and then as soon as they go then it's like ahhh...they treat you as if nothing happened like it's weird!
[Individual Interview]

For Sean the masculine behaviour of The Valley Boiz is clearly a front. He suggests that away from the group these young men act differently and are willing to talk to him and join in with the different conversations

The Geeks have, something that doesn't happen when The Valley Boiz are together. Their written work, a solitary, individual practice, is also remarked on by Sean to be of a good standard and he seems impressed by it. I suggest that away from the glare of the 'team' performance individually Hughesy and Birdy are able (to an extent), suppress the archetypal front performance of masculinity. Studying English enables them to express another performance of masculinity which is more diverse, but full of tensions and is a struggle to achieve. This switching practice was further evident with Brad.

Brad: 'I don't want people to be intimidated'

As the final year in the Sixth Form progressed, Brad began to distance himself from his friendship group and to spend more time with his girlfriend. This was a common trend among the young men (something I will discuss more with Jimmy in Chapter 7), but it was interesting to see how much effect the change had on Brad. I asked Brad if he thought this had altered things with his friends and he gave a thoughtful reflexive response:

Brad: Ah yeah, big time, happened to me, I was a cock big time I was before, I was aye...
MW: Ah that's a bit harsh.
Brad: No, I was like, before like to Lucy, my life was the boys, boys, boys, then I realised who they were and what I had and, ah, I threw it back in her face, I was a cock, but I don't give a shit anymore, I don't care what people think of me, whereas before, I used to think about what the boys thought...but now I don't care, I am who I am!

[*Individual Interview Year 13*]

Brad felt that the transition he had made from privileging his male friends, to focusing on his own relationship with his girlfriend, had had a positive impact on him. It had enabled him to realize that the macho front performance was problematic and that even though it had provided some form of collective identity for him, he had worried about it. When I asked Brad more about this and perhaps how being part of The Valley Boiz group might have been seen by others in his year as a bit intimidating, he offered another insightful response:

Brad: But I don't want people to be intimidated, I don't like that. I don't want that for other people, because maybe in some ways I was intimidated in some ways by other people.

MW: Do you think you were intimated by them because they were quiet or...?

Brad: Na I wouldn't have been, just find it hard to make conversation, I wouldn't be able to have a conversation say with Nixon, I wouldn't know what to bring up, I'll say hello and if I have a sweet I'll offer him one as well, but I wouldn't know how to have a conversation with him.

MW: Right.

Brad: And I wouldn't be able to have a conversation with Sam, I find it hard, because if I do overhear a conversation it's about computer games and I'm like *'ahh mental stress'* (Laughs). It's all I ever hear, he probably doesn't talk about it all the time, but that's all I ever hear, always going on or about school work... so you know... just let him be innit!

[*Individual Interview Year 13*]

Far from being confident in his macho front-stage performance, Brad occupies a contradictory masculine position. These two narratives highlight the pressures and costs to Brad of performing a traditional version of masculinity. He and the other young men in this chapter may seem to be performing a re-traditionalized version of an older form of masculinity, but the reflexive approach displayed here highlights the on-going struggle to negotiate multiple versions of self. By not wanting to appear intimidating and admitting to being intimidated himself by other young men, the inconsistency of being one of The Valley Boiz is clear. Away from the coercive pressures of the friendship group, Brad finds some release, but cannot connect with the different interests some of The Geeks have and ironically becomes marginalized himself. As the following section concludes for others like Jonesy, the pressure to maintain the front of the performance hid deeper problems.

Jonesy: The playboy mansion

On occasions during Years 12 and 13, various fieldtrips or events were organized by the school for different groups of students. The fieldnotes below were made during an information day held at the University of Glamorgan[11] about the Engineering Education Scheme Wales.[12] The scheme was aimed at Sixth Form students interested in engineering careers, and partnered schools and their students with engineering companies to work together on different projects.

The room next to the main conference centre at the university had been set up for lunch and we filed in. Tomo and Jonesy who I was

with, eagerly heaped sandwiches, pasties and crisps onto their plates and we sat down in a semicircle at one side of the room. During the break out session between talks, Jonesy and Tomo began discussing the lack of women in the room and how difficult it would be to go and talk to any that were there. Tomo laughed and said that they should try out Birdy's chat up line about the polar bear. The conversation moved onto Hugh Hefner and the playboy mansion. Jonesy and Tomo exclaimed that he was *'cool'* and a *'legend'* and they would love to be that age and still have *'fit'* girls living with them so that they could *'bang um'* [have sex] any time they wanted. Jonesy mentioned that when he had been in LA he had visited the Playboy Mansion. He wasn't allowed into the house, but told me that he had grabbed a plant from inside the gate and pulled it out. He'd then stuffed it into his pocket and brought it home with him. He said it was to act as a memory of the holiday, but sadly it just turned into a brown lump by the time he'd got home. He said that he still had the memories in his head that wouldn't fade.
[*Fieldnotes*]

I had gone along to the event with members of the A level Physics and Electronics class and during the lunch break, the above discussion had taken place with Jonesy and Tomo. The way Jonesy told the story about his holiday surprised me as up until this moment he had rarely stopped acting like the classic 'class clown'. In school and on nights out he used jokes, did impressions of teachers and other boys and generally messed around to increase his status with friends, but also it seemed, in order to belong. On one occasion during Year 12, some of this disruptive behaviour had earned him almost legendary status. Whilst sitting in the students social space (common room) he had taken this performance to a new level, by urinating into a kettle that was provided for the students and then boiling it, causing revulsion and admiration from those watching. Despite this incident, I sensed something deeper was going on. This conversation between Tomo and Jonesy was more than just Jonesy trying to validate his status through telling a story. I suggest his narrative can be read in two ways. First as another example of fantasy and sexual storytelling (similar to Hughesy's caravan tale) and a heroic narrative of Hugh Heffner's sexual prowess in the form of an imagined other. Here Heffner is seen as 'cool' and a 'legend' something that the boys say that they want to aspire to, but under the surface this story can be read in a second way, and is far more nuanced and contains some of the diverse elements of masculinity that I have already outlined, and an ability to switch between displays. Through the telling of this story to one of his closest friends, the usual portrayal of front had slipped and something else was visible. Jonesy not only illustrates a naivety in the belief that the plant would remain alive, but also there is a sadness and softness to the tale around the memory of a potential holiday of a lifetime that he said would not fade. I felt that if I got the chance to discuss this with him on his own, I could explore this further.

A few days later this opportunity arose, and I could talk with Jonesy alone as we sat in the common room and I asked more about the holiday. The conversation began when we were discussing learning a language and Jonesy mentioned that he wanted to learn Spanish so that he could pull more girls. I said that I did not speak any languages apart from English, but sometimes having a different accent could be a useful conversation starter. Jonesy said that he agreed with me on the accent front and told me that when he had lived in Swindon, he had experienced this. I was confused as I had not realized he had ever left Cwm Dyffryn and asked him more about this. Jonesy then went on to tell me that he had moved there with his mother for about two years when he was around ten, as his mother had taken him away after she had split up with his father. He continued to inform me that he had only moved back to Cwm Dyffryn (to live with his father and grandparents) when his mother had moved to France with her new partner. The holiday to America (which he stressed was paid for by his mother's new partner) had been the last time he had spent any time with her. She had given him her car when she left for France, which he appreciated, but he mentioned that he would rather see her more. He went on to say that this '*probably affected me psychologically*' and that he worried about girls leaving him. His girlfriend had just cheated on him, but even though he had since kissed someone else, this had not made him feel any better about it.

What is clear here was that for Jonesy, away from the wider peer group, his performance of masculinity can be diluted and the front can be allowed to be adjusted and softened. With close friends, one can be more open or, as Goffman (1959: 115) succinctly puts it, 'step out of character'. The front and back displays of a performance can be kept close, but when a front performance is given, the 'backstage or region' is more often than not often hidden away. When Jonesy is 'on stage', he is a joker and always 'having a laugh', but behind it something else is visible and a glimpse of a more troubled and difficult world seems to emerge. This switching process, as I show throughout this book, occurred time and time again with the young men in this ethnography. As the following chapters will outline, this process was slightly different for separate groups of young men, but the process does shows that those studying the gender identities of young men and theorizing masculinities, must be aware that while multiple masculinities exist, individual young men inhabit these at different times, ages, places and spaces and can switch between them.

Conclusion

At the end of the Sixth Form, the future of many of these young men was uncertain. Birdy, Hughesy, Clive and Shaggy finished their courses and made successful applications to local universities. Through family connections, Davies (who had dropped out of school before the end of the Sixth Form), Brad and Cresco had all found employment, the former with their fathers, the latter with his brother in a local recycling plant and Tomo had been successful in gaining a Modern Apprenticeship with an international steel company. Dai, Jonesy (who had also dropped out before completing Year 13) and Bunk were unemployed and looking for work. What this chapter has shown is that de-industrialization has yet to erode the locality's traditional culture and the associated masculinities still live on even when economies change. These practices become damaging as many young working-class men have not the resources to create alternative options. In many ways, The Valley Boiz seemed to resist the subordination of the new global order by a process not only of enduring, but also by re-traditionalizing the industrial heritage of place by reaffirming acceptable gender norms through educational subjects and leisure pursuits (Kenway et al., 2006). However, as I have shown, on occasion different presentations of self would seem evident and newer ways of being a young man from the Valleys operate simultaneously within some contexts and peer groups relations. This then facilitates a discussion of the contradictoriness of identity to be observed and articulated by the boys themselves. This back region seems to develop as they transition through the Sixth Form. The hegemonic masculinity that is performed during some interactions seems to belong to a particular age, and the Sixth Form is a highly contradictory space which influences the cracks and gaps that begin to emerge.

By staying on in education, despite not being typical Sixth Form students, The Valley Boiz were able to begin to break away from the archetypal performance of working-class masculinity and a more complicated picture starts to emerge. Returning to school was a safe and secure choice for these young men, but it also created and allowed for some space to diverge from the 'normal' expectations of what has come to define what being a man from the Valleys is. It allows for some hope to come through and for a return to ideas of self-improvement which were once fostered through trade union and miners' institutions, but have perhaps been forgotten since the loss of industry. Nonetheless, traditional forms of masculinity based on physical strength, heterosexuality and the rejection of the feminine, continue to hold a powerful position and results in the marginalization of other ways of 'doing boy' in the region. In the next chapter, I look at how another group of young men in the area adapted to these industrial changes and negotiated the pathway to adulthood differently.

4
The Geeks: Studious Working-Class Masculinities

Introduction

Education has played a key role in shaping popular conceptions of Welsh society as being relatively open and meritocratic. It has been argued that a higher value has been placed on educational achievement as a way out of poverty and as a means for improving one's own occupational prospects than in other sections of the British population (see Williams, 1960; Lewis, 1980; Rees and Delamont, 1999; Williams, 2003). Whether based in fact or not, popular perceptions of the sons (less so daughters) of farmers, coal miners and steelworkers using educational success as a way into university, professional occupations and as a means of escape have persisted (Rees and Delamont, 1999; Weeks, 2007). Yet in Cwm Dyffryn and the South Wales Valleys more generally, education as a form of social mobility or as a route out of poverty occurred at the individual level, rather than for the collective community and those who managed it were often the exception to the rule.

As I highlighted in the previous chapter, more young men from some working-class families are opting to continue in forms of post-16 education than might have traditionally done so. Here, I outline the lives of The Geeks, another set of working-class boys in the same year group who lived in the same disadvantaged community. In opposition to The Valley Boiz, these young men's front region displays of masculinity were a lot more studious and could be considered as stereotypically 'geek'. These geekier performances of self were characterized through acts of working hard academically to achieve good grades in a range of subjects, but most notably maths, science and technology. Outside school, these acts were accompanied by leisure interests such as reading books and comics, drawing, writing poetry, playing with gadgets and computer games, and appearing less interested in cars, sport, drinking, girls or fashion. In comparison to The Valley Boiz and other young men at the school, they also seemed to publically express less misogynistic and homophobic views than their peers. The performance of a studious, geekier form of masculinity, in an environment where more traditional notions of masculinity were the default reference point, proved problematic and they occupied the lowest status position in the school's social hierarchy, even as they transitioned through the Sixth Form. These performances were seen by others in their year group as 'feminine' and attracted homophobic name calling and bullying from their peers. However, just like The Valley Boiz, other presentations of self could occur. As The Geeks transitioned through the Sixth Form into older masculinities, some contradictions to the front region of the performance were also apparent. The Geeks, in some situations and in settings away from the school and on occasions Cwm Dyffryn, engaged in many of the traditional, sexist, macho practices that they distanced themselves from and criticized others for engaging in.

I begin this chapter by looking at the literature on working-class boys' educational achievement. I focus especially on the role of locality and address how this impacts on the development of a studious performance of masculinity. I then define the peer group and look at what being a 'geek' meant in this context. The chapter then analyses in detail the front displays of this more studious form of working-class masculinity before (as I did with The Valley Boiz) highlighting some contradictions to this display. In other settings, it also became apparent that there were costs and consequences that accompanied these traditional class-based performances.

Working-class educational achievement and the performance of studious masculinities

Social science research that has centred on working-class young people in the UK and elsewhere has tended to focus on their problematic relationship with education. In particular this work has addressed three main themes. First, studies have concentrated on the role of education as a route to social mobility and as a way out of working-class origins. This pathway traditionally occurred through the grammar school system (Jackson and Marsden, 1962; Lacey, 1970). Second, a prominent focus has been on anti-school or rebellious behaviour, poor performances and educational underachievement (Hargreaves,

1967; Willis, 1977; Corrigan, 1979; Brown, 1987; Epstein et al., 1998; McDowell, 2003). Third, this work has begun to look at the costs associated with educational achievement for working-class identity, once one has progressed to university or reached adulthood (Skeggs, 1997; Walkerdine et al., 2001; Weis, 2004; Reay et al., 2009; Wakeling, 2010).

However, some of this research on working-class men has been accused of pathologizing the working-classes, and there have been suggestions that some male authors have been guilty of glorifying oppressive forms of masculinity, such as the 'hooligan' (Skeggs, 1992; Delamont, 2000; Ingram, 2009). Delamont (2000), in particular, has argued that this trend has a long history in ethnographic work and has occurred on both sides of the Atlantic. Alongside these criticisms, some studies have offered a more nuanced critique of the problems and practices associated with being a working-class young man and broadened the concept of masculinity to challenge, exploring male dominance and power inequalities between men and between boys (Connell, 1989; Mac an Ghaill, 1994; Martino, 1999; Reay, 2002; Renold, 2004; Francis et al., 2010). Nonetheless what still appears to be missing from many of these studies, and what the authors fail to engage with, is how the specifics of a locality impact upon what is means to be a man in certain communities and the effect this has on successful working-class boys' identities and intra-class differences. As Morris (2012) found in his study of young men in Kentucky, the experiences and interactions they have in their everyday lives, within their own places and spaces, help form the way young men experience schooling. For some young men, schooling may appear as an extension to one's home life, but for others is may be an alienating experience (Reay, 2002; Weis, 2006; Kenway et al., 2006; Keddie, 2007). Locality and the importance of place are therefore significant when analysing performances of masculinity and attitudes towards education and more importantly, about how particular performances are shaped.

Introducing The Geeks: Educational achievement, subject-choice and family biographies

The Geeks friendship group consisted primarily of Leon, Gavin, Ruben, Scott, Nibbles, Alan, Sean, Ieuan, Sam, Sin and Nixon. Apart from Sin, who was of Chinese heritage, all were white and had been born in the town and, by Year 11, they had the highest grades in their year group. Even though Cwm Dyffryn High School operated a mixed ability policy for the majority of the taught subjects during the compulsory years of schooling, the core GCSE qualifications of English, Mathematics and Science were still streamed from set one to six. It was in one of these top set classes (an English Literature class) that I first encountered some of The Geeks on the opening morning of fieldwork observations when they were revising for an upcoming exam. Some of the young men were spread around one side of the classroom sitting quietly, two to a desk, concentrating on the poems and the past English Literature exam paper they had been given by the teacher. Another group of young men (whom we met in the previous chapter) although smaller in number, seemed to control the classroom space. They did this by shouting out answers to the teacher's questions, laughing and messing around with each other and generally dominating the learning environment and ignoring the commands of the teacher to *'put your hand up'* before answering. In the playground at break and lunchtimes, this marginalization continued. The Geeks, as they were referred to by others in their year group (as they grew older they reclaimed this label), stood or sat around the edges of the playground with their packed lunches. Here they talked about schoolwork and computer games and were excluded from the wider social space where games of football, which spread across the yard, dominated (Table 4.1).

Those young men who transgress a locality's social norms by being academically successful and having different cultural interests, are often bullied and receive labels by their peers such as 'nerd', 'dweeb', 'dork', 'freak', 'brainiac', 'boffin', 'swot' and 'geek' (see Connell, 1989; Martino, 1999; Pascoe, 2007; Zekany, 2011; Mendick and Francis, 2012). While the word geek is a relatively simple term, it is full of ambiguity and has multiple meanings changing from place to place. Nonetheless what these labels all tend to have in common is that those who receive them, are deemed to be stigmatized (Goffman, 1963) in some way or other as overtly intelligent, shy, unattractive social outcasts, who often shun other people who do not share their stigmatized status. Accompanying these labels are particular attributes of personal front which are deemed abnormal, such as unfashionable hair and dress styles, glasses and with reputations for bad personal hygiene. The word geek is likely to be used as a pejorative marker (especially in working-class communities) and to be labelled as such is to be defined as a social misfit (Kendall, 1999; Comeau and Kemp, 2007; Pascoe, 2007). In the extracts below, a 'geek' is described by the young men themselves as someone who does not

Table 4.1 The Geeks: Educational and future trajectories, family backgrounds and sporting interests

Name	Subjects studied Post 16	Parents' occupations	Parents with higher education degrees	Siblings	In receipt of EMA	Team sports	Final exam results year 13	Immediate post-school destination
Sam	A Level English A Level History A Level Media	F: Caretaker M: Supermarket manager (Divorced)	None	Younger sister	No	No	A*, A, A	University of Nottingham, BA, English and Creative Writing
Ruben	A Level Physics A Level Electronics A Level Maths	F: Supply teacher (secondary) M: Midwife	Both	Younger brother	No	No		Cardiff University, BSC Engineering
Scott	A Level Physics A Level Electronics A Level Maths A Level Art	F: Retired mechanic M: Housewife	None	Older sister	Yes	No	A, A, B	University of Lincoln, BA, Architecture
Alan	A Level English A Level History A Level Media	F: Absent, never known M: Administrator local government Step F: Unemployed/bus driver	None	2 older brothers 1 older sister	Yes	No	B, B, C	University of Glamorgan, BA, History
Sean	A Level English A Level History A Level IT	F: Mechanic M: Administrator in a school Separated, never married	None	Older sister	Yes	No	A, D, E	Cardiff Metropolitan University, BA, English and Creative Writing

Name	A Levels	Parents	Siblings	?	?	Grades	Destination
Nibbles	A Level English A Level History A Level Media	F: Absent M: Dead Step F: Steel worker But long-term back injury so cannot work	None	Younger brother	Yes	No	?	University of Glamorgan, BA, English
Nixon	A Level Chemistry A Level Biology A Level Maths	F: Driving instructor M: Teacher (primary)	M	?	No	No	B, B, C	University of Glamorgan, BA, Politics
Ieaun	A Level Chemistry A Level Maths A Level Biology	F: Mineral surveyor M: Housewife	F	3 older brothers	No	No	C, C, D	University of Portsmouth, BSc, Biochemical studies
Sin	A Level History A Level Chemistry A Level Biology	F and M: small business owners (takeaway)	None	Older brother	No	No	?	Returned to Sixth Form to re-take A levels
Leon	A Level Chemistry A Level Biology A Level Maths	F: Teacher M: Secretary in college	F	Younger brother	No	Yes Football	A, B, C	University of Portsmouth, BSc, Chemistry
Gavin	A Level IT A Level English	F: Manager in a hospital M: Housewife	None	?	No	No	D, D	Returned to Sixth Form to re-take A levels

participate in sports and is more interested in video games, films and comics:

Sam: Get a sporting accolade and you're already like the greatest person ever.
Alan: If you don't do sport in school you're like...
Sam: ...a geek...
Sean: ...yeah a geek basically.
[*Group Interview Year 11*]

MW: So do you play a lot of video games then?
Sean: Yeah, I'm a geek I am, I love games!
MW: So are you really a geek like when you say you are?
Sean: Yeah I love all the geeky things, like um games, films um...
MW: ...you're well into your films are you?
Sean: Ah yeah! Graphic novels, comics, things like that.
[*Individual Interview Year 12*]

As Sean indicates here, being defined as a geek was also evident in more subtle ways than just being positioned as academically successful. In Year 11, some of The Geeks were smaller in stature and less physically developed than many others in the year group, making them easy targets for bullying. They turned up for lessons on time with their own pens and pencil cases, did their homework and carried their books and equipment in bags, which others in their year group did not always use. Along with this compliance to rules, they correctly adhered to the school dress code and their uniforms were accompanied by neat haircuts and for some, horn-rimmed glasses or braces on their teeth, completing the stereotypical geek persona. These artefacts then marked The Geeks with their own recognizable identity.

Whilst The Geeks adhered to school rules and policy, others in their year group sought to disrupt uniform policy and replace compulsory items with one's own. It was common practice to replace the standard black V-necked jumper, with a round necked one, because this then meant the school tie could be removed and it would go unseen by teachers. Other attempts by those in The Geeks year group to disrupt school rules included replacing shoes with trainers, wearing hooded jackets and baseball caps and, for some, adorning their bodies with flashy rings, chains and single earrings or studs. Besides these uniform alterations, as I showed in the last chapter, a large group of pupils, who were registered on sports educational programmes, were also allowed to wear a tracksuit instead of the regular uniform. This process not only validated a specific form of masculinity based on sporting prowess by the educational institution itself, but also acted as a symbolic marker of status which The Geeks did not have access to and were therefore 'othered' as a group for not belonging to the sporting elite.

After achieving good GCSE grades, all The Geeks returned to the school's Sixth Form. The subjects chosen by The Geeks to study were predominantly in the arts (English, History, Fine Art), natural sciences (Biology, Chemistry or Physics), Maths and IT. The Geeks had been in the highest sets for all their core subjects at GCSE level and even though they were a close group of friends, they were fiercely competitive over their grades. They also all harboured aspirations to go to university. This is not to say that others in their year group did not aspire to go to university or gain well paid and meaningful employment, but for The Geeks this seemed to be of paramount importance to their projected futures. As Sam illustrates here, he had thought of a course he wanted to study at university and planned on spending a year in America as part of this:

Sam: Journalism is what I'd like to get into at the moment.
MW: Alright.
Sam: And I'd like to go to America as well for my university course.
MW: So you've thought a little bit down the line where you want to go?
Sam: Yeah I have done a bit of research into it and they do offer it in some of the English universities and the exchanges into American universities, so I'll aim for that first... if I get rejected I'll just go lower down the ladder.
MW: So you've thought about going to uni then?
Sam: Yeah [shouts] I am going to uni!
[*Individual Interview Year 11*]

Sam's final statement here, not only shows a powerful sense of agency, but also a commitment that he is not constrained by place and his ambitions clearly illustrate a rejection of the locality and a willingness to move on. His determination to find a way to his goals by attending different universities, if his first choice is unavailable, is also clear. Attending a university for Sam is therefore a way to gain a form of masculinity (Connell, 1995), so often denied him – and other boys like him – who have invested in academic capital in this community.

The Geeks parents' occupational backgrounds give some indication to their positive outlook on academic qualifications and they shared similar, although not identical, family biographies. A few of the boys had fathers and mothers who had some experience of higher education (Ruben, Nixon, Ieuan and Leon) and were employed in professional occupations as surveyors, teachers, secretaries or midwives. Other parents owned their own businesses in the form of motor repair (Sean) and takeaway food shops (Sin) or were engaged in more traditional working-class occupations, such as lorry driver (Scott), caretaker (Sam), in supermarkets or were unemployed (Gavin, Alan). Three of the boys (Scott, Ieuan and Gavin) said that their mothers stayed at home and describing them as housewives. Sadly Nibbles' mother had died when he was 14 and his step dad (his biological father has left the family years before) was on long-term incapacity benefits after being injured in an accident whilst driving a lorry.

Although some of these young men's parents could be seen as employed in middle-class occupations, my justification for using the term 'working-class' to refer to these young men as a group, is because it is important to recognize the inequalities that they experienced by coming from a deprived community and the levels of social, economic and cultural capital they had access to. I suggest that having a parent who is a teacher in a de-industrialized area (with high levels of unemployment, low levels of health and educational attainment and employment opportunities) is very different to having a parent who is a teacher in a more affluent area (see Weis, 1990). It is also important that the geo-demographics of place are considered when defining class and how successful boys from poorer communities experience education (Burrows and Gane, 2006).

The performance of a geeky front: Classroom practices and social interaction

In Cwm Dyffryn High School, the focus on sports was high and for many young men this was a clear way of projecting a successful heterosexual masculine image (see Gard and Meyenn, 2000; Messner, 2001; Kimmel, 2006). This focus on sporting success infuriated The Geeks, and their front performances of a studious masculinity continued to be at odds with the school's emphasis on sport.

Sam: Get a sporting accolade and you're already like the greatest person ever!
Sean: Do you know where the old gym is by there?
MW: Umm.
Sean: Well on the wall outside it, there are photos on the wall of sportsmen from the school, but you won't find any photos of people who done well and that... it's just all sports.

Ruben: Yeah that's a point yeah...
Nibbles: ...yeah...
Ruben: Like with all the past students they got this one played football for, or amateur football, for Wales turns out he's now just a bin man now, but he did play amateur football for Wales once...so have his picture up. Then you've got other people then, who've gone, like Mark Bowen, who recent left he's gone to Oxford to study in Oxford [University] and they haven't got, you know, no recognition of him around the school.
[*Group Interview Year 11*]

The Geeks occupied a difficult position in their de-industrialized community, and as I have shown were often seen as socially deficient. In the extract from a group interview above, they position their own performance of masculinity as superior to that of the school environment, as they felt the institution itself was complicit in producing a form of masculinity based on sporting prowess and physical attributes. Their studious form of masculinity, based on academic interests, is not seen as an essence of 'real' masculinity, forged through industrial labour or associated with specific cultural or sporting practices. It therefore illustrates a more feminized and socially marginalized form of masculinity in the community. Ruben is also aware that some occupations, such as being a 'bin man', have distinct markers of status and class, and that by achieving academically he hopes to be able to distance himself from these lower-class occupations.

The front performance of this studious, geekier masculinity brought with it certain disadvantages. Bullying and intimidation were often problems in Year 11 for The Geeks. Some of this bullying had been physical further down the school years, but it was still present through verbal altercations, subtle gestures and smirking. Sam, in particular, found solace in feeling intellectually superior to others and as a way of combating this bullying.

Nixon: They do try and bully us, or try.
MW: Obviously they're not stealing your dinner money...[group laughter].
MW: So what type of bullying would it take?
Sean: Verbal abuse like.
MW: Alright.
Ruben: I wouldn't say I get bullied by them really, but they do always do their little in-jokes, like '*Nixon, Nixon high five*' and then they expect Nixon to turn around and they all find it funny that Nixon doesn't turn around.

Sam: It's like little smiley little faces...
Ieuan: [talks over the top of Ruben]... it's so retarded that it's funny but it's easy to beat them just by speaking.
Sam: We're more intelligent than them, as you probably all know, so you can just speak, you know just talk really fancy to them and they get annoyed and they just walk off, and you insult them without them realizing it, which makes us feel big.

[*Group Interview Year 11*]

Here Sam and his friends are illustrating a form of what Redman and Mac an Ghaill (1997: 169) call 'muscular intellectualness' (see also Edley and Wetherell, 1997). This was a way for them to combat the verbal altercations that were targeted at them and to seem superior by using their intellectual capital. This front performance helped articulate a form of masculinity that differed to that which traditionally defined being a 'proper' man in their community. It also contradicted much of what the school culture tended to validate through its focus on sports. The development of 'muscular intellectualness' was also evident between lessons where it was common for The Geeks to play Scrabble. Scores were kept and a record of who had won each game was collected. A dictionary was used to check words and cheating was frowned upon. During one game in the school's library, Ieuan had tried to use the internet on his mobile phone to look for a specific word, and, when discovered, this was met with disdain by the others. The value of words in the Scrabble game was a way to symbolize capital and power within the friendship group, but outside it, the capital provided less protection and was not equal to the power held by the more sporty boys.

Sam, who was selected by his teachers to be the school's head boy, also found other subtle ways to promote his intellectual status over those in his year group who had previously taunted him. In the following excerpt from my field notes, Sam makes it very hard for Brad, one of The Valley Boiz, to get help with the homework that had been set. I was sitting in the library between lessons with some of The Geeks when Brad rushed in.

> Brad poked his head in (to the library) and looked really worried and agitated. He asked the boys what homework he had to do for Mr Berry for Friday and as Sam put down a Scrabble tile nonchalantly answered '*reading*'. Brad seeming confused at the advice being given and asked for a second time what this was. Sam again seemingly frustrated at the intrusion, sighed loudly and without turning to look at Brad said

'that chapter from the book we are reading'. With only one brief further comment from Alan about the homework, Brad still seeming confused, groaned and rushed out of the library.

[*Fieldnotes*]

Sam here had a way of getting back at Brad whose performance of masculinity differed to that of The Geeks. He was wearing the sports tracksuit and trainers that were the required uniform for his BTEC course so he immediately stood out from the group who were dressed in school uniform. Sam's reluctance to help and his adoption of a superior position was a way of punishing Brad for what he assumed was a lacklustre approach to the homework. It was also as a way for him to exercise power in this situation where he so often (even being head boy) didn't have it. He had the answers regarding the homework and Brad wanted them.

Whilst the bullying had been reduced as The Geeks had grown older and the year group had grown smaller (at the start of Year 13 only 35 pupils remained out of 134 who finished the end of compulsory schooling in Year 11), Sean still found that Sam wasn't really able to deal well with confrontation:

Sean: Sometimes he (Sam) doesn't really think about other people like.
MW: I remember in Year 11, sometimes boys used to take the piss out of you but most of them have left now, so he used a bit of humour to deflect it?
Sean: Yeah, but sometimes when he does that, it doesn't really help the situation! Like say they're like, you know, casually taking the piss...
MW: ...yeah...
Sean: ...and he'll get really bitchy and snipe at them or something and they'll just get worse and you're thinking by doing that you're making yourself look weirder! Just take it like!

[*Individual Interview Year 13*]

The 'piss take', described here, is a practice with a direct link back to a working-class occupational culture where male chauvinism, racist and sexist humour were a part of the industrial workplace and were accompanied by practical jokes, coarse language, banter and messing around between (male) colleagues (see Beynon, 1973; Tolson, 1977; Willis, 1979; Cockburn, 1983). In Sean's eyes, Sam needed to 'take it' (the piss taking or the banter) in order to stop being seen as 'weird' in front some of his peers. I enquired more about the banter that went on between his close friends and Sam told me: '*We (do) take the mick out of each other, take the piss out of each other, if you fall over or spell something wrong, we laugh at each other.*'

For The Geeks, this banter was just another extension of their academic abilities, where 'having a laugh' came through picking out errors in others' academic work or commenting on their personal faults. The industrial legacy behind the 'piss take' is being expressed in a different way by The Geeks, but it still illustrated the importance and power of it, in determining one's own ability to perform an acceptable version of manhood within the friendship group.

Whereas Sam struggled with other forms of banter, Sean seemed good at this; being really quick witted and in the context of the reduced student number in the Sixth Form, he could answer back with a joke and almost always get a laugh from others around him, even those who were trying to 'take the piss' out of his friends. Alongside his geekier interests (computer games and reading comics), he supported Liverpool Football Club and would regularly talk to others in the Sixth Form common room about whose team had beaten who, and whose team was better. Yet because of his ability to take part in a football discourse and to make others laugh (he could also laugh at himself), I never witnessed any of the 'piss taking' experienced by others. Scott, who was a lot shorter and slighter in statue than Sean and who did not have the quickness of wit, often attracted negative attention for his long hair and beard which grew longer and longer as Year 13 progressed. He was often referred to by others outside The Geeks group as 'Jesus' because of his supposed similarities to the religious figure. Only when his closest friends Sam, Ruben and Ieuan stressed how scruffy and untidy he looked and threatened to physically force him to shave and cut off his straggly beard and hair, did he decide to get it cut. This then prompted much hilarity and questioning when he walked into the Sixth Form common room the next day. It would seem that Sean's ability to perform a traditional version of working-class masculinity by investing in football banter, alongside his geekier masculinity, allowed him to code-shift and achieve something that Sam or Scott were unable to do.

Nonetheless away from the school this ability to code-shift was not so successful. When Sean had finished his A levels and he was waiting for the results, he worked throughout the summer as a receptionist in a local motor repair garage partly gained through his father's connections as a mechanic. He took calls from customers and dealt with enquires about cars and parts. As his time in the workplace increased, it soon became apparent that he was unable to shift masculine codes in order to display the traditional working-class football discourse he had successfully performed in the Sixth Form to protect him from the 'piss take'. Not only was his appearance at odds with the older mechanics he worked with (tall and skinny in stature, long, bleached blonde hair, casual clothes and a spotty complexion), but he was unable to build up a rapport as he was working in the office away from the workshop. Whilst the mechanics were repairing cars as a team in the workshop, he was sitting alone completing administrative work.

On a trip to the cinema with Alan and me to see that summer's big blockbuster film *Inception*, he told us how, on many occasions, he felt left out of the daily routines in the garage. These in particular were the journeys to the local shop for sausage rolls, pies or pasties that he felt he was deliberately excluded from. When he gave one of the mechanics money to buy him something, they often returned empty handed and he was told that they had run out of whatever it was that he had asked them to get. On one occasion Sean had gone back to the same shop to find the shelves were actually full of the product he had wanted. Sean also said he felt frustrated as they expected him to make tea for them, but he never had a cup of tea made in return. Only the previous week he had ventured into the workshop as he was bored being stuck in the office alone and had mentioned he was going out with his girlfriend to the cinema on the upcoming weekend. On hearing this one of the mechanics had turned to him and exclaimed in mock surprise *'girlfriend'?* creating a big laugh from the other men in the workshop in the process. It is clear here that not only was Sean seen as effeminate due to working in the office of the garage (being ignored and often expected to make the tea) but from the not so subtle hints and assumptions made towards Sean, it seems that the other workers thought he was gay. The homosexualization of his gender performance was alien to the mechanics' workplace and the social-economic and cultural heritage of the region that was their default reference point. Sean and The Geeks, by choosing to invest in 'mental labour', saw this as a progression to professional futures. However, by investing in a more middle-class success discourses, they were further solidifying their marginalized masculinities and distancing themselves from their working-class peers. For Sean, the experience of the workplace was like stepping back in time to a different era, when the physical body was valued over mental ability. The transition from school into a space of employment was difficult and, even though it was a temporary position before going to university, it was an uncomfortable and troubled time, and he left before the end of the summer. With limited opportunities for work in the locale, for boys like Sean, these opportunities create valuable experience of the job market. However, the pressures to act in certain ways create extra problems and as in Sean's case, might be too much for some boys to deal with.

Teachers

The Geeks had a lot of respect for certain teachers but seemed to have little or nothing at all for others. In Year 11, they mocked Mr Sharpe for looking like a character from the cartoon *The Simpsons* and talked with scorn about the lack of ability of some teachers to control other pupils in their classes who they thought weren't working as hard as they were.

Sam: They don't bother in class and then they get special help from the teachers to get their work done!
MW: On time?
Sam: Yeah just let them fail and laugh at them at the end...(group laughter)...I'd make a crap teacher!
Sean: It's like Mrs Jayne changed the deadlines with the coursework, a week later they're still using class time to get it done, we had to take the deadlines but they didn't.
MW: What was the deadline?
Sean: Umm can't remember now, but it was like next week next week, it kept changing.
MW: So they try to give more time?
Leon: This one time right, all the chavs in the media class, speak and all that and Mrs Jayne doesn't really do anything about it... and I spoke up cos Mrs Jayne was teaching something... like ridiculous... Mrs Jayne was doing spider diagrams and I said this *'isn't going to get me anywhere in life'*.
[*Group Interview Year 11*]

Sean and Sam adhere to the rules and deadlines set by the teacher, but they suggest that others in their classes do not appear to be as concerned. This brings with it a feeling of intellectual superiority because they have completed the work set by the teacher, but frustration because their peers, who might be struggling or are less interested, receive extra time and help. Leon here not only criticizes the teacher for the classroom pedagogy, but also the way others pupils in the class, who he refers to as 'chavs', are dealt with – placing himself above the behaviour of both the teacher and his classmates. Also by being in the top sets for their compulsory subjects, The Geeks were taught by the most experienced members of staff and had preferential treatment in terms of equipment and books. The hidden curriculum was important as it impacted on the expectations of them by their teachers. This continued into the Sixth Form with the preference of teacher help being given to those thinking of applying to university. Inter-social class differences were appearing here, and The Geeks positioned themselves against others in their year group. This distancing from their peers occurred in other ways too.

Boyishness: The Geeks doing 'mature' heterosexuality

In the school and in the community more generally there seemed to be official and unofficial ways of being male with The Geeks occupying a difficult position as academic achievers, not just in terms of their studiousness, but also in the way they treated the young women in their lives:

Sam: Some boys you know are very boyish!

MW: So between the boys (friends) do you talk like that about your...

Sam: ...no, no I keep my private life private, I've only had one girlfriend and everything I know and everything I have done has been with her, that's it, she is the only person.

MW: Well in some ways I think that it's really nice cos some of the boys the way they talk about it you know *'I was with her last night and cor!'*

Sam: Yeah I know, it's callous, something to do a bit of fun... I know it's as if they treat them, not to sound clichéd, as an object. You know like I've got the latest mobile phone, I've got the latest girlfriend, that sort of thing.

[*Individual Interview Year 13*]

In this interview, Sam criticizes others in the year group for being what he terms 'boyish'. He portrays himself as against the objectification of women, a practice he perceives some of his peers are involved in. The expectation of this objectification, in terms of acceptable manhood practices, is also addressed in another individual interview with Ruben outlined below. He discussed a night out in the town where he had felt under pressure from other young men in the year group to chase after or 'pull' a girl he was friendly with and conform to a heterosexual script. Ruben told me:

> Like when we were in the Harp (pub) with that Jenny... everybody but you, said *'ah go on, get in there Ruben'*, But I explained to you what was going on and you listened. I tried to explain to the others but

they weren't having it, but you understood my side of it.... you've got people expecting you to do stuff, making opinions on stuff, but they don't know what situation you're in... boys think that you only want to talk to girls for only one reason!
[*Individual Interview Year 13*]

As with Sam, in this interview extract Ruben outlines the normal expectations of manhood that he feels are forced upon him by his peers and the pressures that are placed on him to interact with members of the opposite sex in order to create potential sexual conquests. To be simply friends with a girl, without another motive, is viewed as strange and draws criticism from other young men around him.

Whilst Ruben felt the pressure on him to comply with heterosexual norms, Nibbles, the only gay young man in the year group, felt less pressure. As Nibbles began to explore his sexuality and go out to gay bars outside the town and attend gay pride events, he became more of an outsider and drifted out of the group. Whilst chatting about this in the common room one day, he told me that he had come out at the start of Year 11, which had been a particularly tough time in his life as his mother had died around the same time. I asked him if he had experienced any bullying and he told me he often had to put up with some name calling and abusive language. During year 13, I enquired if this still happened, to which he said '*I'm more used to it (now), and so much stuff has happened to me, I'm kind of not bothered.*' I did notice that whilst some of this name-calling tended to occur whilst he walked around the school from younger pupils, it did not occur from his own year group. I discussed this with Tomo and Brad, two of The Valley Boiz and asked what they thought about this bullying. Tomo commented that '*if he's gay, he's gay, no point in going on about it or bullying someone. As long as he stays away from me and don't try and touch me, it's all good.*' Brad laughed and added that there was '*no point in hating someone who was gay, it was childish*', but he also added rather forcefully that if a guy came on to him, he would '*batter him*' (beat him up)'. Thus, the experiences of some young men from marginalized communities who do come out would seem to indicate that homophobia is still something that is encounter in contemporary society.

Whilst Ruben, Sam and Nibbles are trying to be anti-sexist, anti-objectivist and exploring their sexualities in different ways, they have to do so in an environment where more traditional notions of masculinity are the default reference points. Despite these positive outlooks, at other times, their masculinities seemed to be performed in often contradictory ways. Selves cannot be totally created outside the social milieu one is situated within, which can constrain one's actions and shape interactions with others. So despite their front performances outlined so far, The Geeks were far from the one-dimensional stereotype depicted by popular culture. The desire to distance themselves from the area and from an archetype of masculinity was clearly evident, but at other times, their masculinities seemed to be performed in often contradictory ways. I now want to move on to look at some of the contradictions to this studious front that I have outlined so far.

Contradictions and social pressures

The friendship group was based primarily on their educational connections, but outside school The Geeks found it harder to 'hang around' or in the local vernacular 'bother' with each other in Year 11. The school's catchment area was spread between the outlying villages to the north and south of valley around the main town. Sam and Ruben, for example, lived six miles apart even though they attended the same school. Sam lived in a small farming village four miles to the north of Cwm Dyffryn whilst Ruben lived south of the town in a community of densely packed terraced housing which had been built around a long-defunct colliery. Being 16, both were unable to drive and without any income they relied for the most part on their parents for lifts or money for buses. Ruben did cycle, but the six-mile journey, mostly uphill, that he would have had to have made to see Sam after school was impractical. As Ruben informed me, they could only meet up if it had been organized in advance.

The geography of the area played a role in the nature of their friendships, but so too did their investment in mental labour. Those in their year group who played sports, played music in bands (see the next chapter) or attended a local youth club had a collective focal point for their out-of-school activities which The Geeks did not have. This became easier as The Geeks grew older and activities started to revolve around the pubs and clubs of Cwm Dyffryn. For Scott's birthday, Ruben had arranged for a game of 'pub snooker' to be played. Everyone invited had to attend dressed as if to play snooker in ties and waistcoats. A chart, which Ruben was carrying, had been drawn up with the names of all the players (Ruben, Scott, Alan, Sean, Sam, Ieuan, Sin and my name) on one side with the points scored or 'balls potted' on the other, alcohol was to be substituted for 'balls potted'. Pints of lager or cider were the 'red balls' and worth one point each, shots of various coloured spirits were the 'coloured balls' and the more sprits that were drunk, the more points could be earned. In theory, one had to drink a pint or pot a 'red ball' and follow it up with a shot of spirits or a 'coloured ball' progressing through the colours in sequence just like in the traditional game of snooker. As my fieldnotes illustrate this soon got a bit messy:

> When we got to the rugby club the game of 'snooker' was really beginning to get out of control. I had deliberately shied away from drinking spirits so as to last the night, but Ruben who was in the lead and still keeping score, kept downing shots one after the other. Scott the smallest guy in the year group was beginning to slur his words and I couldn't quite understand what he was saying... as the night wore on Ruben got in a bigger and bigger mess and at one point spilt a pint of lager all over the table, himself and the seats.
> [*Fieldnotes*]

Even though a few years previously, they had mocked their peers for indulging in underage drinking and acting out of character when drunk, playing pub snooker provided a way for The Geeks to perform the more traditional working-class masculinities they missed out on by being academic achievers. But remnants of their front display of a studious geeky masculinity are also evident here and not totally discarded. Here the young men are drinking with an aim not just to get drunk, but to also score points and record their achievement in a chart as they went along, in keeping with their geekier masculinities and to gain a form of accreditation for the act. By embracing social practices (e.g. wearing costumes/dressing up) and drinking games of many undergraduates in higher education institutions, they could also be seen as preparing themselves for university life, highlighting how masculine pursuits, such as binge drinking, cut across social class groups (see Thurnell-Read, 2012).

As the following detailed fieldnotes illustrate, on one occasion when The Geeks went out to celebrate Sean's 18th birthday in the capital city Cardiff, away from the town and within their own close friendship group The Geeks were able to further participate in some of the other practices that they criticized their peers for doing:

> Whilst drinking in Wetherspoons before leaving Cwm Dyffryn, Ruben had suggested that when they got to Cardiff that night they should go to a strip club to really celebrate Sean's birthday. The other boys seemed interested and 'up for it'. When we got to Cardiff later in the evening, I never seriously considered that they would go into one, but as we walked down one of the main streets and neared a club

it appeared that we were going in! I momentarily tried to change the decision by saying that is was going to cost a lot of money and it would be better to go somewhere else, but no one seemed to listen and my pleas were ignored. As we paid our entrance fee (£6.00) and descended into the club the boys were rather excited. We were ushered over to a table in the middle of a large room full of comfortable low chairs and tables with floor to ceiling mirrors around the club and a small bar at the back. A small number of older men were spread out across the room with their eyes fixed on the dancer on the stage in front. She was naked apart from a G-string and The Geeks soon started nervously laughing and chatting to each other and pointing at the dancer on the stage. I noticed that there were half a dozen or so young women walking around the floor of the club just wearing underwear and small robes. Until we were served drinks by one of the clothed waitresses, they did not approach the table. Once the drinks and been brought over, a few of the dancers came over to chat to us. The dancers sat on the edges of the seats or stood in front of the seats towering about the seated boys. Some whispered into individual boys' ears or playfully encouraged the others to suggest a dance for one of the group. I was struck by how quickly the boys were persuaded to go off for a 'private dance' with the dancers. Each one-on one dance (costing £10 for three minutes) took place in a private booth. After midnight the prices were increased and the same dance cost £20.

[*Fieldnotes*]

The pressure to conform to heterosexual practices, to hold the male gaze and to objectify women is fully on display here. The Geeks, who as I have shown normally distanced themselves from many of the attitudes that their peers expressed towards women, when away from their home town, felt much freer to indulge in many of the same practices they chastized others for doing. Without the risk of being judged by anyone they knew, or having the contradicting to their usual studious front performance of self challenged, this night out was a chance for them to live the heterosexual fantasy and act like the 'real' men that their marginalized geeky position did not often allow. It can also be seen as an escape from the pressures that being an academic achiever in an area like Cwm Dyffryn brought on them. To end this chapter, I turn to the desperation and feelings of escape that The Geeks often felt in being outsiders and the barriers to these desires that came with occupying a disadvantaged social class position.

Escape practices: University desires and imagined futures

When I first encountered The Geeks, they discussed wanting to escape the valley, which they aimed to do through achieving good grades in their GCSEs and then taking A Levels. Many also expressed a desire to continue to university and to enter middle-class occupations such as medical consultants, journalists and geologists. As noted earlier, Sam had already thought of a course in Year 11 and planned on spending a year in America studying. His aspirations grew and he applied to study English Literature at Oxford in Year 13. Unfortunately he was unsuccessful in his application, failing the entrance exam, and in an individual interview he reflected on this:

MW: And did you feel like you could have fitted in there?
Sam: (Laughs) No, not really, like um I went to like ah an Oxford interview preparation thing, in Bristol.
MW: Right ok.
Sam: Again totally pointless obviously.
MW: No, no I think it's all experience.
Sam: I went there and I felt, I'd never felt so Welsh!
MW: Really?
Sam: Like a lot of people there were Welsh, but they were privately schooled, so they spoke, you know with that really intelligent sounding non dialect accent, that just sounds English.
MW: Ok.
Sam: And everybody just spoke like that I thought I sound so Welsh, there was this part where he said *'do you want to speak in front of the group'*, and I said no I don't.
MW: Because you were conscious about your accent?
Sam: Yeah, I could hear myself, and I don't sound Welsh in comparison to a lot of people around here, everyone was really different is the best way to put it. I mean here it's all camaraderie and you have you group of friends and you don't grass...as the old phrase goes! But there it was dog-eat-dog, you just look after yourself, and there everybody was [puts on upper-class accent] *'I'm very smart, listen to me.'*
MW: And that's how you feel a lot of people were?
Sam: That's how they were yeah, they'd ask questions and then answer them, and jumping up and down or whatever, but when your schools like this and the teacher asks questions, you look at the floor, that's how it goes...

[*Individual Interview Year 13*]

From Sam's retelling of his rejection by Oxford and the experience of the preparation day in Bristol, what comes through is that despite being one of the highest academic achievers in his school, he feels he is unable to compete with other young people he met at this event. He is aware of the accents of others at the preparation day (who he thinks may have been privately schooled) and feels conscious and possibly embarrassed about his Welsh accent, which is shaped by an industrial working-class history. So, despite performing a studious, geekier form of masculinity in his home community (which often brought with it intimidation and marked him out as different from peers), he is unable to feel comfortable in this new environment, illustrating the hidden injuries of his classed position (Sennett and Cobb, 1972). It also impacts on the extent to which he can impression manage his masculinity in this particular setting. He cannot fully shift from his classed position and he struggles with his normal intellectual performance with this different audience.

University for others was further seen as an escape and a way to get out of Cwm Dyffryn. One afternoon towards the end of Year 13, when I walked around the town centre with Sean and Alan, they seemed to vent their frustration at living there. I asked them what they saw as the worst things about it and Sean told me that he hated '*the people, the empty shops and the nothingness of it all*'! Alan said he couldn't wait to get out and go to university, and was desperate to leave. On the walk back to my car, I asked the boys why they thought others did not want to leave the town. To this Sean said, '*well without sounding like a prick like, I think it's down to intelligence in a way. There's nothing here, my dad said Cwm Dyffryn used to be known as the Vegas of the Valleys with loads of clubs and stuff. It's just shit now.*'

Alan and Sean also talked about the ages of people around them in the town and commented how old everyone seemed. The economic restructuring of the town and the valley as a whole, has led to more young people moving out to other areas to find work whilst those who stay are older and continue to get older still. This has meant that the population has slowly decreased, which has had an impact on the school system. Primary schools are closing and the various high schools are due to merge if local authority plans go through. Without any industry to support jobs, the area continues to suffer high levels of social and economic deprivation. As time goes on and more and more young people leave the area to find work or attend university, which seems to be the hailed as the great saviour by the schools, the 'nothingness' of it, especially in the eyes of young people like Sean and Alan will continue. If they return looking for jobs to use the skills they have gained through their academic qualifications, they will not find them in the area that they left to acquire them in the first place.

Conclusion

With the exception of Sin and Gavin (neither of whom did as well as expected and returned to the Sixth Form to re-sit their final year), all The Geeks progressed to university. Sam, Ieuan, Scott and Leon left Wales to study and made the largest moves out of their community. Whilst the rest stayed in South Wales, Ruben and Sean did move to the capital Cardiff to study, so they did make some break from Cwm Dyffryn. While this chapter has highlighted working-class educational achievements, I have shown how these achievements come with risks and those who invested in intellectual labour were bullied for their success and deviation from the norm. I have argued that this studious or 'geeky' performance of masculinity, rather than being a straightforward practice for these young men, illustrates that a high degree of complexity exists in young working-class men's lives. This fluidity must be recognized when trying to understand the performance of young working-class masculinities and it's relation to schooling and achievement.

Whilst there are undoubtedly instances of studious practices of masculinity performed by The Geeks, and the adoption of middle-class academic aspiration, these are loaded with risks. The drinking and birthday trip to the strip club, show older versions of traditional working-class culture (speech, cultural practices and social activities) appear within these narratives. These young men are trying to be successful and embrace a neo-liberal agenda within a globalized workplace; however, they are restricted by the associated expectations of manhood in their community. These working-class 'achieving boys' offer a hybridized form of masculinity, trying to escape but also falling back and feeling the pressure to perform traditional classed masculinities. The implication of this on their ability to achieve their goals is important and illustrates how much harder working-class boys must work than those from more privileged backgrounds in order to be successful in different aspects of their lives.

5
The Emos: Alternative Masculinities?

Introduction

As I have shown in this book, the shift to adulthood for young working-class men in particular was once inextricably linked to labour. However, due to economic restructuring over the past half century, in places like Cwm Dyffryn working-class young men are now no longer likely to directly enter employment after formal schooling, but to continue into post-16 education. In Chapters 3 and 4, The Valley Boiz and The Geeks both highlight different perspectives on these changes and opposing performances of working-class masculinity. The Valley Boiz tended to adopt older masculine practices through selecting specific 'masculine' educational subjects and engaging in risky leisure activities, to maintain a legacy of the industrial past and to ensure they are connected to their community. For The Geeks, their more studious performances of masculinity through academic achievement, was a way to find solace from a community they did not feel they belonged to and an escape route to what they saw as more successful futures. However, as I argued these front displays of masculinity, were also contradicted by other displays depending on the audience around them and the setting they found themselves in, highlighting how a degree of complexity and fluidity accompanied these performances.

In this chapter, I look at another group of young, white working-class men in this year group, who I term 'The Emos' and who at first seemed to perform their masculinities in a very different ways to their peers. Yet, as I go on to illustrate, The Emos, who embraced the trans-global form of youth culture known as the 'alternative scene', continue to evidence many traditional discourses that contradict their own 'alternative' displays. I explore how their contemporary displays of masculinity rather than offering an alternative form of manhood, were in fact another way to re-traditionalize older displays of working-class masculinity, through pain, heroism, physical toughness and acts of homophobia, further illustrating how a particularly form of working-class masculinity in this de-industrialized community was the default reference point across all groups of young men.

The 'alternative scene' and being an 'emo'

The 'alternative scene' revolves around a combination of guitar-based bands stemming out of broad genres of non-mainstream music which transcends the globe (Moore, 2005). 'Alternative,' I suggest can be used as an umbrella term for a music scene with fluid, flexible boundaries, which can incorporate many sub-divisions of punk, different forms of heavy metal, nu-metal (Harris, 2000), hard-core, glam, thrash, grunge, riot grrrl (Moore, 2010), emo (House of Emo, 2010) and the goth scene (Hodkinson, 2002). Multiple forms of dance and violent body movements, such as moshing, slam dancing and crowd surfing accompany the live arena with many of these activities being carried out in spaces known as 'pits' (Tsitsos, 1999). Riches (2014) suggested that these rituals allow for men to play out homosocial relations within an aggressive, physically demanding environment, offering men opportunities to embody and perform multiple masculinities within this interaction space. The broad scene is also marked with different clothing fashions, but these are frequently combined together to make a complex appearance. These incorporate tight or over sized jeans, T-shirts with slogans or band logos on them, canvas or chunky trainers, heavy boots, dark or colourful belts with big buckles, hooded jumpers and jackets. Hair is often straight and long (sometimes pulled down over one eye) and dyed in various shades, but usually black. Tattoos, facial and other body piercings are also popular. Leisure pursuits or 'extreme' sports that are loosely associated with the music, such as skateboarding, BMX riding, surfing and snowboarding, also accompanied the scene. Holly Kruse (1993) argues that the loose term of 'alternative' music also means that 'local identities and traditions interact with relatively coherent translocal frames of reference' (Kruse, 1993, cited in Hodkinson, 2002: 27). The shared task of networks, communications and commerce can connect people with each other.

As with The Valley Boiz and The Geeks, when I first met the key members of The Emos friendship group – Bruce, Clump, Jelly Belly, Jack and Tommy[1] – they were coming to the end their final year of compulsory schooling (Year 11) and aged between 15 and 16. Over the time I was acquainted with them and as their educational pathways changed, other young men and women were introduced to the group. Jenkins, Dai and Billy-Joe became friends with Clump and Jelly Belly at a local FE college and they performed together in different guitar-based bands playing music in pubs and clubs across the region. Brittany and Rosie also became part of the wider group when they became romantically involved with Clump and Bruce and would attend live music events with them, standing in the crowd at the very front of the stage when the different bands played.

In keeping with the alternative scene and Goffman's (1959) framework for understanding social interaction that I have used through this book, one of the ways these young men's personal front performance of masculinity was displayed was through their distinctive style of clothing. When not in school uniform, they tended to dress in baggy or very tight skinny jeans, with dark T-shirts which had their favourite musicians or band logos on them and big hooded jumpers. The Emos tended to have long hair which was dyed a variety of bright colours and sometimes, but not always, pulled down over their eyes. Their bodies were also adorned with piercings in their eyebrows, ears, tongues, noses and even though the base of the neck. Even in their school uniform, they stood out with these not-so-subtle symbolic representations of the 'alternative' scene, and the young men were constantly reprimanded by teachers for breaking uniform policy. As they grew older, ever more elaborate colourful tattoos were also added on their arms, legs and bodies to further enabling them to showcase their allegiance to the 'alternative' scene. However, embracing this scene caused alienation within their schools and colleges from both teacher and their peers. They were often bullied in the wider community because of the way they dressed, their hairstyles and the variety of body piercings and tattoos that made them stand out within the locale as they transgressed accepted patterns of behaviour and masculinity. While this bricolage of styles acted as an unofficial group 'uniform', its contradictions to more traditional working-class culture, highlight the plural nature of young working-class masculinities and how gender is produced and performed within this scene.

Alienation, bullying and intimidation

At school, teachers and their peers referred to the group as 'emos', something the popular press and other forms of media have sought to mock

(The Guardian Online, 2006) and vilify (Daily Mail, 2012) when writing about the 'dangers' of non-mainstream youth (also see Peters, 2010). The Emos did enough to 'get on' in school and achieved a mid-range of GCSE grades (see Brown, 1987; Roberts, 2013). However, they all said that they hated the way they were treated in school and the majority of the group left after their GCSEs to undertake a variety of music and arts-based courses at an FE college. Although Bruce and Tommy did opt to return to school to undertake A levels (arts-based subjects, such as music, graphics design and fine art), they continued to feel out of place. This feeling of alienation resulted in Tommy leaving school before he has completed Year 12, so only Bruce remained. The disaffection Bruce felt from school was now further amplified and he tended to spend most of his time with Brittany his girlfriend and things began to get serious between them. During the summer between Year 12 and 13 he proposed to her over a picnic on the mountainside above the town and they planned to marry when they had finished school. Brittany was a year younger than him and because a combined Sixth Form programme existed between the different schools in the area, he was able to spend the majority of time with her during his final year. Bruce even took on an additional chemistry AS level course so that he could spend more time with her. Nonetheless when Brittany wasn't around, he stayed in the rooms of the art department working on his art projects or playing his guitar and practising songs to music by bands that he liked such as Lamb of God, Kill Switch Engage, Bullet for my Valentine and Funeral for a Friend. When I asked him if he was lonely, and why he didn't mix with the others who were still in school he said *'I prefer being on my own'* and would not sit in the common room, eat or attend social events with the others. With only Bruce remaining in school, my own contact with the friendship group became harder to maintain, and as a consequence I was unable to continue to follow their progress as closely as others in this book.

Alongside the alienation which many of the group felt within the school, The Emos also indicated that they felt they did not fit in with the town of Cwm Dyffryn. Their involvement with the different aspects of the 'alternative scene' (as noted above) attracted unwanted attention within the locality.

Jack: Yeah, it used to be bad, and used to be annoying, because everyone hated each other but it's a bit better now cos everyone's grown up a little bit now.
Clump: Yeah used to get heaps of shit everyday in like Year 7...

MW: ... Who did?
Bruce: Us, cos we're different to everyone else so we just got shouted at ... called names, but now in Year 11 we get hardly any of it.
MW: So do you think you're different to these other guys?
Bruce: Yeah I suppose, like with the drinking thing we don't like it but we do enjoy ourselves more than them like. They get drunk and won't know what they're doing tomorrow morning and tomorrow morning we can look back at the things we done last night and say yeah we done that and it was amazing!
Tommy: It's like whoever drinks most gets the most respect like.
Jack: Yeah, which is stupid!
[*Group Interview Year 11*]

Jack, Clump and Bruce here try to play down or minimize any bullying that occurred to them, but it is also possible that the bullying could have diminished as the rose through the age hierarchy and occupied the position that the bullies once occupied. They frame it as occurring in the past and therefore make it safe by indicating that is 'used to be bad' and that now, as they and others are older, they *'get hardly any of it'*. In this way The Emos are also able to distance themselves from any negative feelings associated with this bullying or how it may have affected their self-esteem and attitudes to school in general. It is interesting that Bruce discusses the issue of not drinking alcohol, and how he feels this marks him and his peers out as *'different'*. As I showed in the previous chapter, drinking large amount of alcohol was a key marker of masculine respectability in the community and a connection to the cultural pursuits of an older industrial era. This tradition was continued by the young men in this book and something Tommy himself is aware of and points it out here. Through deciding not to drink alcohol, this creates another form of alienation to their community.

Outside school the bullying took a more violent turn, and The Emos talked further about how their hobbies brought them into conflict with other young people in the area down the local skate park.

Clump: It is like a gathering area it's like we skate down there and now we only get like one bit and it's always full of people sitting on it with crates and tipping beer all down it ...
Tommy: ... and then they hang their jumpers off the sides and they go to us *'watch our jumpers, watch my jumper ... '*.
MW: Well the answer would seem to be to move your jumper out of the skate area!

Hendrix: Stuff like that though if you're not going down to skate or Bike it's pointless you going in there like.
[*Group Interview Year 11*]

They explained that on certain occasions when they were out at night, they felt threatened and intimidated when they came across other young men drinking alcohol in parks or in the street.

Jack: Like, yeah, wherever we go out, cos we don't wanna go out drinking round the street, say we wanna go up the country park sitting on the swings like that and a load of piss heads (drunks) will walk up like.
Bruce: Yeah I can guarantee that you'll go out on a Friday night and you're guaranteed to see loads of um.
Jelly Belly: It's like they can't enjoy themselves.
Clump: Like drink after drink just to get smashed and...
Bruce: [cuts in] the bad thing then is that you're walking through them you are a bit wary of things.
Tommy: You walk past some of um and they'll go [change of tone] 'can I have a fag en butt' (can I have a cigarette then) and if you don't have a fag you're fucked!
Bruce: Yeah that's it like, no fag or lighter they start on you!
Jelly Belly: Me, him [Points at Clump] and Jenkins [not present] right got jumped on down the skate park because we didn't have a fag or nothing, they kept shouting at us, about 15 of um coming on to us.
MW: Did you manage to get away?
Jelly Belly: Well all them lot, Jenkins and Clump run off!
Clump: Yeah I had to! I got head butted!
MW: Really? Hang on, start again!
Jelly Belly: Well as Jenkins and Clump run off they all chased um, I stayed there for a little bit and they all went, then when I jumped down [off the skate ramp] they were all round the corner, about 14 of them and then I got jumped again!
[*Group Interview Year 11*]

What these highly charged discussions show quite clearly here, and in keeping with other studies of marginalized masculinities (Connell, 1995), is that The Emos were subordinated by others for not adhering to the normative masculine practices of the region and in the spaces where these practices were played out. The boys used the focus groups and interviews over the period to voice their concerns and had angry discussions of the bullying and harassment they received. Nonetheless, as can be seen in the defence of their actions when they were 'started on' (a verbal or physical altercation) for not having a cigarette in the skate park, instead of seeing themselves as victims, The Emos try to frame their experiences as forms of heroic narratives. As Jelly Belly states '*15 of um coming on to us*', it is clear he sets himself up as trying to battle back against the odds in the face of intimidation and to hold onto his pride. He also doesn't talk here about any of the pain that these beatings may have caused him physically or emotionally, again adding to his heroic narrative and proving he has the ability to suffer and take a beating. This is potentially also about the reinforcement of a minority marginalized status through the numerical terms of the bigger group of 'them' versus the smaller outside group of 'us'.

The Emos strategies for performing non-normative ways of being against the dominant notions of masculinity in Cwm Dyffryn, produced a troubled and risky subject position. However, in this final section I again focus now on how these positions were quite often contradictory. These young men who were 'othered' by their peers, often tried to maintain their position or justify it by exaggerating their expulsion. These contradictory ways that Bruce, Clump, Jelly Belly and the others adopted as part of their front displays of masculinity, were in many ways like The Valley Boiz in Chapter 3, re-traditionalizing older discourses of class and gender and a claim for power, where there was none.

A real 'alternative'?

The following extracts illustrate how strongly The Emos felt about some issues which defined their difference, but also how, by engaging in practices, such as skateboarding (which were not allowed by the school) and surprisingly American Football (although through observations this never amounted to more than a casual throwing around of a rugby ball), the traditional masculine values of the locale were reborn or re-traditionalized through 'alternative' performances of pain, heroism and physical and verbal toughness:

Tommy: The only games played are like football and rugby...
Hendrix: Like the normal games.
MW: So that controls what you can do and that's what annoys you?
Hendrix: They don't like listen to opinions of other people...like us we hate football!
MW: Yeah, yeah...

Hendrix: Like we'll have a kick around, but stupidly not so seriously like we like American football that's fun but they won't let us do it.

Jelly Belly: (talked over by Hendrix) Kids take it too serious football like.

Jack: We even asked once if we could bring our skateboards in once.

MW: Why did you say American Football though?

Hendrix: Cos its fun, you like get to munch people like.

Tommy: It's different innit more running...

Jack: We even asked if we could bring our skateboards in at one point for games lesson but they wouldn't let us....

Tommy: [talks over Jack]...it's an extreme sport that is...

Jack: But they wouldn't let usn.

MW: Have you guys ever tried and I know it's hard because it's uphill to the school, but skated to school?

Various: Not allowed...we're not allowed, they take the boards off us. We're not allowed to do it!

[*Group Interview Year 11*]

In the narratives these young men told of their lives, a collective identity emerged which saw them positioning themselves away from their peers by not participating in certain sports. Jelly Belly thought these were taken too seriously by others who he saw as 'kids' indicating that he felt more mature than others for not doing so. However, by Tommy referring to skating as an extreme sport a hyper-masculine discourse would seem evident, which of course connects with the dominant game of the locality, Rugby Union. So while these young men perform their masculinity in different ways through clothing, and bodily styling, they still adopt some cultural masculine norms of the locale by becoming involved in activities such as skateboarding which require a 'tough' or 'brave' element to the sport.

One afternoon in the music practice room at the school, whilst trying to learn a variety of guitar riffs from their favourite bands, Bruce and Tommy discussed how they liked to spend their EMA on going to see live music events (gigs) or on musical equipment. Instead of tales of drunken antics (which they saw as a waste of money) or watching sport, these young men talked about going to see the music they liked and participate in, jumping around in the 'mosh pit' at live music events in clubs and the festivals that they went to. Tsitsos (1999) describes these as practices and forms of dance and body movements which are violent and aggressive. This particular space was one where they could connect with other young people with similar interests to them, but also perform older discourses of masculinity displayed through acts of physical toughness in the mosh pit. In the final section of this chapter, I now turn to look at some other ways more traditional masculinities attitudes were performed by these young men.

Hetero-normativity and homophobia

The position that the young men took on some aspects of sexuality also seemed connected with the traditions of the locale, and they emitted older attitudes and notions within their language and speech patterns. When they talked about sexual difference when discussing another young man from their school (Nibbles) who was gay, the contradictions were made clear.

Bruce: He deserves a right fucking slap...
MW: Why does he deserve it?
Bruce: Cos he's GAY... I got... no... I haven't got a particular thing against gays but why? I mean why?
Clump: They walk past and you know they are looking at your ass and stuff you know it's wrong like
MW: Why do you think that then?
Clump: No it's just the possibility that they could like...
Bruce: And if there was a so called god do you think that they'd want males together!
Tommy: Stopping the race innit!
Bruce: I know it's up to them but keep it to themselves like, behind doors like.
Jack: It's like in Glyn Neath [a nearby town] before I went fishing with my dad and my Nan we went down like that and there was cars everywhere and just two blokes or blokes going in and out of the bushes like we pelted it away [ran off]...

[*Group Interview Year 11*]

In other recent studies with a range of young men in various educational settings, some authors have proclaimed that contemporary masculinities are become much more complex, fluid and different to what came before. While the picture I present here certainly highlights the complexity of contemporary masculinity for young working-class men, I would suggest that not all young men are changing. The expectations of masculinity in particular places and spaces have a huge impact on manhood and the performances that are then displayed, link back to these traditions. As I have noted, the attributes of the 'alternative scene' might make The Emos stand out and in some cases become victims of abuse, but by projecting a strong heterosexual/homophobic stance they could distance themselves from the harassment that was regularly aimed at them for being 'emo' and expresses attitudes of the white, heterosexual, heritage of the region in relation to masculinity. This display also allows The Emos to validate their own heterosexuality by positioning themselves against another form of 'other' which they proclaim to be unnatural as it was 'stopping the race', being gay was deemed as undesirable or occupying a lower place than their own marginalized position. By using this homophobic discourse, they were also able to distance themselves further from being seen as a source of desire by other men.

Conclusion

In light of economic transformations, while class and gender boundaries have become less important for some (Beck, 1999), in a global economy in the former industrial places they remain a major form of social inequality. In this chapter, I have discussed the ways in which one group of white, working-class young men from a deprived community, who I have termed The Emos, displayed an 'alternative' version of working-class masculinity. I have argued that the experiences of those who embrace a trans-global form of youth culture known as the 'alternative scene' are often alienated, bullied and victimized, both within the school arena and outside of it, for their apparent non-normative masculinities. However, as the locality's traditional culture is linked to a specific form of classed work, the masculinities that are played out within this youth scene are undergoing a re-traditionalization process, reconnecting to these older forms of identity and are not as 'alternative' as they may be first proclaimed by the young men themselves and others. These young men are trapped between two strong gender cultures, one of the traditional working-class masculinity, and the more ambiguous masculinity of the scene they embrace. This is particularly evident through their personal front displays which are performed through certain fashion tastes and other aspects of the scene that I have highlighted in this chapter. As with the other young men throughout this book, they were not the total free agents that neo-liberalism proclaims and holds others to be. Their 'alternative' subjectivities were still bound to the classed and gendered codes of the former industrial heritage of place. Nonetheless, on a more optimistic note, the youth scene they embraced, offered these young men a refuge and a source of solidarity from the marginalized position they continually found themselves in.

6
Working-Class Masculinities in Vocational Education and Training Courses

Introduction

We have seen how The Valley Boiz, The Geeks and The Emos performed different versions of working-class masculinity in Cwm Dyffryn High School. I also looked at how their masculine identities were further constructed through different social interactions and leisure activities beyond the school gates. I argued that these young men are adapting to insecure times in different ways and emphasized how historic legacies of space and place and their family biographies impact upon their educational decision-making and leisure interests. In this chapter, I explore the way young masculinities are performed in other educational spaces. Continuing with three young men from the same cohort – Bakers, Ian and Frankie – I focus on the performance of masculinity in three different vocational educational courses (VET) at three different FE colleges outside Cwm Dyffryn. Two 'masculine' courses – motor vehicle studies and a Modern Apprenticeship in engineering – are compared with a more 'feminine' subject, equine studies.

Through these three young men's narratives, I explore how spaces of VET frame and validate traditional forms of working-class masculinity (based on physical skill, bodily sturdiness and camaraderie through jokes, story-telling, sexist language and banter) but can also provide a space to enable alternative forms of masculinity to be displayed. I do this to illustrate not only how masculinities are performed in vocational spaces through the interaction order in different situations, but also how masculine practices are displayed, perpetuated and can be changed through the situatedness of experience. Finally, I look outside the vocational spaces where these performances are displayed and returning to a theme I considered in Chapter 3, the role of car culture in these young men's lives. Are these speedy 'leisure pleasures' (Kenway and Hickey-Moody, 2009) spaces of masculine production which act as discourses and symbols of masculine status, or are they forms and spaces of escapism for marginalized young men?

The gendered and classed nature of vocational education and training

The FE sector in Wales and the UK more widely is a complex area, offering a large variety of academic, vocational and training programmes some of which (like the Modern Apprentice scheme) are situated within industrial environments (see TLRP, 2008; Jephcote, Salisbury and Rees, 2009; Salisbury and Jephcote, 2010). Brown and Macdonald (2008: 19) suggest that VET (which makes up the vast majority of courses in FE) refers to 'learning that addresses the concepts and understandings relevant to a wide range of work environments and develops in young people the skills, knowledge, competencies and attributes needed for employment'. Although supporters of VET suggest it is a way of attracting some young people to continue in education who might otherwise not have done so, others have suggested it contributes to a dual system of academic versus vocational qualifications (Reay et al., 2005; Connell, 2008).

The experiences of young people in these sectors are far less documented than those in other phases of education (Delamont and Atkinson, 1995). During the 1980s and into the 1990s, however, a few ethnographic studies began to show how VET played an important part in the construction of social class, ethnicity and gender identities and how these helped formulate potential careers (see, for example, Valli, 1985; Weis, 1985; Skeggs, 1986; Bates, 1990, 1991; Riseborough, 1992; Bates and Riseborough, 1993; Haywood and Mac an Ghaill, 1997). More recent studies have suggested that not only do many VET courses fail to give students who undertake these forms of qualifications the broadening of opportunities envisaged, but that class, gender and ethnic inequalities continue to persist and are a determining factor in an individual's future life chances (Arnot, 2004; Weis, 2004; Reay et al., 2005).

Even though there have been changes in girls' and young women's occupational aspirations over the past three decades (Arnot, et al., 1999; Francis et al., 2003; Francis and Skelton, 2005; Baker, 2010), boys and young men still tend to avoid jobs and courses seen as stereotypically feminine. Girls are more likely to work in caring professions, while boys opt for technical, scientific and business jobs (Fuller, et al., 2005;

Madden, 2005; Osgood, 2005; Osgood, et al., 2006). However, as I show in this chapter, there are some small indicators that young people post-16 are beginning to enrol on non-gender traditional subjects (see also Miller and Budd, 1999; Archer, et al., 2007) but that stereotypical choices and future career directions still persist.

Subject frames

VET in the UK (and elsewhere, see, for example, Weis, 1990; Brown and Macdonald, 2008) has followed a typical format. As Parker (2006: 695) explains, the apprenticeship, in particular, was originally linked to male-dominated craft occupations, such as building and printing, but 'by the early 20th century it had become an altogether more pervasive form of training across a variety of workplace settings including both broader manufacturing locales (e.g. engineering, shipbuilding) and the domestic trades' (see also Cockburn, 1985; Gospel, 1995; Fuller and Unwin, 2003). During the 1970s and the 1980s, economic restructuring and the increase in neo-liberal policies saw a decline in apprenticeships being replaced by Youth Training schemes[1] and in 1994 the Modern Apprenticeship was launched. This was an initiative designed to increase the skills of young people through the expansion of work-based learning and to increase the participation of underrepresented groups (Hodkinson and Hodkinson, 1995). However, the Modern Apprenticeship has attracted criticism because these schemes are said not to compete adequately with programmes overseas and lack currency with young people (Ryan and Unwin, 2001). Further, as noted above, they continue to reproduce class and gender divisions of labour (Fuller et al., 2005). They are also qualifications that the middle classes are less likely to adopt, and choosing them impacts on the range and possibility of choice of courses and options of progressing to higher educational institutions (Reay et al., 2005).

As I have shown throughout this book, for Goffman (1959) performances can be 'disrupted' and contradicted as matter of course. These performances of self (and therefore gender) take place not only within social interactions between individuals but also within the wider culture of a given social setting. It is these frames that construct the meaning and interpretations of a given situation. I suggest that Goffman's (1974) 'frame analysis' can be especially applied to VET subjects. Here the forms and content of the courses, alongside the interactions between students and teachers, frame and therefore sanction and validate performances of masculinity and femininity more intensely than in other post-16 educational courses where distinct ways of being a man are valued and promoted over others (see also Connell, 1989; Mac an Ghaill, 1994). Nonetheless, there are some possibilities for subverting gender norms by parody, displacement and re-signification (Butler, 1990). It would seem possible then for gender norms to be also challenged and subverted through studying non-gender stereotypical vocational subjects. As Brickell (2005: 36) puts it, this could be a way 'to reorganize or supplement these frames and schedules in ways that may encourage new forms of subjectivity'. However, what does it mean for working-class young men who try to perform 'alternative' masculinities in de-industrialized communities? Are there limits to these alternative performances of manhood outside the VET space?

I now introduce the young men, their family backgrounds and outline their course choices in more detail. I then move on to look at how Bakers' and Ian's narratives highlight how similar performances of a traditional working-class hegemonic masculinity are displayed and refined within their mechanical and engineering courses. I then turn to look at the case study of Frankie, to illustrate how he attempted to subvert the gender norms of the locale, through participating in a more 'feminine' equine studies course.

Introducing Bakers, Ian and Frankie

I briefly introduced Bakers, Ian and Frankie when I was outlining the family biographies of The Valley Boiz in Chapter Three. Whilst they were part of this wider friendship group, I am drawing on their stories separately here in order to illustrate some different post-16 possibilities and ways of performing young masculinities in the region. The three young men came from similar but not identical backgrounds. They shared equivalent educational experiences, perspectives on their futures and had family biographies that indicated a history of working-class occupations in auto-trades and farming in or around Cwm Dyffryn. Bakers told me he wanted to be a mechanic, which was an interest he shared with his father who was employed at a car body repair chain (and grandfather before him). His mother, with whom he lived (he was an only child) after his parents divorced a few years previously, was a housewife. Ian lived with his younger sister and parents, on a small farm situated on the outskirts of the former coal-mining town and wanted to move into an engineering career. Frankie was the middle child, with an older and younger sister, and lived with his father, the manager of a small electronics company, and his mother, who worked as a secretary at a local school. Frankie aimed to work in the equine industry and owned his own horse called Gypsy.

While I am presenting these three young men as working-class, I acknowledge that their families occupy an ambivalent class position. Some of their parents show signs of social mobility through becoming directors of companies; however, none of the young men's parents had any experience of higher education, with Frankie's older sister being the first in his family to go to university. They also seem to indicate a more privileged subject position than many of the other young men in this study; Ian's family, for example, owned their own land. In contrast, Bakers and Frankie (who were also best friends) lived in small terraced houses a few streets away from others like Ieuan, Scott, Nixon, Bunk and Hughesy, and all three participated in the same social activities as other young people in the area. Also, while Bakers and Frankie had been born and brought up in Cwm Dyffryn and lived close to each other in the town centre, Ian was originally from the South of England and had moved into the area only as a teenager with his parents to help run the family farm and his different accent marking him out considerably. Their positions then could be seen to indicate that their working-class identities were not homogeneous or static and demonstrate the complexities, struggles and possibilities on their performances of masculinity when the dynamics of a place or locale are integrated into the analysis.

Despite Frankie having initially had plans to leave the area to train as a jockey after he completed compulsory schooling (which I explain in detail below), all three boys returned to Cwm Dyffryn High School after their GCSEs. Bakers enrolled on a BTEC first diploma course in Motor Vehicle Studies and an AS in ICT; the other two studied for AS levels, Ian doing Physics, Maths and Electronics and Frankie opted for Physics, Electronics and Chemistry. However, during Year 12 all three started to look at options outside the Sixth Form and left after their first year to attend different courses and training programmes. Nevertheless, they remained friends with many of their former class mates and continued to 'hang out', or in the local vernacular 'bother', with The Valley Boiz on nights out in Cwm Dyffryn. Bakers and Frankie were also very close to Jimmy, who we meet in the next chapter and whose narrative brings together many themes and issues from this book.

Bakers and Ian: Reaffirming traditional masculinities in VET

After completing Year 12 at Cwm Dyffryn High School, Bakers went to work as a motor repair garage for a few months. However, he admitted that he was bullied at the garage and after an incident when a colleague had thrown a spanner at him, he left and enrolled on an Institute of Motor Industry (IMI) National Certificate in Vehicle Maintenance & Repair course at Eastside FE College, around 10 miles from Cwm Dyffryn. The course consisted of both practical and theoretical classes on aspects of the motor industry and was conducted over a 20-hour week. The students on the course were all young white men aged between 16 and 21 and drawn from towns around the college.

Whilst happy with studying at school, Ian wanted to progress to a paid Modern Apprenticeship rather than go to university. During Year 12, he applied for different training schemes and was accepted on a Modern Apprenticeship programme with NPower, a national electrical supply company. The scheme involved working at a power plant and studying for a BTEC National Diploma in Operations and Maintenance Engineering at Southside FE College which was approximately 30 miles from Cwm Dyffryn.[2] NPower paid its apprentices a monthly salary of around £800 (tax free[3]) and also provided free hotel accommodation near the college and power plant during term time. Each apprentice was also given meal vouchers to supplement their wages. One of Ian's lecturers explained how competitive the scheme was:

> They have a huge number of applicants each year, it's like ah... a 300–1 chance of being accepted. This college is the only centre south of Rotherham that NPower use to train its apprentices. Only 20 are accepted into the scheme and the apprentices [all male] who come here, come from all over the UK.
> [*Ben, lecturer at South Side College*]

The scheme was competitive, required good grades at GCSE and experience was preferable. Final choices were made on the basis of interviews and presentations by applicants before they were accepted on to the scheme. The NPower apprentices were drawn from across the UK, aged between 16 and 19 and the scheme was generally a white, male only affair like Bakers' course. Out of all the young men in this study, Ian seemed to be in the most advantageous position at this stage of their life course, receiving a wage to study full time, as well as being provided with meals and accommodation.

In the previous chapters, I illustrated how schools as institutions offer a range of ways of being male which often draw on the localized resources available, regulating and producing idealized forms of masculinity through the 'official' and 'unofficial' curriculum of the school. In *Frame Analysis* Goffman (1974: 11) argues that performances of self and the definition of the situation in which they appear, occur through frames, defined as 'principles of organization which govern events – at least social ones – and our subjective involvement in them'. I now turn to show how through these vocational frames that Bakers and Ian learnt to become future workers and where traditional forms of working-class masculine behaviour were adopted and sanctioned. It was here that practices that define what it is to be a specific type of man were sustained and where versions of gender identity are performed in line with dominant stereotypical expectations within a locale's heritage.

Practical performances

Each course had substantial opportunities for practical work and for a performance of masculinity based around manhood acts fostered through rituals and traditions of manual workplace cultures. Even though each course differed in content, there were huge similarities between the subjects. The following extracts are drawn from my field notes, which were taken during participant observation within these settings.

As an apprentice Ian was expected to work within a small team and was set 'jobs' under timed conditions.

> Ian and I, along with the other apprentices, entered the workshop and headed to the locker room so that they could change into their overalls and work boots. I noticed that NPower must have provided their overalls as they had the company's logo and their own names embroidered on to them. As we entered the large workshop, the smells of oil, and grease hit me. It was an open plan room, with a low ceiling, few windows and with dozens of metal workbenches, pieces of ancient machinery and equipment laid out in rows. Ian introduced me to the tutor, Ben, who was taking this session. Ben told me that this lesson was to run until about 7pm and was a practical session where the apprentices would have to strip down a V Twin Compressor, change the paper gasket then re-assemble it.
> [*Fieldnotes*]

These notes that record my observations of the setting, show that the apprentices were provided with a uniform (overalls and dust jackets), and that course's defining tasks as 'jobs'. These processes help maintain a direct link to the motor and engineering industries and symbolize that a specific version of working-class masculinity was being performed.

Working-Class Masculinities in Vocational Education and Training Courses 113

In the extract from my fieldnotes below this was further illustrated through the instructions given by the tutor Jon in Bakers' vehicle and maintenance and repair course:

> Jon gave the boys a 'job' which entailed taking off the outer casing of the engine on the buggy and getting into the engine itself to work on the timing disc. To do this other parts of the engine had to be removed first so that this could be achieved. I stood on and watched and helped where I could by holding a big industrial torch so they could look into the engine. After some initial difficulties with the problem about the timing on the engine, Jon came back over and took the boys across to part of an engine that was on a stand at the front of the garage. Here he explained the crank shaft rotations and talked about other processes the boys should know. After the process was explained, Bakers and his partner went back to the buggy to try and get on with whatever it was that they needed to do. They wrote nothing down (indeed nobody wrote anything down, apart from me) for the whole four hours I was in the garage.
>
> [*Fieldnotes*]

Here we can see that by using the body to solve problems physically, working in an environment of oil, grease and machinery, Bakers was accessing a space through which to perform and reformulate a specific version of masculinity. No written notes (apart from mine as a participant observer) were taken, illustrating how the expulsion of 'mental' labour (and its associations with femininity) which Willis (1977) once stated was rejected by the 'lads', was a key feature of this process of masculinity making. However, on Ian's apprenticeship things were a little different and a contradiction to the traditional manual working practices appeared. These subtle differences are made clear during a practical task in the college workshop.

> The group was separated into teams of two; they collected the compressors they had practiced on last week and moved to separate benches. By 3:35pm Ian and his partner Miles has begun to strip down the compressor laying out the bits they were taking off the compressor in order on top of the bench. Ian then whispered to me that he hadn't fully put it back together like the others had done last week, so it was easier to take apart! I noticed that they had to keep a written track of what they were doing as they went along, which differed to the young men enrolled on the vehicle repair course, who didn't write anything down in the garage. I asked Ian about this and

he told me *'we have to do this in every lesson, they like us to show our workings out and that... it's what we gotta do in the plant as well, show our steps like'*.
[*Fieldnotes*]

In this extract Ian was encouraged to write notes as he went along, so this was something which was seen as a requirement of the 'job' he was given. This course seemed to be preparing and enhancing both practical and theoretical (written) skills of the students, which were need when they progressed into the 'field' after graduating. Whilst these written skills were essential, the practical is much more valued than the intellectual and it was another example of shaping gendered expectations of future workers. These gendered expectations were further framed through the theoretical parts of their courses.

Theoretical (re)production

In the workshop and the garage, Ian and Bakers were using the space to reformulate and frame a specific version of working-class masculinity. This was achieved through an investment in physically working with machinery, using tools, climbing into and around cars or taking apart components and interacting with teachers and student in these environments. In the classroom, where the theory aspects of their course were taught, stereotypical gender values continued to be reproduced. My fieldnotes from these lessons show that the masculine environment continued to be reinforced through the use of gendered and sexist teaching examples and coarse 'humour' by lecturers during theory lessons:

> I copied down the following from the board; 'the rack and pinion is geared to give the driver "feel". This allows *him* (my emphasis) to make the major adjustments required to steer the vehicle and know where it is'.
> [*Fieldnotes*]

During a theory lesson, these notes show that one of Bakers' motor vehicle lecturers, Jack, clearly emphasizes the embedded gender imbalance of the subject by referring to 'him' in reference to the driver during this technical example shaping stereotypical gendered expectations of behaviour in the frame. On Ian's course too, lecturers would often use gendered examples when explaining problems and the masculine, heterosexual environment of the engineering world was reinforced.

> During a discussion about car insurance and buying a new vehicle the teacher emphasized that the sales *men* (my emphasis) would target

him with different cars than with boys. This was because he said *'you boys want different cars for cruising*[4] *and pulling the chicks'* which made the class laugh.
[*Fieldnotes*]

A certain amount of humour is evident here in these fieldnotes and is used in this all male environment to build a level of rapport between the lecturer and the students. However, the lecturer is also maintaining a heteronormative environment and traditional 'macho' values around male domination through finance patterns and patterns of behaviour and sexuality. This ultimately validates which performances of manhood are acceptable or viewed as 'normal'. Furthermore during theory lessons on the mechanics courses, one lecturer, Jack, whilst using gendered examples in his teaching, also kept up a constant flow of jokes during his interactions with his students.

I sat at the back of the room in between Bakers and another boy. As the class settled down, Jack asked how I was finding the college. He told me and the rest of the class that *'the beauty of Valleys life is that you can get divorced from a women and she's still your sister'*. This continued throughout the lesson with Jack cracking further jokes and stories to keep the class entertained. When he told the class *'my friend who had a glass eye was in a car crash, I told him he should have drilled a hole in it so that he could see through it'*, there was a general groan from the young men present and Bakers rolled his eyes at me. As Jack waited for the class to copy from the board, he talked about how he hated women drivers. He suggested that the *'girly button'* on some cars (the button which acts to make the steering on the vehicle lighter for city driving) were designed for women in particular because they couldn't reverse. This was then followed up with another joke to the class about how breweries have started putting female hormones into beer these days as it now means he can't drive and talks rubbish.
[*Fieldnotes*]

These practices are a direct link back to a working-class occupational culture where male chauvinism, racist and sexist humour were a part of the industry and accompanied by practical jokes, coarse language and the 'piss take' (see Beynon, 1973; Willis, 1979; Cockburn, 1983; Weis, 1985; Haywood and Mac an Ghaill, 1997; Maruzsa, 1997). During one lesson I asked a lecturer why he thought there were so few girls on his Modern Apprentice course, and he replied that it was because *'girls' bone density doesn't agree with engineering'*.[5] The performances of a traditional working-class masculinity away from the practical sessions might have been refined and relaxed from the young men's perspective (they weren't carrying out physical dirty work, didn't wear the uniform of the workplace), but a culture of machismo was still being constructed by their lecturers. Through his behaviour Jack is continuing to display a traditional version of working-class masculinity to the young men he is teaching. The gendered examples and sexist language served to structure and frame the interaction order Ian and Bakers found themselves in, and acceptable displays of masculinity, which they would eventually take with them into the workplace.

However, VET course also provide the opportunities to try out different identities. As I did with The Emos in the last chapter, I turn now to look at what it means for working-class young men who try to perform an alternative version of masculinity in a deindustrial community. I explore in this final section how traditional versions of masculinity can be challenged by looking at the case of Frankie who was enrolled on a more 'feminine' VET course which has the potential to be a more gender neutral space.

Frankie: A tortured masculinity?

Whilst there is some literature on the historic significance of horses and masculinities (for example Weil, 2006; Latimer and Birke, 2009), the dominance of men in the role of breeding and showing horses at farming events (Hurn, 2008), the enduring mythology of the Wild West cowboy (Connell, 1995; Birke, 2007; Gibson, 2014) and various pieces of research documenting the professional 'masculine' world of horse racing, these have not tended to focus on the actually performative aspects of masculinity in these areas (Cassidy, 2002; Larsen, 2006; Butler and Charles, 2011). There also appears to be a distinctive gap in research on young men (and women) in what Birke and Brandt (2009) define as the more feminized 'horsey world' of dressage and the experiences of those who are enrolled on FE courses related to the equine industry (see Salisbury and Jephcote, 2010 for some insights into a general animal care FE course). However, as Dashper's (2012) insightful ethnographic research into equestrian sport illustrates, even these areas which are predominantly female and which are linked to female activity in popular association, have a much older masculine tradition (Birke, 2007). Dasher (2012) suggest that equestrianism as a discipline developed out of farming communities, military customs and has links to the upper-classes and rural gentry, therefore even though the sport is now more popular with women, the history of equestrianism is still strongly linked to upper-class masculinity, power and wealth. It would seem then that studying equestrianism with a predominantly female cohort (Dashper also suggests that there are high numbers of openly gay men in these areas) and the upper-class underpinnings, could provide an opportunity for a young working-class man like Frankie, to perform an alternative masculinity to one of his peers and the traditions of his community. Yet, is this necessarily an 'inclusive' or 'softer' masculinity because it is a female dominated space?

At 16, Frankie was already a confident rider owning his own horse and working part-time in a local riding stable. Following this interest in horses he had enrolled on a prestigious jockey apprenticeship course at The British Racing School at Newmarket.[6] Being small in stature, thin and with a passion for horses, he was ideally suited to the course. After he had gained his GCSE results, he had left for Newmarket with his sights set on becoming a professional jockey. However, things didn't quite go to plan. Enrolled on an initial nine-week introductory course, Frankie found the work and the long hours tiring and admitted to missing home; he only lasted a short time before returning to Cwm Dyffryn. In an individual interview, which was conducted almost exactly two years later, Frankie was quite reflexive about his decision and regretted coming home:

Frankie: I should have stuck it out, I say that all the time, I should have stayed there.
MW: Yeah but at the time you weren't happy so you got to think about that.
Frankie: Yeah but I think it was more about the fact that I missed...mates...home
MW: But it's a big thing to do mate when you're 16.
Frankie: But if I went back now I'd think stuff this, I'm not going back to Cwm Dyffryn ever again and I probably wouldn't, but it just proves what two years can do, I'd be happy now, to go to Newmarket do the four or five weeks or whatever it was come back for the weekend, then go carry on with it, cos that weekend I'd see everyone and then it'd be see you in another month like.
[*Individual Interview, Year 13*]

Here we can see that the pull of home was strong and Frankie returned to the town he grew up in, but his regret at this decision is evident and he has come to realizes it was a missed opportunity. He began working again at local stables, and went back to school to start Year 12, but he found returning a difficult experience as he had to keep explaining to other students and many of his teachers, why he wasn't at the racing school in Newmarket. He also struggled with his subjects and didn't do well in his AS exams, so he left at the end of the year and decided go to Westside FE College to do a BTEC Level 3 Diploma in Horse Management. In the following September he began the new course involving working with horses.

Into the arena

The experience of a typical riding lesson, aimed at enhancing students' riding abilities, horse control skills and show jumping expertise, are outlined in the following notes I took whilst watching from the viewing platform. In addition, these notes also illustrate the gendered nature of the multiple bodily acts which are required during such a performance and like the 'masculine courses that I have outlined so far, help to frame what is expected during this vocational course

> I walked through the stables, which were rows of metal cage like blocks filled with hay, but were for the moment empty of horses. As I rounded the end of the last small stable I came across the big gate to the arena. The arena was a large sheltered hangar about the size of a football pitch, with a flat surface and a spectator stand running along the length of one side with the gateway to the stables on the other. At either end of the hangar were two large gates leading to the outer yards. The teacher was standing in the gateway shouting orders out to nine students who were sitting on horses in front of her. With their riding gear on (helmets, body guards, boots) I couldn't make out Frankie until he waved at me with his riding crop. The lesson centred on show jumping, so I trudged across the surface of the arena – which was made up of a weird mixture of sand and little bits of rubber – to the other side to sit in the spectator stand to watch. I walked through the spectator gate and climbed over a few rows of seats so I could sit at the back.
>
> As the horses milled around the teacher began to set up some jumps in the centre of the arena. Frankie was jumping last, after his jump the teacher praised him and told him 'nice line' as he pulled away. On Frankie's second jump he again drew praise from the teacher who said he had a *'good canter'* and a *'good jump'* and on his third jump he was told it was *'really nice'*. A few of the other riders were having problems but Frankie seemed to be at ease with it. A second set of somewhat higher jumps was set up. This time the teacher seemed

more critical with phrases being repeated to many riders such as 'rubbish line' 'rubbish turn' 'insecure length'. Apart from the interaction with the teacher, the whole class seemed very individual. Each rider was involved in a relationship with their horse and there was not much talk between students/riders. Three jumps had been set up for the riders and Frankie was again jumping last. On the first jump he was criticized and told that his *'canter was wrong'*. On the second jump the horse refused to jump, which was the first refusal by a horse to jump all session. He turned the horse and tried again but the horse pulled up short again and just didn't seem to want to go. It whinnied and made a strange noise and Frankie pulled it over to one side and tried again and it still refused to jump. The teacher came over and moved one of the poles making up the fence and Frankie came back for a fourth try and jumped it with ease. The final fence was jumped first time and the teacher told/shouted at Frankie to keep the horse walking around, it wasn't 'allowed to nap' after its poor performance on the jumps. The teacher asked the students to bring the horses back into a line across the middle of the arena and after some general talk about what went right, and what went wrong during the last hour, the session ended and the horses were led back to the stables through the doors on the opposite side of the arena.

[*Fieldnotes*]

There are several similarities here to the practical spaces of Bakers' and Ian's course. Frankie had to adopt a certain uniform for riding, was responsible for a task and had to listen to instructions. The riding instructor, like Jon in the mock garage, used subject specific language and offered advice and support to students using this discourse. Whereas Jon had asked about *'top dead centre'* on an engine, this teacher talked about *'insecure length'* and playing around with the feel of the horse to *'activate it or steady it'*. The teacher also mentioned a few times about being *'brave'* with the horses. If a horse is not ridden properly the rider could be thrown and possibly killed. Although an alternative 'feminized' form of masculinity is being performed here by Frankie, a contradiction in this performance becomes evident. The notion of bravery would more often be linked to industry or manual work, where 'real' men are employed and stoic forms of masculinity are forged through physical work. The male environment Ian and Bakers studied in would not appear to be this dangerous, and risk of serious injury and death was highly unlikely. Nonetheless there is a very strict set of rules and expectation to be followed here with riders being very submissive to the order of the teacher and the discipline in terms of what is acceptable. Through his on-horse display Frankie is actually continuing an older upper-class masculine tradition of bravery through horsemanship and one that is steeped in power and prestige.

The stables

Alongside the frame of interaction, performances of self operate in different ways, the performer can therefore 'drop his front, forego speaking his lines' (Goffman, 1959: 115) in different settings. Frankie begins to drop some aspects of this alterative performance of masculinity as soon as he leaves the arena.

> I crossed the strange floor of the arena once again and exited through the side door and into the stables through the back rather than the main gate. The controlled atmosphere in the arena from the last hour was totally different to what was happening here now in the stables. The students were really busy putting the horses away and taking saddles off and beginning the process of cleaned up. I walked down the centre of the stables looking for Frankie, dodging girls walking past me carrying saddles, buckets of water and containers holding sponges and brushes. Frankie and the other students were just as responsible for the horses now as they had been in the arena. The duties they had to perform, I realized were just as much part of the lesson as had been the riding.

> After taking off the horse's saddle, putting on a blanket and taking off his own riding helmet Frankie walked to the other end of the stables and put the 'tack' and the saddles into the storage room. In the storage room Frankie started chatting and laughing with two girls; one of them happily told me quite loudly that the other girl was *'Frankie's girlfriend'* which both Frankie and the other girl looked quite sheepish about. We left the tack room and collected some water and a container holding different brushes and combs and headed back to the horse. Here Frankie sponged down the horse, which didn't seem too keen on being touched and kept moving around. The teacher came into the stable and mentioned to me that it was probably best that I stand outside as the horse had a bad habit of kicking out at people. After Frankie had sponged down the horse, (I was quite surprised by how much it had sweated) he put a blanket on it and closed the stable door.

> Frankie said he was heading down to the changing rooms to get out of his riding clothes, so I walked with him. On the walk to the

changing rooms Frankie discussed how he hated having to wear jodhpurs whilst riding, as other boys in the college took *'the piss'* out of him. He had an agreement with the course leader to be allowed to wear tracksuit bottoms whilst not on the horse and around the college. Once Frankie had changed we walked back up to the stables and back to clean out the horse and get it *'ready for the night'*.

Whilst I was standing outside the stable looking and feeling again like a spare part and dodging the others walking around with brushes and wheelbarrows full of hay two students started yelling at each other. This just seemed to me like a bit of banter between friends, but when one girl shouted out *'fuck off'*, the teacher, who was standing near me, screeched for both of them to stop what there were doing. She issued a severe reprimand to both of them about their language and behaviour. She said to that the language was *'not very ladylike'* (expressing the gendered stereotype of dressage riders) and that there should be *'no swearing'* in the stables. The stables were now silent and everyone had stopped what they were doing and were watching, to this audience the teacher expressed the need to have *'discipline in front of a visitor'* i.e. me. I wonder if Jon had tried to enforce this rule in the garage or his classroom, how well this would have gone down? Something else that disturbed me a little was the fact that the teacher was also drawing me into the conversation.
[*Fieldnotes*]

In the stables behind the scenes and away from the 'audience' (which is normally the general public and competition judges), dressage riders and these students engage with horses in a different way. They get dirty, have to lift heavy hay bales, use trucks, tractors, handle spades, brushes, get wet, cold, get physically hurt through interactions with horses and get calloused hands. But once the riders leave the yard to compete, the front of the performance occurs and markers of femininity become more important. Frankie has to expand his masculinity here to incorporate aspects of femininity, such as the uniform (tight fitting jodhpurs, riding boots, colourful shirts) which he felt brought harassment from other young men around his college. Thus performance in the dressage ring is not just about the ability to jump and carry out routines and movements, but the uniform itself also frames performances of femininity and masculinity. Thus, when observed by judges on the horse, and when the rider receives marks during a competition, the top winners tend to embody the highest forms of femininity, such as delicacy, elegance, style, poise, good posture and the ability to be submissive to these demands. For Frankie to be successful in the industry, his front performance requires markers of femininity, these can slip in in the yard or stables, but the gender divisions must be worked at and performed in the public domain (Latimer and Birke, 2009).

Away from the arena and stables, Frankie continued to contradict his on-horse performance and maintain his male privileged though the subordination of his female classmates. The course was made up of around 20 students aged between 16 and 18 and Frankie was one of only two men (the other being openly gay) on the course. One evening, when discussing college life with him and his friends in The Harp in Cwm Dyffryn, Bakers told me that he would much prefer to be on Frankie's course as he had lots of female students, as he put it *'he's got the pussy, we've just got the nuts'*. Frankie therefore received a considerable amount of attention from many of the girls on his course. He used his heterosexual identity to his advantage and slept with a few different girls, boasting about this to his male friends and telling them in detail what sexual practices he had engaged in and appeared to be interested only in his own image and sexual pleasure. Through these tales, he was able to emphasize his heterosexual prowess and display the reformulation of a working-class hegemonic form of masculinity beyond the college, where his performance of masculinity expands to fill the space. However, it is also clear that Frankie feels he has to compensate for the feminized form of masculinity on the horse, by showing his hyper-masculinity off around the others boys. This incident illustrates the continued pressure to perform multiple forms of masculinity that the young men in this study seemed to experience and the complex work Frankie was engaged in to keep two different parts of his identity together. This more 'feminine' frame offers great potential to young working-class men like Frankie to try out different presentations of self and divergent career opportunities, but the overall pressure to maintain an acceptable working-class masculinity based on a heterosexual script, and traditional 'macho' values, means these opportunity might not be fully accessible.

Outside their vocational courses, one particular leisure activity that further illustrated the display of a hyper-masculinity, was that of car culture and in particular the 'boy racer' subculture. The role of car culture for Bakers, Ian and Frankie (some of The Valley Boiz were also heavily invested in it) was an important symbol of their masculine identities and highlights how their leisure interests were further embedded and embodied across the locale.

Outside college, performing masculinity through car culture

As I noted in Chapter 3 when I outlined some of the driving practices of The Valley Boiz, investigations into young men and their relationships with their cars (especially outside major towns and cities) have tended to point out the tragically high levels of injury and mortality rates, increasing levels of drink-driving and instances of auto-theft that accompany youthful car cultures (Hartig, 2000; Walker et al., 2000; Carrabine and Longhurst, 2002; O'Connor and Kelly, 2006; Kenway and Hickey-Moody, 2009). As Kenway et al. (2006) point out in their study of young masculinities in Australia, car culture has an important place in the lives of young men outside the major cities not just because it provides a way of getting around often large distances when there is a lack of public transport, but also because it is integral to interaction between males within and across generations. In the UK those who participate in this leisure-pleasure practice (Kenway and Hickey-Moody, 2009) are often referred to as 'boy racers' and there is a 'moral panic' (Cohen, 1972) surrounding their behaviour.[7]

The 'boy racer' is generally a young man, driving a modified car with an enhanced engine and with bodywork that has been adapted to include bigger spoilers, flashy alloy wheels and lower suspension. These adjustments to the vehicle are further accompanied by large noisy exhausts, lower 'bucket' type seats, blacked out windows and sound systems that blast out loud music. The 'cruising scene' that accompanies the culture occurs in retail parks, industrial estates and outside fast food chains (Bengry-Howell, 2005; Bengry-Howell and Griffin, 2007) and provides an area for young people to get together in their cars and to socialize with other like-minded individuals, comparing modifications and testing out their driving abilities. However, these spaces are also a place where illegal activities such as speeding, racing and tricks such as doughnuts[8] are performed, bringing attention from the police and seen by older adults as a social problem (Hartig, 2000; Lumsden, 2009). Although it is a largely male-dominated arena, a growing number of young women are also increasingly likely to participate and become involved in the culture (see O'Connor and Kelly, 2006; Lumsden, 2009).

I suggest in this last section that car culture can be seen as another area or frame where the performance of masculinity for some of the young men in this book is displayed. Whilst as Hartig (2000: 37) explains 'there is nothing innately masculine or feminine about driving a motor vehicle', the activity in which one participates and the people who are involved in this activity, such as cruising or driving modified cars, help to construct a localized version of an acceptable form of masculinity, which is then performed in specific places and contexts. However, in an interesting contradiction it also enabled young men like Bakers, Frankie, Ian and others to escape and resist some of this hyper-masculinity and retreat into their own safe space with close friends.

Cwm Dyffryn's youthful car culture tended to centre on the local McDonald's and in large supermarket car parks. Bakers and Frankie sometimes joined in with these meetings, but on the whole tended to stay away from the wider 'boy racer' community just driving around with each other or occasionally with some of the other The Valley Boiz or their friend Jimmy. Ian distanced himself totally from the scene and rarely used his car for cruising or driving around the area without a purpose. All used their cars for getting to their respective colleges which were a considerable distance away from Cwm Dyffryn. But for Bakers and Frankie their cars were not just vehicles to move them from one point to another, more importantly they also enabled them to 'be seen' around the town.

> I arrived around 9.30pm and met Clive outside the rugby club who was chatting to Frankie and Bakers who were sat in a black Ford Ka in the small car park at the front of the club. I said hello as Clive was telling them how 'crap' the party inside was and warned me that it would be a waste of time me going in. Bakers and Frankie had been in the town's theatre watching Bakers' girlfriend perform in a local play and weren't going to bother with the party. They told me that they were just *'driving round town'*. Bakers then asked Clive if he wanted a spin and replied *'why not'*, they also asked me if I wanted to join them. I briefly hesitated before getting in the back of the car. I wanted to get into the party, but I also didn't want to alienate these boys and I think Bakers wanted to show off his car to me. As I got into the back alongside Clive, Frankie asked me if I'd rather be in the front as I was bigger, but I said no it'd be ok. We sped through the town centre and Bakers fulfilled every stereotype of a 'boy racer'. His driving was erratic and he tore around the street corners with 'banging or pumping' dance tunes coming out of loud speakers with the windows down and he and Frankie shouted out abuse to people as we passed. Over the loud music I asked Clive who sat in the back with me if he liked this sort of stuff and he said it was *'shit'* and that he preferred more indie stuff.
> [*Fieldnotes*]

The fieldnotes above are taken from one evening when I was invited along to a party at a local rugby club that a lot of young people from the town were attending. Both Bakers and Frankie appear to be uninterested in it, preferring their own company and uniting through a more risky leisure practice than drinking and dancing. As The Valley Boiz did in Chapter 3, they used the vehicle here as a front symbol of a hypermasculinity, driving laps around the town at high speed, showing off through their driving and playing loud music and shouting abuse out of their windows at pedestrians. Through sound and speed Bakers, Frankie and Clive, who was there along for the ride, were able to imprint their identities in the local space. The car is an integral part of this display and acts as a symbolic signifier of who they are to others in the area. Their ability to roam around the town shows a degree of control over what they do when outside college and enhances their masculinity status.

As usual Bakers talked quite a lot about cars. I do struggle with these conversations as I don't really know that much about them. He showed me a video clip on his mobile phone that he had taken of his speedometer whilst driving. The short clip showed his speedometer reaching over 110 miles per hour when he was on a motorway travelling to Swansea.

[*Fieldnotes*]

Bakers had an enormous amount of knowledge about cars. He spoke quickly and used a lot of technical language to describe what he had done or what he wanted to do with the car. When he showed me the video clip of him speeding, I asked him if he was scared when he drove at such high speeds and wondered if he thought about how dangerous it was. Bakers said that he knew he was a good driver and that he would never speed in an area where it wasn't safe to do so. On the motorway he felt in control and although he was aware of the dangers of driving fast, he suggested that the real danger came from others who might be around him who were driving with less concentration. His connection to cars and machinery both through his course and outside of it was an interest he shared with his father, and they often spent time together fixing or tinkering with their vehicles. This not only had a direct influence on his chosen career plans and what it meant to be a certain type of man, but was a way to spend time with his father who he no longer lived with, after his parents' divorce.

Car culture is full of competitiveness and for some marginalized young men in Cwm Dyffryn, it was a way of displaying skill and agility though speed and allowed for a degree of power to be exerted over others and the town. However, it was also a way of bonding and cars could be used as a form of escapism and freedom. In my fieldnotes below the inside space of the car allowed Bakers and Frankie to relax some of the hyper performance displayed whilst driving or when they were with other young men. Inside their cars (both tended to ride together in one car) their friendship become quite close, engaging in intimate conversations about thoughts, feelings and problems they were going through.

> On the journey up to Cwm Dyffryn, Bakers expressed how happy he was that he was now single. He told Frankie and me that he had dumped his ex because she had said that he wasn't good enough for her. He talked about the phone conversation he had with her when he had *'ended it'* with her. Frankie and Bakers then continued to tell me about how Bakers had real *'anger management'* issues. Bakers said he had gone to the doctors a few times and had been given *'pills'* to try and subdue these problems. However, the pills had made him depressed and he had *'chucked them out of his car window'* one day so that he didn't know *'where the fuck they were now'* and didn't take them anymore. I asked him if he could remember when it had all started, but he seemed to think he had always had it. People he didn't get on with or *'wound him up'*, made him angry or created what he called a *'rage'* or a *'feeling'* inside him that made him react and freak out. This had meant that he had starting carrying a knife for his *'own protection'* as he put it, which worried me a little, but he quickly said that he didn't carry one any more. Feeling a little disturbed by some of these issues Bakers had mentioned I tried to ask if he had been offered counselling for any of it and he said he hadn't. He said he didn't talk about it much not even to his parents, but they did know about his problems as once when he was shopping with his mother in a nearby town, he had head butted someone who been trying to sell something to his mother in the street!
> [*Fieldnotes*]

The safe space inside the car is an area for Bakers to share some real intimate parts of his life. He talks about his depression problems and the anxiety he faces when around other people without feeling as if he will be openly judged or ridiculed. However, there is not a clear demarcation line between when he is being open about issues that affect him and moderating the story by emphasizing more macho acts, such as head butting someone, even with his close friend. Multiple presentations of self are going on within the confines of the car and it is possibly the only space where these thoughts and feelings can come out at all and he can begin to articulate himself in a different way.

Conclusion

At the end of this study while many of the other young men received their final exam results and prepared to go off to university, Bakers, Ian and Frankie were due to return to college to complete their courses. In Ian's case, his apprenticeship would last for another three years. For Bakers and Ian the 'masculine' VET courses they were enrolled on continued to promote the rituals and traditions of a working-class culture of industrial workplaces. The subject frames (e.g. the interaction order within these environments, course material and spaces of learning) reaffirm a localized hegemonic version of working-class masculinity through future (skilled) manual occupations, despite the lack of opportunities post-graduation and high levels of unemployment in these deprived communities.

Frankie's narrative highlights other challenges and the conflict that accompanies studying a less traditional course. I highlighted the strategies he underwent to adopt multiple subjective positions, to decrease the threat of becoming bullied at college by other young men and alienated from his friends outside it. It is not only the dominant versions of masculinity that Frankie feels he has to adopt which are disturbing. What is also disconcerting about his story was that he couldn't fully achieve his goals and future desires by moving away to attend the prestigious British Racing School at Newmarket and the consequences that this might have for his future life chances. It is clear that while some working-class young men are beginning to explore alternative masculine positions by enrolling on traditionally female dominated VET courses, these do not come without risks and for young men like Frankie, can be extremely tortuous. The pressures of a locale's history on gendered and classed expectations is important and the impact this has on successful futures needs to be recognized. In times of economic hardship, the skill these young people are learning in these environments might have to be transferred to other industries to gain meaningful employment. However, the gendered practices they take with them might not.

Alongside their educational courses one of their main leisure-pleasures that I have discussed in this chapter was that of car culture. Here a showy, hyper-performance of masculinity was displayed through the risky driving practices of the 'boy racer' and being seen around town in their cars. This enabled them to imprint something of their identities on the locale. Interestingly, what I have also shown is that the inside of these cars also acted as a space to escape from the very macho displays that their driving and some aspects of masculinity their courses fostered. It was a space to relax from the tension of having to perform a specific version of a masculine self and be with a close friend in a space of their own away from other people. Highlighting again the multifaceted nature of masculinity that the young men throughout this book seem to display. The next chapter attempts to bring all these factors together through Jimmy's story.

7
Jimmy the Chameleon: Multiple Performances of Self

Introduction

In this book, we have seen the diversity that existed between a large group of young men within a de-industrial community. I have argued that in a variety of settings, spaces and in different social interactions, multiple regions of masculinity are displayed by these young men. These contradictions highlight the pressures that an industrial and cultural legacy of a specific geographic area, places on young men to conform to ideals of manhood. This chapter further explores the issue of multiple aspects of self, with a detailed case study of one working-class young man called Jimmy and his transitions through post-compulsory education. I explore how the challenges of working hard academically and aiming to be a successful athlete are simultaneously met with other pressures to achieve a socially valued form of masculinity through engaging in risky leisure practices, such as drinking large amounts of alcohol. I use this narrative to introduce the term 'chameleonisation' of masculinity to capture these complex processes, and I suggest that this metaphor is a useful step forward for the field of study as it enables the multifaceted processes young men have to navigate whilst growing into adulthood to be illustrated.

Code-shifting and multiple performances of a masculine self

There have been multiple studies involving boys and young men over the past few decades that have focused on the practices and processes that construct dominant or hegemonic forms of masculinity and the pressure to perform masculinity in certain ways. Other recent studies conducted with young men both inside and outside school have illustrated that young men's identities can be quite fluid and complex, and that there are possibilities for constructing alternate masculinities which are not necessarily subordinated or oppressed. In contemporary society, as some authors have documented, men might actually be developing softer or more 'inclusive masculinities' (Anderson, 2009; Roberts, 2014), demonstrating a real shift in attitudes and practices among men. However, as Heward (1996: 41) has argued, a difficult question that arises when looking at changing masculinity is 'the extent to which individuals are constructed by their structural contexts and how far they can build alternative identities despite their stigma'. Jimmy is dealing with such a tension.

Goffman (1959: 45) suggests that 'when the individual presents himself before others, his performance will tend to incorporate and exemplify the officially accredited values of society' and that these values can change from group to group.

> The self, then, as a performative character, is not an organic thing that has a specific location, whose fundamental fate it to be born, to mature and to die; it is a dramatic effect, arising diffusely from a scene that is presented, and the characteristic issue, the crucial concern, is whether is whether it will be credited or discredited.
>
> (Goffman, 1959: 245)

This can perhaps best be summarized by saying that there are many aspects to one's self which can be altered in different situations. Nonetheless, as I have shown in this book, some of these aspects of self are more prominent in some situations than in others and actors must work hard not to reveal certain characteristics in front of the wrong audience.

Influenced by Goffman, Elijah Anderson (1999) in his ethnographic study of an inner-city neighbourhood in the USA, where most of the residents were poor African Americans, found that younger members of the community characterized themselves and each other as coming from either 'decent' or 'street' families. Those from 'decent' families (those more likely to be financially stable) were socialized to accept the values of hard work, to have respect for authority, a deep religious faith and a belief in education as a way for self-improvement. Those younger people from 'street' families were more likely to lead lives less secure than their 'decent' street counterparts, with drug and alcohol problems, and where violence was a part of everyday life. However, Anderson also found that some young people behaved in different ways according to the situation they found themselves in. Anderson (1999: 98) therefore suggests that 'the child may learn to code-shift, presenting himself one way at home and another with his peers'. He found that 'decent' young people saw the ability to code-switch, to play by the code of the 'street' with the 'street' elements and by the code of 'decency' when in other situations, as crucial to their survival in a violent inner-city neighbourhood. Those most associated with the 'street' see little value in gaining middle-class knowledge. How far the young people went to become 'street' depended on their socialization at home, their own opportunities and their own decision-making processes and life chances.

Although not directly drawing on the symbolic interactionist tradition, Reay (2002) illustrates many of the same processes as Anderson (1999) in her study of Shaun, a young working-class man from an inner-city social housing estate in London. The case study explores how Shaun had simultaneously to balance his academic school side with also trying to also maintain a local version of hegemonic masculinity based on violence (Connell, 1995; Connell and Messerschmidt, 2005), which, as in Anderson's study, is needed for young men to survive in the community they inhabit. Yet as Connell (2001: 8) has further suggested there are 'fixing mechanisms that limit the fluidity of identities', with class, as Reay (2002) indicates, being one such mechanism that can limit the effectiveness of young men to display or perform masculinity in different ways that are deemed acceptable in all situations. A second 'fixing mechanism' as this book has made clear is the importance of place, as individual choices are geographically and historically specific and differentiated sets of opportunities develop. Nonetheless, as Goffman (1974: 573) reminds us, the 'self, then, is not an entity half-concealed behind events, but a changeable formula for managing oneself during them': so despite the social-economic barriers Jimmy faces, this young man was still involved in a constant practice of code-shifting which as I will show, results in a form of what I term 'chameleonisation' occurring.

The chameleonisation of masculinity

The young masculinities literature over the past few decades has illustrated how masculinity is performed in different ways and in different settings, something which this book draws on and adds to. However, there is little in the literature on how individual young working-class men alternate between masculinity identities (see Reay, 2002 for a notable exception) or how the pressures to conform to specific ideals of manhood, often termed hegemonic, are juggled with other demands to perform alternative displays of masculinity which are defined by place (Morris, 2012). I propose that young men are capable of acting out different performances across multiple fronts, but that the success of this depends on a complex set of classed, racial and territorial processes. I suggest that one way of capturing and understanding switching between different front displays of masculinity is through a process of chameleonisation. We find that chameleons are a distinctive and specialized species of lizard that are famed for their ability to change skin colour.[1] Although not all species of chameleon can actually change their skin tone, and there is a base colour for all, most can camouflage themselves to fit in with almost any habitat (Le Berre, 2009). The metaphor is therefore useful for trying to understand and make sense of how multiple performances of self are attempted in different situations. As I will go on to show, Jimmy switches between academic and athletic performances in order to create successful future options for himself and to adapt to different situations, but this act of chameleonisation is hindered by what are deemed acceptable forms of masculinity fostered by the working-class industrial heritage of the region. Ultimately, his defence against being ostracized from his community and peers by indulging in risky leisure practices impacts on the success of his academic and athletic life and his future is uncertain.

Being Jimmy

His teachers first introduced me to Jimmy during the initial phase of research at Cwm Dyffryn High School, in the spring of 2008. He was in the top set for most of his subjects and a promising athlete competing at both cross-country and track events (800 and 1500 metres). The local newspaper had written about him and tipped him to appear for the Welsh Commonwealth team in the near future. He was one of the oldest in his year group and lived with his parents and younger brother in a small terraced house a short distance from the school on the edges of the town. Jimmy's father was a train driver and his mother was a ticket sales assistant at a nearby railway station. Both were born in the town and had left school at a young age, neither having been to university. Jimmy was short at around 5ft 7in, slim, with blonde streaks in his stylish quiffed-up hair, which, coupled with his good looks, meant he bore a resemblance to the America teen actor Zac Effron.[2] This similarity was a source of humour between him and his best friends Bakers, Frankie and Ian, but it was something that he said did not bother him too much, as it tended to bring him attention from girls in the town.

Jimmy was polite, softly spoken, well mannered and seemed popular with teachers and the majority of his peers. His main interest outside school was his running, which connected him to his father, with whom he went training with on occasions and who had also been a successful long distance runner in his youth. As the study progressed Jimmy, supported by his father, began to run for different clubs and took part in competitions both at regional and national level.

His other interests included music and, along with learning to play the guitar, he told me that he liked a wide range of music spanning different decades and this was a key part to his identity. Outside school he usually dressed in T-shirts with the names and logos of different rock bands on them and often went to watch local bands play in the pubs around the town. During the summer holidays between Year 12 and 13 along with some friends he had also been to the Sonisphere heavy metal music festival.[3] He still wore the entrance wristband months after the event, which he said was to remind him how good it had been. When I asked him about his favourite bands he told me:

> Well I like Metallica, Jimmy Hendrix, Black Sabbath, Led Zeppelin, ah The Beatles they got to be in there, ACDC... ah there's too much choice man, Avenged Sevenfold, also don't mind a bit of Bullet... Joe Bonamassa.
> [*Individual Interview Year 13*]

During the early stages of the study Jimmy was constantly changing girlfriends and had a reputation amongst his friends as being a bit promiscuous or, as they termed it, a 'player'. This was something Jimmy always denied, stressing that he was only really looking for 'the one', and that it was girls who tended to mess him about, not the other way around. Towards the end of his time in school, things became more serious with one girl, Rhiannon, and as he began to spend more time with her, he distanced himself from his male friends and saw less of them (for a similar discussion of the retreat from friendship groups, see Frosh et al., 2002). I now address these different areas of his life in more detail, drawing out the tensions that came with performing multiple masculinities across separate fronts.

The academic achiever

Jimmy had done well in his GCSEs, achieving 10 A*–C grades, and returned to school in September 2008 to study Biology, Chemistry and Physical Education (PE) for AS and subsequently A level. His best friends left at the end of Year 12 and he began to find school a difficult place to be, especially as many of his other friends with whom he had played with in different Rugby Union and football teams, were not taking the same subjects as him.

Jimmy: It's not as good as the old days when you're in Year 9 or 10 like.
MW: Why do you feel like that then?
Jimmy: Because like Frankie and Bakers and that aren't here cos they were the ones I used to bother [hang out] with the most...
MW: Right.
Jimmy: And like when Hughesy, Birdy all that come in...when they come in it's fine like...but the problem is they hardly come in to school.
[*Individual Interview Year 13*]

Jimmy was expected by the school to do well and he wanted to go to university to study sports science, with the eventual aim of becoming a professional athlete or a PE teacher. However, without his close friends in school and with many of his other former sports team mates in different classes to his own A level ones, Year 13 became a struggle. As these field notes illustrate, he found himself increasingly alienated and alone during his A level classes.

> The chemistry lesson only had a small number of students present. The class was made up of Sam, Ieuan, Leon, Nixon, Sin, and Jimmy, whilst Abby and Carys joined the class from another school in the area as part of the combined post-16 educational programme. Jimmy was sitting on a work bench on his own in the middle of the classroom, whilst the others were clustered around the front bench. I sat next to Jimmy and we chatted whilst the homework was passed around by the teacher. He suggested that life had got a bit better for him since he last saw me, but still didn't feel like he was free enough, and wanted to leave school as he felt like he was in limbo.
> [*Fieldnotes*]

We can see from these fieldnotes that Jimmy was sitting alone, a regular practice in his A level science lessons. As Jimmy got older and his former certainties had been dislodged, he had fallen out of place. His friends had moved on, but there was tension between him and those who remained around him. As his final year in the Sixth Form progressed, he later told me that he felt rather irritated by some of the others in his class. When I asked him more about this he told me he found the attitude of his class mates towards him annoying.

MW: You were telling me about science, didn't you say that you don't feel comfortable in there sometimes?
Jimmy: It's just that there's an attitude from um, like Ieuan and that, they are looking down on me type of thing, like when I get a question wrong or something a snide comment comes out and they kind of go [sighs loudly] and they put their heads down [on the desks]. Come on we're 18 now... also it's trial and error, you're not going to get anywhere if you don't try...
MW: Do you feel that if you shout something out and you're wrong, you think some people may have a dig or a go at you?
Jimmy: Um I know they'll dig at me...but it still won't stop me. Half the time I know some of the stuff the teacher's on about so it don't bother me.
MW: So is that the same in PE then?
Jimmy: Ah no it's tidy there like, good boys I got in my class, cos I think they are into sport as well. You know you get that like sort of sport personality if you get what I mean, extrovert whereas the non-athletic types are a bit um...a bit ahh...all for themselves I find. You got to do what they want to do type of thing; like the other day when I was in the library I was just minding my own business and I heard Alan say that Sam called me inferior because I'm doing lesser subjects than him sort of thing!
[*Individual Interview Year 13*]

As we have seen despite the area's industrial decline, to be a 'proper' boy or man from the South Wales Valleys, an archetype of masculinity associated with this older world of industrial labour and 'masculine' ideas of male embodiment are still the default reference points. However, Jimmy felt that in his science class his classmates belittled him when he tried to answer questions asked by the teacher and he was also mocked by Sam for his choice to study PE, which, as a subject that uses the body, could be seen as a direct link to a manual world of labour. Of course, this is the very area where he excelled and the sporting sphere, where he felt comfortable, was a space which most of his classmates avoided and distanced themselves from. It was also clear how insightful Jimmy was in recognizing the different forms of masculinity that were on display where he discussed with me the differences between the 'sports personality', e.g. local hegemonic form of masculinity (Connell and Messerschmidt,

2005), and those who he referred to as 'all for themselves', e.g. the individualistic, academic achieving, middle-class aspiring geek. Jimmy then proceeded to tell me how he felt his subject choices were further criticized by some of his peers.

MW: Do you think there's a type of snobbery then?
Jimmy: Yeah... definitely.
MW: So the subjects you do in school, other people either look up or look down on you maybe?
Jimmy: Yeah apart from in PE like, it's a good subject... and there's more to PE than those boys think as well! Cos I still get comments off um saying that PE isn't a subject mun, you know...
MW: (laughs) Who said that then?
Jimmy: Ha well them again really, Ieuan, Sam and them in Biology.
MW: Even though you do a lot of Biology as part of PE don't you?
Jimmy: Yeah and history of sport... there's a lot, I can't wait to get out of here!
[*Individual Interview Year 13*]

As I showed in Chapter 4, Jimmy's A level science classmates (members of The Geeks friendship group) are illustrating a form of what Redman and Mac an Ghaill (1997: 169) suggest is 'muscular intellectualness' (see also Edley and Wetherell, 1997). This front performance helped articulate a form of masculinity that differed to what traditionally defined being a 'proper' man in their community and normally it was not equal to the power held by the more sporty boys (see also Mac an Ghaill, 1994 for a similar process); however, for Jimmy trying to cross between these two spheres was not easy, and he felt he was judged and without his best friends in his class he was open to ridicule and felt out of place. He did not fully achieve the chameleonisation process and couldn't quite fit in.

Jimmy continued to work hard with the hope of being the first one in his family go to university. However, when discussing his future and university options, it became clear that Jimmy was adamant that he wanted to attend somewhere local, despite initial ideas about applying to universities further away from Cwm Dyffryn.

MW: So um when you decide to leave school you're going to go to uni?
Jimmy: Yeah.
MW: And you're going to go to UWIC [University of Wales Institute Cardiff[4]]?

Jimmy: Hopefully yeah.
MW: And what other choices have you...
Jimmy: Um... Glamorgan[5] is my um (click fingers) insurance is it?? And I turned down Swansea.
MW: Ok... and where else did you apply?
Jimmy: Um well just those three.
MW: Ahh right... cos you had six choices didn't you?
Jimmy: Five I could choose yeah.
MW: Five right...
Jimmy: Um cos I wanted to go to America like but...
MW: Right.
Jimmy: But I didn't bother in the end.
MW: Maybe you could...
Jimmy: ...didn't bother applying or nothing like...
MW: Because you mentioned Bath to me a while back didn't you?
Jimmy: Yeah I was thinking of Bath Uni... but it don't entertain me. UWIC's just as good as... it's on your doorstep innit... Welsh people... and this is my home like, do you know what I mean?
MW: Yeah, do you feel then that they would be a bit different up in Bath then?
Jimmy: (Laughs) Um well you know what it's like when you go to a different country, also different sense of humour... like with UWIC or Glamorgan, I just do my work, come home chill out around here...

[*Individual Interview Year 13*]

Jimmy seemed to be trying to reconcile his aspirations to go to university with his desire to stay at home in a place where he felt comfortable (see Lucey, Melody and Walkerdine, 2003 for a discussion about working-class girls who also feel this pressure). As illustrated above, Jimmy struggled with the environment of the A level science classroom and his classmates' attitudes towards him. From his experiences it is clear that he does not fit in with the others, who are themselves marginalized in the community for being academic achievers, but what it further showed is how his potential is hindered by his experience of studying without a close friendship group for support. Jimmy felt lonely battling against his classmates, whilst trying to succeed in the subject in order to progress into higher education. Although social class is not overtly mentioned here (nation in fact replaces it), what Jimmy does refer to in his decision making is that he would rather stay local as a 'different sense of humour' would exist elsewhere and he feels he wouldn't fit in. A 'sense of humour' could be read in terms of class, as the studying environment in Bath would be vastly different to that of the socio-economic conditions he is under in Cwm Dyffryn. His choices represent his desire to study with people he is familiar with and also show that his chameleonisation is perhaps limited to the local level and that he cannot take this into other environments.

The party boy

As Year 13 wore on, Jimmy went out at weekends and during the week drinking and partying at night. He also bought a car from Ebay and took to driving around the town at high speed with Frankie and Bakers. However, when he went out at night during the week, this affected his academic performance in class. As the extracts from my fieldnotes below show, trying to burn the candle at both ends, or to perform a more macho masculinity, alongside a more studious position in the classroom, was not always possible.

> When I walked into the registration classroom I joined a group of boys sitting at the back. Jimmy, Brad, Bunk, Tomo and Birdy were chatting about a party they had been to in the town's rugby union club the previous night. Jimmy was looking quite hung-over with a white face and dark bags under his eyes and was explaining to the others who had also gone out the night before, how bad he was feeling.
>
> Biology was the first lesson of the day and the class contained Jimmy, Ieuan, Leon, Nixon and two girls, Abby and Carys. The lesson was based on the human life cycle and sexual reproduction. From the beginning and throughout the lesson Jimmy struggled. This seemed due to his hangover and not having done the notes he'd needed to do in order to catch up, as he'd missed the previous lesson. After around 50 minutes into the lesson the teacher suggested that Jimmy was half an hour behind everyone else which caused the others in the class to laugh. It appeared that Jimmy's 'party boy' image, and his attempt to be popular with everyone, certainly wasn't helping today. His hangover seemed to be affecting his work and he had to ask the teacher and the others for help. Whilst they were waiting for Jimmy to finish off the diagram from the board, Leon showed the teacher his revision notes and the teacher marked the electronic register.
>
> At 10.00am the teacher stopped the lesson for a 10-minute break and the majority of the class headed to the shop just outside the school gate. Jimmy followed a few minutes later after finishing the diagram.

When he arrived at the shop, he bought a can of coke and before drinking complained that he felt really ill and stated how hung-over he was. On the way back to class Jimmy and Leon started discussing some chords from a song they had both been trying to play on their guitars, but when they returned to the classroom Leon went back to his place on the front bench and the conversation was cut short. The teacher resumed the lesson and continued to go through other parts of the reproductive process and the lesson continues as before, with diagrams on the board and the students making notes and answering questions. Towards the end of the lesson with Jimmy still showing signs of struggling due to his hangover, Carys mentioned that this would be worthy of a Facebook status update which made the others laugh and she criticizes him for always drinking.

[*Fieldnotes*]

As these fieldnotes show, this 'party boy' image not only had an effect on his schoolwork, but also alienated him from The Geeks in his A level class. This is not to say that his classmates did not go out at night (as I showed in Chapter 4) but they tended to go out on weekends or during the holidays when it would not impact on their school work. These practices acted to police and regulate their behaviour, something which Jimmy could not do if he was to maintain his standing with his wider peer group, and an acceptable form of masculinity with them: so he began to fall behind in his academic work. Drinking alcohol was a way to maintain an acceptable symbol of manliness and a connection to the heritage of the locale from which he was in danger of becoming disconnected from by his investment in academic labour – and the hangover he was suffering was a symptom of this pull. His drinking also began to have an impact on his running and performance as an athlete.

The athlete

Jimmy took his running seriously. After spending so much time with him and discussing and reading about his continual progress in the local newspaper, I was interested in watching him race for myself. When a trial for the Welsh schools team was held at a nearby athletics track towards the end of Year 13 I went along to support him.

I parked my car just behind the running track and as I walked into the stadium, asked the people at the table by the entrance gate what time Jimmy was due to start. As the events were running ahead of schedule, the race was to begin shortly, so I quickly found a seat at the back of the spectator stand to watch. As I sat looking over the track to where the ten or so runners were lining up for the 3,000 meters, I caught sight of Jimmy. He was wearing a black and yellow vest with the number 22 pinned to the front and standing in the middle of the athletes behind the starting line. When the gun sounded he took off at speed and from the beginning of the race he was out in front with another competitor and left the rest of the field far behind. Coming into the final lap he was still leading and holding the other runner off, but as the contest neared its climax, the other athlete was too strong and made a surge for the line and took first place. Sitting high up in the stand and looking down on Jimmy, I couldn't help but feel more than a little disappointed for him. He had told me in the morning that this was his last chance to get into the Welsh schools team. I left the stand and walked to meet Jimmy at the end of the track. Jimmy's father was there and he seemed slightly frustrated at Jimmy's second place. After briefly chatting to Jimmy I left him to it as the atmosphere between Jimmy and his father seemed rather tense.

[*Fieldnotes*]

During an individual interview we talked about the pressures he felt to go out and socialize and to run. However, as can be seen in the race described above, to do both was not always successful.

Jimmy: Doing pretty well in my running like you know running for Wales and stuff but umm...in the past four months I'd say there has been a lot of socializing going on outside of it like...drinking and all that...but I got to get myself back on track been a week now. I know it sounds like I'm an alcoholic speaking but...but you got to start somewhere.
MW: So you know when you're running and that, how many days do you run?
Jimmy: Six days a week I reckon.
MW: And what or how much are you running?
Jimmy: About 10 miles or well about 8 miles a day on an average day, don't want to do too much too soon.
MW: So you want to increase distance or speed or?
Jimmy: Um both really got to push yourself past your limits.
MW: Um when you're running like cross-country distances, what's your distance?

Jimmy: Four mile normal... but when I reach twenty it'll be um six miles.
MW: OK... and how fast are you doing it?
Jimmy: Um for cross country it don't really matter about time like... just position, but um when track season comes now, time will matter
MW: And you do six minutes on the track is it?
Jimmy: 800, 1500 and 3,000 metres. Yeah.
MW: So when you do the running though, do you think it's a good way of coping with everything else that's going on?
Jimmy: Um because I've been doing it for so long I don't really think about it like that, but thinking on it or reflecting on it does help. Just switch off, get into a rhythm and don't think about anything else.
[*Individual Interview Year 13*]

While the running was a form of escape for Jimmy and he said that when he was doing it he could stop thinking about other things, drinking alcohol was again having an impact on his performance, this time his athletic ability. He talked with knowledge about his sport and seemed to know what was expected of him as an athlete; however, drinking with his friends impacted on how good a sportsman he could be. Also, as Connell (1990: 86) notes in the life history interview with the water sports iron man Steve Donahue, being successful as an athlete should have prevented 'him from doing exactly what his peer group defines as thoroughly masculine behaviour: going wild, showing off, drink driving, getting into fights', but the temptation to participate in these activities was strong. This is also made clear below when I asked him what his father thought about his drinking:

Jimmy: Um he hasn't said much but he said it won't help your running, let's put it that way!
MW: Do you find though that it does mess it up a bit?
Jimmy: Ahhh yeah definitely you just feel tired all the time, can't be bothered to do anything.
MW: Must be difficult like when the boys are drinking?
Jimmy: Yeah yes it is, but um touch wood I won't do it for a long time now.
MW: I think if you balance it though, it should be alright?
Jimmy: Humm, yeah just like you know not every weekend like, it's going to be hard let's put it that way! Well I want to get in good shape for the summer now... so if I start now, it'll get easier.

MW: It must be hard when all the boys are going out...
Jimmy: Yeah I'll have to start going out and not drinking like which is going to be hard like.
[*Individual Interview Year 13*]

Jimmy's constant chameleonising took a huge amount of effort to maintain, and the contradictions in his multiple performances of masculinity were clear. As I have shown through this narrative, Jimmy experienced various obstacles in performing his masculinity across the different educational and leisure settings. As an academic achiever, by investing in 'mental labour' (Willis, 1977), Jimmy would be perceived by some in the community to be in opposition to what constitutes a dominant or hegemonic form of masculinity. But by investing in sports and also by going out drinking and partying, he could maintain an acceptable form of masculinity to offset this and chameleonise between these two worlds. However, a major consequence of this was that Jimmy could not truly fulfil his academic goals and he suffered within the more studious environment and had conflict with his classmates there. The overall consequence of this seems to be that he doesn't really fit in comfortably with either position. I turn now to look at a final area of his life where he tries to juggle these positions further – that of his friendships with his close male friends and relationships with girls.

Friendships and girlfriends

Although Jimmy had a large group of acquaintances spanning across his school, sporting and social life, he had a relatively small circle of close friends. As noted above, these were Frankie, Bakers and Ian, whose lives I have already outlined in some detail in the previous chapter. After they had left the Sixth Form, Jimmy still spent a considerable amount of time with them through other activities, such as meeting up with them at night to drive around in their cars together, or by going to the pub. During Year 13, alongside his schoolwork and his athletic training, Jimmy was also employed at a local sports hall as a receptionist during weekday evenings. He revised during these evenings and found it a place away from distractions. However, on some nights his friends would call in, often uninvited, to see him and disrupt him.

> As we entered the corridor of the sports hall Jimmy exclaimed '*what are you doing here?*' and was shocked to see us. Frankie and Bakers said they'd come to surprise him and keep him company for the last

30 minutes of his shift before going onto a party held in a nearby club that had been organized as a fundraiser for another schools' end of year prom. Jimmy and I sat on a table outside the reception area of the sports hall, whilst Bakers and Frankie starting kicking a football back and forth in the corridor. Soon after this we went and sat down in the reception room and the boys discussed which girls were going and began to talk about whom they wanted to 'pull' at the party. As I sat on a chair at one end of the small room, Jimmy leaned against the desk which had the computer, his abandoned books and revision notes spread across it. He was wearing a white T-shirt with a picture of Jimi Hendrix on the front with grey baggy jeans and trainers and said he was going 'casual' to the party and not bothering to change. Bakers and Frankie, who by this time had started messing around with a hammer and a screwdriver they had found on a nearby shelf, were dressed rather differently. Frankie had put in a silver earring in his left ear, spiked up his hair and was wearing a grey trendy cardigan with tight skinny jeans. Bakers was wearing a black Fred Perry polo shirt with the collar turned up, alongside the same sort of tight skinny jeans that Frankie was wearing, both had obviously tried to make the effort. After taking the ball out of the computer mouse and throwing it around the room much to Jimmy's annoyance, Bakers proceeded to stick the screwdriver into the wooden floor and hammer it in with the hammer! The handle of the screwdriver then split which caused him to stop and laugh. Jimmy at this point tried to say with as much authority as he could muster that *'enough was enough boys, this is my job here like'* and wrestled the screwdriver off Bakers.

At around 9pm after the last customers has left, Jimmy closed up the sports hall and the two of us got into his car, which was parked outside. Jimmy had recently purchased his first car off EBay for £1,500 and was proud of it, which like Frankie's car, was the typical 'boy racer'. As we prepared to move off a plastic bottle hit the side of Jimmy's car. Jimmy got out and shouted at the other boys who had driven a little way across the car park. I don't think it was deliberately meant to damage the car or even if it had been thrown by the others (who denied it) but it annoyed Jimmy and when he got back into the car he said he was *'pissed off with how childish they were being tonight'* and as we drove to the party he wished that he wasn't going, but because this girl he liked would be there, he felt he had to go.
[*Fieldnotes*]

During the evening Jimmy was again caught between his school studies (revising whilst working) and his loyalty to his closer mates who had left school and, as the last chapter made clear, were all enrolled on vocational college courses. The messing around with the screwdrivers and the mouse ball, which Jimmy calls *'childish'*, impacted on the time he had to catch up on his school work given his other commitments such as his running and social life. It is these other commitments, however, that distance him from the majority of his fellow A level classmates and make his school life quite miserable. He also indicates, at the end of the fieldnotes here, that he was only going to the party all three were heading to, because there was a girl he liked there. The pressure to maintain a heterosexual masculine identity was a constant anxiety for Jimmy and he had to again switch between multiple performances of masculinity.

During Year 12 and into Year 13, Jimmy had had an on-off relationship with a girl a few years younger than him, but when she broke off the relationship he found it a difficult time and turned to going out on the 'pull' with an attempt to move forward. In order to maintain the presentation of a heteronormative self and gain peer group status this strategy of 'hyper' masculinity was adopted, but it seemed to be a selective process that would change depending on the situation and who he was with. But this promiscuity had created a reputation of him as being a bit of a 'playa', or a 'man slag' which brought admiration from close friends and with The Valley Boiz, but disapproval from The Geeks.

One night whilst I joined them in the sports hall the topic of how they had lost their virginities came up. Whilst Frankie and Bakers were quite open and very brash about it, Jimmy remained quiet and would not be drawn into the conversations, playing with his phone whilst the others talked.

> As we chatted Frankie told me that they knew one girl who had apparently slept with over 30 boys at the age of 17. I asked if this would be ok for a bloke and Frankie said *'yeah course'* and laughed, but Bakers was more reserved and didn't seem to think it was that good a thing. This then led into a conversation about sex in and out of relationships and first times. Jimmy remained quiet and didn't offer much to the conversation, but Bakers was happy to tell us that he'd first had sex aged 15 with an older girl on holiday in Spain. He stressed it had been an awful experience from what he could remember as he had been really *'hammered'*, but that as *'any hole's a goal'* he was glad he had done it as when he starting seeing a girl later that following week back in Cwm Dyffryn, he knew what to do. He mentioned that

he thought he had waited 15 years to have sex he admitted it had been 'shit'. I asked did he think sex was better in a relationship and he said yes he thought it was, but usually hated the cuddles and stuff that came after sex with a girlfriend. There was only one girl that Bakers had been with whom he had liked doing this with and said that the whole night (they'd watched a film, had a takeaway and kissed for ages before going to bed) had been cool. Normally he said that the first thing he wanted to do after sex with a girl was to *'wash his dick'* even if he had been wearing a condom. Frankie added that he always had to wash his hands straight away after and hated having to lie there for ages until he could get up and wash them.

Frankie said that he had lost his virginity in a field behind the riding stables where he worked part time. He said that the girl he'd slept with had told him that she had had sex with three other guys before they *'did it'* but when they had started she mentioned she hadn't actually been with anyone else either. Similar to Bakers he told me that it had been an awful experience and that neither of them *'knew what they were doing'*. He stressed that he hadn't even *'met her'* before or during sex. *'Met'* as I have come to understand it means French kissing and I couldn't believe this could be true and asked why not. Frankie said it was because she was *'hangin''* and a *'minger'* stressing the lack of emotional attachment that he felt towards the act. He said he had tried to have sex with her from behind but as it was both their first times *'it didn't seem to work'* so they had given up on this position. I was struck with how honest they were both being about it all to me and each other and how they both seemed to moderate the stories between bravado and naivety.

[*Fieldnotes*]

Wood (1984) argued that a desire for a relationship could stem from the unhappiness of the male peer group. While Walker and Krusher (1997) further highlight how young men see a girlfriend as an escape from banter and machismo and also as a way of developing a more self-confident persona, so a private and a public sense develops. These multiple selves are therefore contradictory because, as Walker and Kusher (1997) found, those boys who had public identities that seemed linked to the macho attitudes privately expressed anxieties about their public selves. However, Jimmy's anxieties and those of his close friends did seem to be expressed with each other. The front and back performances are therefore closely connected and intertwined and this close friendship allows for this to come out.

Even though Jimmy received a lot of attention and he was always texting and arranging to meet girls on his mobile phone, he always felt troubled and uncertain of these relationships. He always seemed to want to talk about these relationships with me and seek reassurance, but he never seemed truly happy, worried constantly about whether a girl liked him and was desperately seeking a steady girlfriend and a committed sexual relationship. One way of coping with this was through listening to music.

MW: So when you listen to music does it help then?
Jimmy: Well I can relate stuff to it especially with Beatles songs, it helps me make my decision if anything
MW: Oh right?
Jimmy: Like there was one girl I didn't see much of as you know
MW: Yeah...
Jimmy: ....And there was a song by the Beatles, called 'You won't see me'... which sounded like what I was thinking at the time...
[*Individual Interview Year 13*]

Jimmy's anxieties continued even when he had begun his second serious relationship with Rhiannon. He spent less time with his friends and more time with her. In fact, he retreated so far from his friends that he rarely saw them and only tended to go out when Rhiannon had other plans.

> When I entered the pub, I was a bit later than I wanted and Jimmy was sitting alone drinking a pint of blackcurrant and watching the Spain vs. Paraguay world cup quarter final match. After I'd bought a drink and sat opposite him on the table, we chatted about how quick the year had gone and how he felt different now with Rhiannon and admitted to saying he loved her and that he'd never told another girl this before. Jimmy stressed that he couldn't believe all the time and energy that he wasted on different girls, and said that he was happy now. As we chatted Jimmy mentioned that Rhiannon was in Cardiff that night on a friend's Hen Party and questioned me on the types of clubs she might go in and what sort of men might go to these place.
> [*Fieldnotes*]

During a drink in a pub towards the end of my fieldwork and before Jimmy received his final exam results, he again talked about his feelings to me. As the notes capture above, while he talked about how happy he was in his relationship, there appeared to be some insecurities around the relationship and it didn't appear like his completed trusted his girlfriend, as he questioned me about nightclubs and where she might come into contact with other men when away from him on a night.

As I have shown through in the chapter, Jimmy's multiple performances were not fixed dualities, but were fluid and changed in specific spaces and in different interactions. Jimmy had the ability to chameleonise, to be able to present himself in different ways and to shift the cultural and local ideology of what it means to be a man in diverse situations, to varying degrees of success. Nonetheless, most of Jimmy's anxiety was attached to the hyperperformance of his heterosexual masculinity. The ability to chameleonise into the dominant masculine performances produced the most difficulties and was accompanied by a high level of stress and uncertainty, ultimately impacting on the more studious performances and potential future life chances.

Conclusion

After completing his final exams Jimmy received an A in PE and two Cs in his sciences subjects. Despite getting the grades, he rejected his first choice university, instead opting to go to a university which was closer to Cwm Dyffryn. His rationale for this, he told me, was that this way he could keep his part-time job at Domino's Pizza, be close to his girlfriend Rhiannon and remain living at home. His running had petered out and although he planned to start again when he went to university the following month, I felt that this would be difficult with the new pressures he would face as an undergraduate with an even busier social calendar.

Jimmy's story draws together many of the other themes that have crisscrossed this book. I have shown how those who adopt different pathways to the traditions of the locale, like Jimmy, face demands to adopt multiple subjective positions to decrease the risk of becoming alienated. His performances of masculinity alter or, as I have termed it, he chameleonises his masculinity across different spheres, within and outside the school gates. What is disconcerting is that his goals and future desires, due to his disadvantaged social class position and the pull of the locale, appear in danger of not being fully achieved. Nonetheless, there are glimmers of hope in his story, as he had a very close relationship with some other young men and, despite acts of macho bravado, this is a small platform for discussing many of the issues he found troubling in his life. In detailing some of these issues and problems, this chapter, and book as a whole contributes to the literature on young masculinities by outlining how we must begin to think about young men having the ability to display multiple masculinities at various times, and are therefore not the bearers of one all-encompassing masculinity that is always, and everywhere, the same. This could help educators and others working with young men, to combat some of the more negative or damaging aspects of masculinity and recognize how working-class young men in particular are under pressure to adopt multiple identities in order to appear successful across different fronts and still fit in to their home communities.

8
Conclusion: Growing Up into Uncertain Futures

Introduction

The restructuring of the economy and the de-industrialization process that has occurred during the last 40 years has altered traditional transitions from school to work across the global north. These economic changes have been accompanied by a set of common held assumptions that men are the new disadvantaged, and that there is a 'crisis' in contemporary forms of masculinity. This supposed 'crisis' is evidenced in political rhetoric, public policy, high levels of educational underachievement, violence and suicide rates, mental health problems, absent fathers and a lack of male role models. However, these changes have not impacted on all men equally and it is the lives of white, working-class men in communities where heavy industry has not been replaced, who have suffered the most. As an alternative pathway to adulthood and to cope with changing job markets, qualifications and progression into higher education have increasingly been since by governments as the solution to many of these issues for young people. Yet in de-industrialized communities, these contemporary pathways to adulthood that young men have to contend with, are quite different to the traditions of their fathers and grandfathers. With a lack of employment opportunities, the relationship between class and gender has been greatly affected, challenging assumptions around what it means to be a man and what defines masculinity. These changing assumptions have further influenced the relationships between men and women and the spaces and places young men inhabit, deeply affecting the factors that shape the ability to form new identities to deal with such change in contemporary society.

Given this background, in the introductory chapter I explained how I was interested in the ways in which young men's masculinities, within a specific Welsh locality affected by such changes, were performed across a variety of educational and leisure spaces. I focused in part on how Erving Goffman's work on the performance of self, social behaviour in public places and the framing of social identity were central to the theoretical basis of this book. Through a longitudinal ethnography, this study has shown how living in a community of social and economic deprivation, demanded multiple masculinities to be performed within different educational and social contexts. I have also explored how history and place have a great bearings on the formation of masculinity and future decision-making.

I asked the following research questions:

1. How are young working-class men living in the Valleys adapting to change in insecure times and making sense of their position as they make the transition to adulthood?
2. When young men are left with the historical legacy of industrial labour, do they perform and articulate traditional forms of masculinity in particular ways and by different means?
3. In educational contexts, how do academic and/or vocational subjects impact upon specific classed masculine subjectivities?
4. What are the broader social and spatial networks within the community (e.g. family, sports, nightlife, fast cars, music, sex) that mediate the identities of these young men and how do space and place impact who they can be and become?

I conclude by drawing out the following key arguments and discussions. First, my ethnographic work addresses the multiple, nuanced ways young men's lives are lived in a specific de-industrialized place. I have explored the demands on a cohort of young men to perform multiple masculinities in a variety of settings and spaces and through different peer group interactions, as they make different transitions through post-16 education and into the world of work. However, I have suggested further that there is also a degree of chameleonising occurring, where individuals can adjust and alter performances with different audiences. Second, I have shown that different academic and vocational pathways frame the definition of the situation for these young men, learning what roles are expected of them when studying a certain subject or course and what is also expected of people around them. This ultimately results in classed and gendered implications that have an influence on their future life chances. Third, I have argued that outside education institutions, the legacy of the region's industrial past and the working-class cultural milieu of the locale, were re-embodied and re-traditionalized in different ways across other local sites and spaces. I conclude by showing that these young men continue to carry the legacy of industrialization and that, to truly understand their lives, it must be acknowledged that masculinities are relational, shaped not only by social, economic and cultural forces, but also by the specificities of place and the spatial features of the South Wales Valleys.

Front and back regions and the chameleonisation of masculinity

One of the most interesting and significant findings that has emerged from this book is that in the de-industrialized community of Cwm Dyffryn the performance of masculinity, for these young men as they progressed into adulthood, was a difficult and often frustrating experience. This had varying consequences for them and others around them. While I acknowledge that there are limitations in using typologies or friendship groups (see also Francis, 2000; Swain, 2006; Mendick and Francis, 2012), they have been drawn on as a starting point for outlining these young lives and employed as a heuristic device in order to act as a cross-referencing point to the wider field of masculinities research. In Chapters 3 and 4, for example, I used this approach to centre on two broad white working-class friendship groups which I termed The Valley Boiz and The Geeks, whose lives seemed to highlight oppositional positions in the school hierarchy which also continued outside the school gates. The Geeks were the academic achievers of the year group and performed a version of masculinity that was seen as non-hegemonic in the locale. This geek masculinity was based on educational success and was combined with an interest in reading comic books, and playing computer games. They appeared less interested than some of their peers in drinking heavy amounts of alcohol, driving fast cars, playing sports, and presented themselves as more anxious about their futures. For many, educational success offered a way to get out of Cwm Dyffryn and to escape the rootedness of 'place'. The other group of young men I identified were The Valley Boiz, who performed a more traditional localized, hegemonic form of masculinity (Connell, 1995; Connell and Messerschmidt, 2005) and at first glance seemed in opposition to the previous group. They tended to study more vocational or non-exam based qualifications, enjoyed playing sports and participated in other spaces of working-class masculine production such as drinking large amounts of alcohol, going out 'on the pull' and engaging in 'risky' leisure pursuits such as fighting, driving cars very fast and taking soft drugs. In opposition to The Geeks' higher educational aspirations and desires to escape, The Valley Boiz sought to preserve the industrial heritage of place by performing their masculinities through re-traditonalizing discourses (Adkins, 2002).

While character types exist and are useful as a starting point, I have argued that this detailed ethnographic work has shown the complexities and multiple ways working-class young men's lives are lived out. As Schrock and Schwalbe (2009: 282) indicate 'learning to signify a masculine self entails learning how to adjust to audiences and situations and learning how one's other identities bear on the acceptability of a performance'. As I showed, it was possible for one of The Valley Boiz, for example Jonesy, to re-traditionalize older forms of working-class masculinity through risky leisure pleasures and certain educational subjects but to also perform a 'softer' side through intimate stories with close friends. I have also shown that it is also possible for The Geeks to be seen as academic achievers and to be perceived as more studious and therefore as a subordinated group, but to still perform (within certain contexts away from the glare of the larger peer group and confines of the school and town) a more traditional form of masculinity similar to that performed by The Valley Boiz from whom they often distance themselves. For example, as I highlight in Chapter 4, on one occasion The Geeks visited a strip club on a night out celebrating an 18th birthday, thereby performing a more traditional, hegemonic form of masculinity accompanied by compulsory heterosexuality, machismo acts and the objectification of women they had paid to dance for them. A shift between a front presentation of self and back performance seemed evident in different ways by both groups of young men. This shows that while front performances of masculinity may shift and adapt to living in new times (Dolby, Dimitriadis, and Willis, 2004), older legacies of masculinity still endure and weave in and out of their narratives. These legacies not only have implication for the young men themselves and their projected futures, but for the girls and women around them.

At the individual level, these implications can be further broken down and the consequences and difficulties of trying to keep both multiple performances close and to occupy numerous subject positions are illustrated in Jimmy's story. I suggested he tried to chameleonise between performances and tries hard to hold his fragmented self together across different spaces whilst being pushed and pulled in different directions by competing transitions (see also Lucey et al., 2003; Walkerdine, 2009;

Conclusion: Growing Up into Uncertain Futures 153

Walkerdine and Jimenez, 2012). His story highlighted the dilemmas faced in trying to achieve academically and gain entrance to university, to work hard beyond the school by trying to become a successful athlete and to also achieve a socially valued form of masculinity that enabled him to fit in with his wider peer group and keep him connected to his close friends. For Goffman, reality is context dependent, which then bounds or frames experiences and shapes the self or performance of self in different contexts. I propose that this could be one reason why young men who operate in or across multiple frames need to chameleonise their masculinities to a greater extent than others. Jimmy, for example, performs his masculinity across multiple frames of experience (academic, sporting, musical, etc.), so within one body he has multiple, simultaneous points of reference from which to interpret experience and shift from one version to another. Yet this process is extremely difficult to do and not all young men can achieve it.

What is clear from this study is that despite structural inequalities, the performances of these young men's masculinities are played out in different settings with different people (peers, family, teachers and the researcher!), and some are able to chameleonise their masculinities to greater degrees of accomplishment than others. Using ethnographic methodology has proven a valuable tool for enabled the performances of young working-class masculinity to come through, highlighting how an interview-based study alone would not have been unable to obtain the richness of the data collected. Ethnography captures reality as it is happens, whereas interview-based studies are only participants' accounts of events, rather than actually observed situations. In terms of analysing and theorizing contemporary forms of masculinity, I suggest that the chameleon metaphor is a useful step forward for the field of study as it enables the multifaceted processes young men have to navigate whilst growing into adulthood to be illustrated. Young men can operate through various masculinities, they are not always locked into one way of 'doing boy' and, through various acts, could be seen as 'inclusive' in some contexts, while maintaining traditional forms of masculinity and the ideas associated with those attitudes in others. The chameleonisation of masculinity thesis builds on Connell's work by showing how masculinity is 'done' in a micro context through interaction, but also how these pressures are linked to global economic changes and how critical studies of men and masculinities can understand how young marginalized men deal with such social change (Beasley, 2012).

Academic and vocational 'frames'

I have taken the perspective in this book that these young men's performances of masculinity are played out as dramaturgical tasks. However, these performances of self (and therefore gender) occur not only within social interactions between individuals but also within the wider culture of a given social setting. It is these frames that construct the meanings and interpretations of a given situation and how we assume we should present ourselves at any given time and the performance or performances that are required for this context. This therefore allows us to see how we 'do gender' (West and Zimmerman, 1987) through social interaction and how this social interaction is framed through specific contexts alongside wider social, economic and cultural histories. In general, therefore, it seems that Goffman's 'frame analysis' framework can be applied to both academic and vocational courses, where the forms and content of the courses, alongside the interactions between students and teachers, frame and therefore sanction and validate performances of masculinity and corresponding educational subjectivities.

When this research began I was interested in the different school subjects that the young men took as part of their GCSEs. As they grew older and progressed through their post-16 educational pathways, I wanted to investigate the impact of these choices alongside the formation of their educational subjectivities further. Throughout my time at Cwm Dyffryn, it became clear that different school subjects elicited different meanings for the young men. In Year 11 academic subjects such as English, Mathematics and Science, supported by languages (French and Welsh) allowed The Geeks to display their academic capital through achieving top grades which gained teachers support and favour. The vocational subjects that the school offered such as the BTEC qualification in sport, GCSE in Physical Education and Design Technology allowed others such as The Valley Boiz to adopt a hegemonic position and to subordinate others by drawing on traditional discourses of masculinity, such as sport and certain 'macho' behaviours, such as intimidation and bullying. As the young men moved through the Sixth Form, these choices again divided the year group, even though the numbers were much smaller.

In Chapter 6, I moved away from the school to show how three different vocational courses provided frames for the construction of masculinity in different ways. For Ian and Bakers, their vocational courses, both mechanical subjects, provided the platform for the affirmation of a specific form of masculinity based on the shop-floor culture of industrial workplaces. The language used by teachers was often sexist, with gendered examples used within the learning environment both in vocational classes and the more theory-based lessons. In Frankie's case, I showed how the subversion of masculine identity was possible in one particular 'feminine' course, equine studies. However, beyond his course, Frankie used other ways to reaffirm his identity by indulging in a showy, hyper-performance of masculinity displayed through the risky driving practice of the 'boy racer'. By focusing on both academic and vocational routes at post-16 level, this study contributes to our knowledge of young working-class men's educational choices in the context of social transformation (McDowell, 2003; Nayak, 2006; Richardson, 2010). It also shows how these subjects continue to reproduce outdated examples of gendered practices.

Beyond educational institutions and the legacy of industrialization

As has been evident in this book, the legacy of Cwm Dyffryn's industrial heritage was played out beyond schooling in different ways and was re-embodied and re-traditionalized across other local sites and spaces. Although the concept of what it means to be a man from the South Wales Valley has altered over time, the localized hegemonic versions of white working-class manhood still exists, despite the complete closure of coalmining in the area. It would be a mistake to think that just because, in the occupational sense, times have changed, symbolic associations with the industry have disappeared. As we have seen with The Emos in Chapter 5, through their investment in an alternative youth subculture there are also consequences for those who do not perform their masculinity in a way that is acceptable by their peers, by diverging from the script.

Young men like Hughesy, Tomo, Brad and Davies continued to display the traces of the locale's industrial culture that was socially embedded through other cultural values and leisure pursuits that interlinked with their educational aspirations. Their family biographies show the history of manual work in the region and were an influence on some of their future aspirations. For others, like Bakers and Frankie, their cars were used as a way to rework traditional masculinities and their reckless driving and speedy pursuits enabled an exaggerated performance to take place. Those who wanted to escape the area by being academically successful, like Sam, Sean and Alan, had to do this alongside the pressure to conform to 'normal' expectations of manhood and deal with the pressures to drink large amount of alcohol, take part in heterosexual discourses and deal with the working-class signifiers they carried with them on university preparation days. Those, like Bruce, who invested in a specific music scene, also had to deal with these 'normal' expectations, and when his friendship group broke up as they got older, he was alienated and isolated within the school and it became a lonely place for him. What is evident for all is that place-based identities continue to be of significance for these young men. By situating the performances of these young men within a spatial context, I have shown that place is centre stage in the performance of young men's masculinities, something which other studies with young men do not always consider.

Implications for policy and practice

This study has gone some way towards enhancing our understanding that the performance of young masculinities is a highly socialized and complex construction. Despite some evidence of agency in the narratives presented here, more dominant versions of masculinity cannot be negated and influenced how the young men saw themselves. A culturally dominant version of masculinity, based on toughness, heterosexuality and physical capital, was the overriding default reference point, but what was also clear was that these boys could, when given the chance, also be articulate, thoughtful and expressive. I suggest that enabling them to talk more in educational spaces about how masculinity is constructed could provide further opportunities for boys to negotiate and renegotiate what it means to be a man and to reflect on social conventions. The chameleonisation of masculinity metaphor that I have put forward could help those working with young men to address issues and challenge damaging behaviour by suggesting that there are alternatives ways of acting, and to also draw on the positive side that exists to masculinity, such as the closeness of male friendships and the support network this can provide in time of trouble.

Another implication of this study is that education and wider youth policy needs to consider the specificities of place in young people's educational decision making. In the current economic climate, employment opportunities for young men from deprived communities like Cwm Dyffryn are limited at the local level. I feel there needs to be a greater link between those who work hard within schools to get their students into higher education and those practitioners who could assist them to discuss a wider range of further opportunities beyond education, even if unfortunately this means leaving the locale. Policy makers also need to recognize the enormous potential that young men can exhibit if given wider access to opportunities that they are unable to afford themselves. Furthermore the changes to the 14–19 curriculum in Wales, which were first instigated over ten years ago, still fall far short of providing students with clear guidance for their futures once they have gained their educational qualifications and, despite the promises of providing a holistic education, there is still an academic/vocational divide.

Finally if there continues to be a lack of real investment in the area, then those young people who can will have no option but to leave and look elsewhere for work and create lives outside the Valleys. This outward migration could then have a drastic effect on these communities. There is a real need to understand what this means to young men themselves and for future generations.

Final thoughts

In this final chapter, I have drawn together the main themes of the book. I have argued that there are diverse ways to be a young man within the community of Cwm Dyffryn, in South Wales. I have suggested that to understand the performance of young masculinities, masculinities must always be understood in time and place and that while new times demand new ways of being, not all young men transition easily. The ability to shift and hold the contradictions of multiple performances together rests upon some complex familial, social, cultural and historic dynamics. The main point I draw out in this book is how being a young man, and thus masculinity, cannot be achieved so easily from educational pursuits as from the former employment practices that shaped the area. Whilst there are undoubtedly instances of 'softer' practices of masculinity being performed, what is always present is the heritage of an industrial and cultural legacy which shapes acceptable forms of manhood. This must make us rethink the argument that more traditional forms of masculinity are on the decline. What this book clearly shows is that despite social transformations, a re-traditionalization of older masculine discourses is occurring within groups of disadvantaged working-class young men. While many are aware of the multiple performances they must undertake in different settings and with different audiences, this has consequences for their futures and the wider communities they live in. I owe a debt of gratitude to these young men who let me follow them around and write about them, coming in and out of their lives over two and a half years. I hope this account does them justice and goes some way to representing what life is like for a young man in a de-industrialized community and the difficulties they face growing up into uncertain futures.

Epilogue

The 35 young men that made up the core of the study have had a mixture of futures since the fieldwork ended. Three were to leave school before the completion of their courses (Jonesy, Steveo and Davies) and two of these were to return to the Sixth Form again to resit some of their subjects (Sin and Gavin) due to poor final grades. Out of the remaining 30, 15 went on to university, 13 to study for degrees and two to study for HND qualifications. Four of this group left Wales to study (Sam to Nottingham University to study English literature, Scott to the University of Lincoln to study architecture and Leon and Ieuan to Portsmouth University to train to become pharmacists); the rest (11) stayed in South Wales. Ruben went to study engineering at Cardiff University; Birdy enrolled on a geography course at Swansea University; Sean opted to take English literature and creative writing at Cardiff Metropolitan University; whilst Alan, Nibbles, Nixon, Jimmy, Hughesy, Clive, Bob and Shaggy went to the local university, the University of South Wales. Unfortunately, after his first year Clive dropped out followed by Jimmy and Sean at the end of their second years. Sean returned home to Cwm Dyffryn and went to work in McDonald's. Similar to other studies with working-class young people, only two of this group went to Russell group universities which appear to offer more opportunities than other higher education institutions (for a discussion of the importance of this see Ball et al., 2000; Reay et al., 2005; Breen and Jonsson, 2005; Bradley and Ingram, 2013).

Of the 15 who finished their courses and did not go to university, there was rather a mixed bag of different routes. Bruce and Scud returned to education and went to different FE colleges. Tomo was successful in gaining a highly competitive paid apprenticeship with a national steel company and others boys entered a variety of jobs. Some of these entailed working with their fathers in different trades such as tiling (Brad) or with siblings in a recycling plant (Cresco). Others went on to become a bus driver (Stig), charity donations collector (Rhys) and a teaching assistant (Dai). Bunk and Ed were unemployed and the positions of the remaining five (Scooter, Simon, Freddy, Carr and Spud) were unknown. Frankie, Bakers and Whippy all returned to complete their courses.

Tragically as I made clear at the start, one of the young men in the book died just after his 19th birthday in a horrible car accident whilst driving fast to work one morning, illustrating painfully the risk and cost of driving at high speed and performances of risky masculinity. On a happier note, four of the young men (Tomo, Cresco, Stig and Bruce) have become fathers.

Appendix 1: 'Doing' Ethnography: Understanding, Researching and Representing Young Working-Class Masculinities

The setting and participants

As I have acknowledged, this study was conducted in a similar district to that in which I grew up. However, I wanted to create a little distance between myself and my participants, so I made the decision to select a community that I was familiar with, but was not my own. Initially a list of schools was compiled in the area that would be suitable for a pilot study to be conducted in the spring school term of 2008. I also hoped that there would be opportunities to explore other areas of young men's lives by going beyond the school gates, if I could return for further research and if funding was granted over a longer period of time (it was).

After an initial search of secondary schools (ages 11–18) in the area, I found 12 schools suitable for further consideration and letters of introduction to head teachers were sent. I excluded all faith-based schools and Welsh medium schools because of access issues and my own (embarrassing) inability to speak the Welsh language. Two community schools were selected for final consultation. One of these was Cwm Dyffryn High School and it was chosen for two key reasons; first, it fitted in demographically with my research aims as it was situated in a largely white, working-class area in a former coal mining town and had a high proportion of pupils on Free School Meals (FSM) and entitled to the post-16 Educational Maintenance Allowance (EMA), indicating high levels of social and economic disadvantage. Second, and most importantly, it was selected because of the overwhelming support and encouragement from Mr Simpson the head teacher. Without Mr Simpson's interest and continued support over the two and a half years of the research period, this study would not have progressed as it did.

The school

The school was located a few miles outside Cwm Dyffryn at the top end of the valley, built overlooking the towns and villages below and surrounded by terraced houses, a small shop, a few pubs and a large graveyard. Opposite the school was a large FE college that backed onto the open mountainside. The site had been used since the 19th century for a variety of educational purposes, including providing technical education and later as an all-boys grammar school. In its current form, the school had been in operation since the late 1970s providing a single sex and, more recently, a mixed, comprehensive education. A gateway just off the busy main road was the entrance to the site with a large car park separating the entrance from the main building where the reception, senior staff offices and assembly hall were located. It was here that teachers left their cars and where buses and parents stopped to drop off children who attended the school. Behind the main building, grassy banks and a large playground were flanked by other school buildings, built at different times over the past few decades. On one side stood a large three-storey structure, rather worn and run down, with different classrooms, technology workshops, and the small Sixth Form common room and library. On the other side of the playground stood another block of classrooms that included the language and science labs and the school dinner hall. On the site, there was also a multi-purpose sports hall, funded through the National Lottery and used by the wider community during evenings and weekends.

Once access was gained, I drew on inspection data from the Welsh inspectorate *Estyn* to provide some information of the demographics of the school. There were around 700 (male) pupils on roll with 22% of these being in receipt of FSM. At the time of the inspection, there were 134 pupils in Year 9, who by the time this study began, would have progressed to their final months of compulsory schooling in Year 11. All year groups were further divided up into five mixed-ability form groups with further special educational provision for other pupils. The GCSE subjects were then streamed into ability sets. After completing their GCSEs, pupils had the option of returning to the school's Sixth Form (Years 12 and 13), which was part of a wider consortium of five schools and a local FE college in the area, that provided joint post-16 provision.

In theory, the consortium allowed individual pupils access to a wider range of subjects as not all schools offered every subject. These ranged from traditional academic A level courses, vocational school-based BTEC qualifications and, through links with a local college, a variety of other vocational subjects such as health and beauty, motor mechanics and bricklaying. The consortium offered free transport between school sites and a single timetable was operated across the different Sixth Forms and the college, to allow continuity. It also provided students with the ability to meet and mix with others from outside their own 'home' school. However, in reality there were sometimes difficulties in the smooth running of the consortium. Students were regularly late for the beginning of lessons as buses between sites (schools were spread over a large area) were delayed and in order to accommodate individual subjects and teachers, subjects were split between teachers at different schools. This often caused confusion between students (as on occasion they were taught the same part of the curriculum twice) and problems for individual teachers, as they were unsure of which parts of the curriculum had been covered by other teachers. Also, in most cases, students tended to stick with friendship groups from their 'home' school and were discouraged by teachers from lingering in Sixth Form common rooms in other schools, so interactions between pupils from different schools were minimal (Table A.1).

Participants

As the table outlines below, in the spring term of 2008 I conducted the first phase of fieldwork, which consisted of participant observation of classroom and sports based lessons, school assemblies and break and lunchtimes. Originally Years 11, 12 and 13 were considered, but I took the decision to refine the study to include

Table A.1 Research phases

Dates and location	Type of data collected	Participants
Phase 1 March–June 2008 Cwm Dyffryn High School Final term of compulsory school	Participant observation and fieldnotes of – Classroom lessons – PE lessons – School assemblies – Playgrounds – Dinner Halls Focus group interviews	Young men from Year 11, Year 12 and Year 13. After the first week, research focus shifted to just Year 11 (134 male pupils). Pupils from different subject sets, form groups and friendship groups. The Geeks The Valley Boiz The Emos
June 2008–September 2009 Cwm Dyffryn High School	Ethnographic conversations during intermittent visits One-on-one interviews	Year 12 (56 male pupils) who had returned to school after their GCSEs.
Phase 2 September 2009–June 2010 Cwm Dyffryn High School	Participant observation and fieldnotes of: – Classroom lessons – Form room at registration – Sixth Form common room – School fieldtrips – University open days – Parents evening – Prize Nights One-on-one interviews	Year 13 (35 male pupils remaining)
October 2009–December 2009 South Side, East Side and West Side College	Participant observation and fieldnotes – Classroom lessons (theory) – Workshops lessons (practical) One-on-one interviews	Bakers Frankie Ian Other college students
October 2009–August 2010 Outside educational institutions	Participant observation and fieldnotes – Pubs and nightclubs – Car and car parks – Cinemas – Shops – Places of work – Facebook	Young men from both school and college Friends and girlfriends Other family members

just Year 11 after the first week of observations in order to increase the richness of data collected in the short space of time available. At the end of the period, before the year group broke up for a period of study before GCSE examinations, I conducted three focus group interviews with different groups of young men based on friendship ties that had become apparent over the period. I also felt these different groups of young men were performing their masculinities in quite distinctive ways.

Questions asked during these interviews ranged from: *What do you think would be your best/worst memories up until now that you'll take away from school? Any plans for the future when you leave Year 11?* and *Have you any educational or vocational (work) goals?* Discussions also centred around more personal issues, such as what other influences the boys had in their lives within and outside school. Due to the small-scale nature of the project, it was impossible to involve everyone in the year group so selection was made on a voluntary basis and through invitation. Consent forms were signed by the young men and their parents to take part in the interviews. All group interviews were then subsequently digitally recorded and transcribed. The analysis of this data was then written up in my Master's thesis.

This first phase of the research was then the basis for the more in-depth, multi-sited intensive year-long study that followed between September 2009 and August 2010. This was conducted in the same school's Sixth Form and across other educational institutions that some of the young men opted for after their GCSEs. This enabled me to explore how some of the same boys performed their masculinities across different post-16 educational pathways and over a longer period of time. When I returned to the school, and as the research period progressed into FE colleges, this again included observing and actively participating in different lessons (on one occasion I helped change a tyre on a car and on another groom a horse); 'hanging around' in the Sixth Form common room and various canteens during break and dinner times; playing Scrabble; and attending school events such as prize nights, parents' evenings, school trips and sporting occasions.

In order to extend the gaze of research and gain a more meaningful and intricate understanding of how the young men understood and experienced their world, a major aim of the study was to go beyond their educational institutions. Once the young men invited me into these other areas of their lives, research was undertaken across multiple arenas. I was then able to spend time in a variety of different settings in order to gain a deeper understanding of their performances of masculinity. These included sitting in cars in car parks and driving around the town; attending sports events and nights out in pubs and night clubs in the town centre and in the larger cities of South Wales; going to live music events such as concerts or 'gigs' and the cinema; shopping; birthday parties; frequenting takeaways and cafes; playing computer games; going to university open days and visiting places of work (such as sports centres, bars and supermarkets). I also used the social networking site Facebook as a means of keeping in touch and being involved in organized events. I only become 'friends' with the young men in these spaces, once they had invited me to do so.

As Appendix 2 makes clear, from the original year group of 134, 56 boys had returned to the Sixth Form at the start of Year 12, around 46% according to the head teacher. By the start of Year 13, 35 remained enrolled on a variety of

A Level and BTEC courses. Many of those who had participated in the Year 11 focus groups, but had not returned to the Sixth Form, were now enrolled on other courses at local FE colleges. These included most of The Emos friendship group. As I spent more time hanging out with those from the Sixth Form on nights out, I also became reacquainted with three other young men, Frankie (who I had interviewed in Year 11 with The Geeks) Bakers and Ian from the original year group. They had all returned after their GCSEs to the school's Sixth Form, but had subsequently left once they had finished Year 12 and were enrolled on different vocational courses, at different FE colleges around South Wales. After another round of letters, emails and telephone calls supported again by the ever-helpful Mr Simpson, I was granted permission by the individual colleges (Frankie, Bakers and Ian having readily agreed) to conduct participant observation and shadow the three boys on their different courses.

I tried hard to avoid 'going native' (Junker, 1960; Pearson, 1993) by over identifying with any one group or particular participant. For example, Cusick (1973) in his study of American high school youth subcultures, spent more time with the sportsmen or 'jocks' than other groups of young people. Willis (1977) also famously sided more with the 'lads' than the 'ear oles' in his study, so with this is mind, I tried hard to balance up the time I spent interacting with different groups. However, just as Coffey (1999) found with her participant 'Rachel' in her ethnography of an accountancy firm, and as Everhart (1977) found in his study of a junior high school with 'Don', I did develop closer friendships with some (Jimmy, Ruben, Sean, Alan) more than others (Carr, Scooter, Ed). In many cases this was simply because they were around the school and the town more and also because we were 'friends' on the social networking site Facebook.[1]

Individual interviews

Even though many hours were spent in the school and elsewhere carrying out participant observation and multiple ethnographic conversations (some online), to build a biographical picture alongside these observations, more formal interviews were also conducted with key actors across different subjects towards the end of Year 13. Interviews provided an important way of understanding individuals' stories and were particularly useful for bringing Jimmy's narrative (see Chapter 7) into focus. Other interviews were conducted with Sam, Alan, Sean, Ruben, Scott, Bunk, Clive, Brad, Cresco, Stig, Tomo and Frankie. Each interview took place on a voluntary basis, which meant that not everyone was interviewed in a more formal structured way. All interviews were digitally recorded and transcribed fully by myself. I also took the step of providing all interviewees with a transcript of the interview after we had met. This enabled participants to comment and discuss any issues they may have had with the narratives produced. In addition, I saw these interviews as a way to explore further the findings emerging from my fieldwork as a participant observer. The interviews gave the young men an opportunity to talk to me away from the bigger group and explain their lives, problems and experiences without being distracted by others. Some interviews were conducted in empty classrooms or offices at the school or college, whilst others were carried out in canteens, cafes and pubs.

These interviews involved asking the young men to tell me about their lives both within the school and outside of it. Some of the topics we discussed involved why they had taken certain subjects after their GCSEs, what their opinions, attitudes and hopes were for the future and what they thought they might miss about school. Discussions also centred on girlfriends, hobbies, where they went on nights out and their feelings toward 'mates', families and Cwm Dyffryn. I used unstructured interviews as I believe it enabled the young men to give their own accounts of what was important to them without me overly guiding conversation. Also, as I had adopted a very casual and open approach in the field, I did not want to alter the trust and rapport that I had built up by taking up a more formal approach when interviewing, which I thought might not generate such rich and useful data.

I also got to know other young people who were friendly with those I have introduced here and had conversations with them. I met other male and female friends on the college courses and on nights out in the town – girlfriends, brothers and sisters, and some parents. The number of young people I spoke to over the period could have been in excess of a hundred, but I have had to narrow down the narratives to those who I spent more time with, so as to bring some order to the data.

Managing field relationships

Practicalities of note taking and writing up

Taking fieldnotes is an integral part of ethnographic research but so too is deciding when to write and when not to write (Denzin and Lincoln, 1994; Emerson et al., 1995; Atkinson et al., 2007). Before starting the first phase of research I had been aware of classic stories within the literature of ethnographic researchers retreating to toilets to write up brief notes, or even using toilet paper itself on which to record details (see Ditton, 1977). This tactic has been adopted by fieldworkers because they have either felt uncomfortable writing in front of participants or the process of note taking has been impractical (see also Cahill et al., 1985). Initially, this seemed rather a silly idea and I could not quite see myself doing this. As most of the lessons I observed were classroom based and writing was an integral part of these lessons for the pupils, it seemed perfectly acceptable to write in a notebook. For sports lessons that I participated in, where it was impractical for me to take notes whilst running around (I was more concerned with not looking like an idiot), I wrote notes up after the events. However, as the research progressed and I started to observe different settings, I encountered other difficulties about how to record conversations. I had bought a digital voice recorder but felt nervous about using it, fearing that it would look more intrusive than a notebook and sometimes it just seemed impractical.

I persevered and experimented with the recorder using it in class and asking those I was talking with if they minded me recording something as we were chatting. But again this seemed intrusive and even though the recorder was small, similar to a mobile phone in size, it seemed to stifle conversation and I found the boys kept looking at the recorder. As the classrooms were often noisy places, surrounding chatter would also be picked up so I soon discarded the recorder and it was not used again apart from recording the more formal focus group interviews.

When I returned to the field for the second phase I again took copious notes during the lessons I observed. Here I recorded details about the specific subjects that were being taught, the layouts of the different classrooms and the interactions between the boys and between them and their teachers. As I became more familiar with the young men, these notes became more refined and the focus narrowed to how individuals experienced lessons and interactions within friendships. In some practical lessons at the various colleges, I felt I got in the way slightly, especially when I was with Bakers in the workshop. I got around this by trying to help where I could on different tasks.

As the weeks went by, I spent less time in lessons and more time in the common room, often just 'hanging out'. I took the decision early on not to write notes in these less formal settings, but to write up events afterwards as best I could. As the research became more in-depth and I spent more time in the field, I began to realize that maybe the classic ethnographic stories of writing notes in toilets were not so silly after all. I often retreated to my car if the boys were in lessons, or not around, to write up brief notes if I thought something was particularly important. When I started to go outside the school gates, note taking became erratic. There was a running joke between the boys and me when we met up in pubs about me bringing my notebook along. Fearful of losing the book, I left it in my car or at home. It was here that I often used napkins to scrawl notes on, often getting the young men to write things down themselves.

After a day in the field, I tried to write up my notes each evening, but I found the fieldwork a lot more tiring that I thought it would be. On some occasions in the colleges, where I was on my feet a lot in workshops or in the stables trying to dodge horses, I found the process of note taking and talking to different people particular exhausting. During my time at the various colleges, as I was less familiar with the procedures and ways of operating, I shared written up notes about the setting and the technical aspects of their vocational courses, with Frankie, Bakers and Ian via emails to make sure I had observed things correctly. Ian was especially good at this, and the notes I took from my time spent working alongside him are almost a collaboration where he refined some of my writing and added detail about the more technical side of his Modern Apprenticeship.

I developed a routine that I stuck to religiously unless I had been out late at night and had had a few drinks. After returning home from school or college I would sit and write up my notes on my laptop that I had taken in my field notebook that day. This often took me hours, but regardless of how tired I was, I felt each day needed to be written up and this routine was more or less adhered to throughout the whole research period. At first, my written notes were often less than a 1,000 words, but the notes from the second phase of the fieldwork were more detailed often running over many pages. Overall I ended up using five small notebooks and wrote well over 200,000 words. Apart from note taking, I also took other practicalities into account.

Dress

I consciously paid attention to how I dressed in order to 'impression manage' my fieldwork relationships with people ten years younger than myself. It was obvious I could not dress like the boys in school, as a uniform policy was still in place; however, I did not want to dress like a teacher or be mistaken for one. So I decided on a different uniform to help adopt the 'least adult' role (Epstein, 1998). I chose to wear casual shirts with floral patterns, checks or stripes on them.

I never wore a tie with these, something that was pointed out by the deputy head of the school on one occasion. My shirts were accompanied by jeans and dark trainers or, when it was raining or cold, boots. I made a point of almost always wearing a hooded jacket, as they were banned and against school uniform rules. Pupils were disciplined for wearing 'hoodies' to school (even in the Sixth Form), so this was a double strategy to avoid being seen as a teacher (no other teachers seemed to opt for the floral shirt ensemble anyway!) and also to be seen as a little bit of a rebel, as I knew no teachers would ever ask me not to wear one. I always carried a hard-backed notebook in my pocket, with a pen, a digital recorder and when at the school a visitor's badge that I had to wear pinned to my shirt. Whilst visiting Frankie, Bakers and Ian at their separate colleges I was also required to wear certain clothes in the workshops or stables, so I had to purchase overalls and safety boots to be allowed access. When not at school or college I wore much the same – maybe a t-shirt to the pub instead of a shirt sometimes.

Age

Even though I was only ten years senior to those in the study, at times I felt a lot older. In the early days of fieldwork when the boys were still in Year 11, I sometimes played football with them during lunchtimes and during PE lessons. I do not really like football and I am not at all good at it, but I joined in as I was asked repeatedly to play by some members of the year group. I was even left 'in charge' by the teacher for a brief period during one PE lesson. On some occasions I think I was taken pity on and given easy passes to help me to score or put into a team as an extra player so others could cover me. By the time I returned, many of those with whom I had previously played football had not remained in school, but some of the same boys who did, and were now in Year 13, had (luckily for me!) grown out of the habit of lunchtime football and thought themselves too grown up to play it in the playground.

In Year 13 as the fieldwork progressed and the boys became legally allowed to drink in pubs, I was often invited to nights out in Cwm Dyffryn and the age difference would again become apparent. One evening when we were sitting in the local pub, chatting and drinking (I will return to the issue of alcohol in a moment) with Jimmy, Hughesy, Tomo and Bunk, it was my turn to put money into the jukebox, or in the words of the young men to 'feed the pig'. I looked through the choices on offer and selected songs I hoped wouldn't make me look too out of touch and from artists that I knew the boys I was with liked. These included songs from bands such as The Killers, Bullet for my Valentine, Funeral for a Friend and Muse. Having had a few beers and feeling quite happy with the way the evening had gone I could not resist adding a song choice of my own, 'Born to Run' by Bruce Springsteen. When the song eventually played ten or so minutes later, my choice was met with a chorus of boos, jeers and comments from around the table such as *what the fuck!* and *who put this on?* which were jokingly directed at me. As the boys laughed and I tried to explain that I had been trying to educate them in classic rock songs, I was told in no uncertain terms that this was *old* or *dad's* music and to get a round of drinks in as a forfeit for my 'uncool' behaviour.

Appendix 1: 'Doing' Ethnography 169

Negotiating masculinity

Morgan (1992) suggests that the field of men and masculinities is fraught with difficulties and that men who study men must recognize patriarchal inequalities and challenge (and potentially change) men's practices within it. However, whilst conducting research, male researchers should also recognize how one's own gender influences or restricts the development of relationships within the field (see Warren and Hackney, 2000; Ortiz, 2003). As I began my fieldwork, I did not expect my gender to be a particular issue. I assumed that as I was an older man from a similar community, I would be able to easily talk with other men (albeit a few years younger than myself) and would have little problem in building rapport and trust. Nonetheless, the rapport building and the trust I gained over time took longer with some than others. I learned that I had to adopt different strategies with different individuals and to negotiate my performance of masculinity in different ways (Goffman, 1976; West and Zimmerman, 1987). I found that with some young men such as The Geeks I had to rely on my status as a university student to gain trust, whilst with those young men who seemed more interested in sports and cars, I had to be able to code-shift and discuss and talk about practices which I often knew little about. Whilst I stopped short of joining in with misogynistic or sexist jokes and stories, at first I did not openly challenge their views and opinions for fear of being seen as judgemental and ruining rapport. Over time, as I got to know them and they got to know me, I did begin to ask why they said some of the things they did and behaved in certain ways. The negotiation of my own masculinity continued throughout the fieldwork and I discovered the success of the project would depend on me finding appropriate displays of masculinity to enable me to successfully impression manage my field relationships.

A balancing act

Ethnographic research is often a balancing act where researchers try to become immersed in their fieldwork to better understand a culture, without becoming too immersed or 'going native' and losing one's focus (Delamont and Atkinson, 1995; Delamont, 2002). As I indicated above, I went out to pubs and clubs with the young men on numerous occasions to experience aspects of their lives other than school in order to discover some of the broader contemporary networks that impacted on their performance of masculinity. Very much like Hobbs (1988), I not only worried about spending research money on alcohol, but after drinking sessions with participants the following morning, I regularly woke up with a hangover and it was often a case, as Hobbs (1988: 6) put it, of deciding 'whether to bring it up or write it up'! Occasionally I also felt torn between being a researcher and participating in what was happening, or feeling responsible as an adult who should take control when things were getting out of hand. On some nights out I participated in rounds of 'shots', the practice of drinking or 'downing' neat alcoholic sprits, quickly. At other times I was more cautious. During Scott's 18th birthday night out I was invited to go out with him and his friends, The Geeks of the year group (see Chapter 4 for more details of this event). A lot of alcohol was drunk and some of the boys overindulged and fell ill. Although I did not do it on this occasion, on other nights out I deliberately stepped in to try and minimize the damaging effects of drinking too much alcohol had on the young men. On another 18th birthday night out, this time in Cardiff, I thought there was a particular need to assert some authority over the situation and as a researcher, I had an ethical responsibility for my research participants' safety and well-being:

> As we came into Cardiff we got off at Cathays train station and walked through the city finishing off the cans and bottles we had had on the train and headed to the Old Library pub. There was a live band on in the pub playing cover songs, so it was hard to talk with the loud music. Ieuan ordered a round of Jägerbombs and we knocked them back to celebrate Sean's birthday. A Jägerbombs is a cocktail that is mixed by dropping a shot glass of Jägermeister (a strong dark liqueur) into another glass containing the energy drink Red Bull. The drink tastes revolting but has to be knocked back as quickly as possible and the glass then slammed down onto the counter. Leon was looking a bit worse for wear after two bottles of wine, the drink on the train and now the Jägerbomb. Even though I was technically just along as a researcher and friend, I still felt somewhat responsible and attempted to play the adult card and wanted him to drink some water, which once I'd ordered it for him from the bar, he did.
> [*Fieldnotes*].

Researcher as vampire?

Ethnographic research has been described as a 'messy business' that can be both unpredictable, chaotic and emotional (Pearson, 1993; Hammersley and Atkinson, 1995; Denzin and Lincoln, 2005). It was not until I became fully involved in the field, that I became aware of how complicated things could get. At times, during fieldwork, I felt very much like a vampire, trying to suck information instead of blood from my participants or victims. One example is shown quite clearly in my early fieldnotes after I was told about Tomo becoming a father:

> We were sitting at the front of the room and I asked about a love bite on Tomo's neck. Tomo (quite a tall boy with short dark hair who wears designer zip up jackets, studs in his left ear and white trainers which are not part of the school uniform) said that he had fallen down the stairs. To this Ruben replied *what in a bungalow* and Bunk laughed and repeated the line. As we talked about Tomo's girlfriend, under his breath Bunk seemed to say something about being pregnant. Ruben smiled and I asked Bunk to repeat himself as I'd missed it, but he mumbled something again which was still too quiet for me to catch and I got the feeling he didn't want to tell me. Tomo then told me that his 16-year-old girlfriend was pregnant.
> [*Fieldnotes*].

Sadly for Tomo and his partner they suffered a miscarriage the following month. After Tomo's girlfriend had lost their baby, we had chatted about it for a few hours one night on the Internet using the social networking site Facebook. When I saw him the next day he told me that it had been nice to talk about it all with someone he felt he could trust and who was removed from the situation. He said he had not really wanted to talk about it with anyone, especially not his parents, but he was really glad he had told me about how he had felt and that is was a lot easier using the Internet, as he felt less pressured to explain himself without worrying about it.

The boys' reflections on the study

At the end of each individual interview I took the step of asking each interviewee what they had thought about the whole research process, which proved quite illuminating:

Sean: ...I've found it enjoyable, interesting to be honest like it's nice to have like it seems that someone is taking an interest kind of thing. I know it sounds a bit weird but um, you get the feeling that most people around here especially adults in this school, they don't really care kinda thing.

Sam: ...it's interesting, like a counselling session.

Alan: Yeah it's been good, I sort of uh got a few insights into myself about talking to you.

MW: Oh yeah...like what?

Alan: Well you know sometimes we'll be talking and um I'll come out with something and I didn't realize I thought that.

Ruben: Um well I think it was weird for Year 11.... and then we came back and it was like oh yeah it's Mike, it's good to talk to you about stuff you're the only male person I know I talk to about this stuff.

Sean, Sam Ruben and Alan found the experience interesting, but they also found it helpful to talk with someone about issues they were facing. Others in the year group were less reflexive, but still seemed to find it enjoyable.

Jimmy: Don't really notice you're there...we see you as a mate.

Frankie: It don't bother me, you're like one of the boys to me, it don't matter.

Brad: ...we just know you as Mike now, one of the boys kinda thing, once you're in the group kinda thing you just talk, you don't think you're that guy who comes in, you're just one of the boys kinda thing, join in with the talks.

MW: Ah that's nice mate.

Brad: Ah it's alright mun, I'm not lying, you come out with us, speak to the boys now and again and you got to be who you are.

MW: And since I've been doing the interviews and hanging around with you has it been ok?

Clive: Yeah, you've been accepted as one of the team.

Cresco: More the merrier in it!

For Jimmy, Frankie, Brad, Clive and Cresco I was just 'one of the boys'. Alan also commented on this and shows how by going beyond the school, the rapport developed further.

Alan: Yeah, I think cos you come out, outside of school as well, maybe if it was just inside school, sticking to your questions all the time, but you're a mate more than anything now I suppose.

Tomo's reflections were particularly insightful:

Tomo: ...you're quite sly, like sit here for like five minutes and then I realize what I just told you, shit I wouldn't sit down and tell anyone that!
MW: Oh right (Laughs).
Tomo: Got a bit of a gift for getting information out of people, you'd be a good spy (Both laugh). And when I listen to other people talking to you, they are slagging other people off like to you and that's brilliant that is how you can just sit down with someone and make friends with people really easy can't you?
MW: Right, yeah I suppose.
Tomo: Yeah like you're an outsider aren't you, like you're outside this group if you told someone in this group it would move around the group, but you're not going to go to someone else and tell um all about it, it's nice to have someone like that about for us as well as yourself.

This brief snippet from a much longer conversation shows how surprised I was at being viewed in this way in his eyes. I was conscious of having to try and talk to as many different people as I could, but I hadn't realized how others interpreted this. Of course Tomo had already confided in me around the issue of the miscarriage, but still this illustrates how significant trust and confidentiality was to him and also how comfortable these young men had become with me.

Interpretation, data analysis and ethical considerations

Data analysis

As outlined before I had analysed and written up the initial phase of research for my masters study and presented some of these findings at various conferences, so I was already familiar with the participants and the analytic process when I came to writing up the final document. However, the practice of analysing the data from the fieldnotes and interviews was not straightforward. Quite early on I constructed a simple spread sheet with a register of all those who remained in school and the subjects they were studying updating this with key information gained as I went along. I kept a field journal and used it to write a plethora of analytic memos and added diagrams and sketches of classroom layouts to these notes. When writing these fieldnotes, I also began to look for recurring themes and tried to make sense of the data being generated. I also got into the habit of writing reflections on my day in the field, to support my typed field notes. As the second phase of fieldwork became more demanding and took over other parts of my life, this was not only part of good ethnographic practice, but I found it helpful as I could re-evaluate what had happened that day or evening and make connections between the data.

Despite the initial approach, as the fieldwork continued I was cautious about beginning to analyse the second phase of data and still had some concerns about portraying my participants' lives adequately. In order to give myself some breathing space between having conducted the research and turning it into a written manuscript, I did not begin the real in-depth analysis of my fieldnotes (which were the bulk of the data gathered) until a few months after the end of the fieldwork. The analysis was therefore split into two stages and I first turned to typing up the interview transcripts (all were digitally recorded) from the individual interviews and began the process of coding the data here.

This indexing and coding was carried out using the CAQDAS package NVivo, which helped me to organize the data into further key themes. These interviews provided me with an opportunity to increase the biographical information about each participant and highlighted issues that I had previously observed in the field, identified in the background literature and what had formed my original research questions. These included talking about the performance of hegemonic or softer masculinities, the different uses of space within the school and the wider community, the impact of place on future decision making and it allowed me to explore the ability of young men to impression manage their own masculinities and perform different presentations of self to different audiences (Goffman, 1959). Once I had transcribed the interviews, the second stage of analysis began, which involved coding my fieldnotes, whilst referring back to the individual interviews and cross-referencing some of the data. I was interested in looking for behaviours which were recurring and which could then indicate the emergence of a particular trend; these were then further coded according to events, the participants involved, the physical settings events took place in, and the times and durations of these events.

Ethical considerations

Ethical guidelines often outline that research participants should be informed about any research they are involved with, in a clear and understandable way in order to give consent before the study begins. With this in mind, when conducting this study all participants involved in the research were openly informed of my presence and I made every effort to clarify why I was there and what I sought to investigate. I provided teachers and parents with information sheets and gave out postcards with information on it to the young men and their friends. I often found these were scanned quickly and stuffed into bags, pockets or left discarded on tables, but became invaluable when attending the colleges with Frankie, Bakers and Ian as I met so many new people and the information was enough to quickly satisfy the curiosity of others.

Whilst it had been my intention to inform all the young men and other people I came into contact with about my study, as the ethnography progressed and I met more and more young people outside the main cohort, this became impossible. On nights out in nightclubs and pubs, it was not only totally impractical to inform everyone in these establishments that an ethnographic study was going on, it was also difficult to articulate and explain why I was conducing it, so unless anyone asked outright who I was, it often went unmentioned. In relation to harm and exploitation, I was also often concerned that because some of the practices and activities that the young men participated in (both legal and illegal) were potentially dangerous, I tried hard not to place either the young men or myself in vulnerable positions. To go some way to protecting them, all participants involved have been anonymised as far as possible along with changing the name of the town to Cwm Dyffryn. Most participants selected their own pseudonyms; however, others were reluctant to do so as they wanted their real names to appear in any publications. It was often hard to explain that even though I was writing about their lives and the issues they faced, I still had to try and protect their identities.

When I began the research I was also an FE lecturer so I had undergone an enhanced Criminal Records Bureau (CRB) check. I was therefore aware of the privacy and confidentiality issues that came with working with young people. All young men who were formally interviewed (individually and in the early focus group interviews) had to return signed consent forms before participating.[2] Each participant was also aware that the interviews were being recorded and I mentioned to all those participating that the recordings would only be heard by me and that all transcripts would be kept in a locked filing cabinet. I was therefore consciously deliberating whether or not the information I gained would compromise anyone in the study or cause harm or embarrassment. However, I also feel that this research raises many issues about these socially marginalized young men and was therefore important to share with others.

Appendix 2

Table A.2 Young men enrolled at Cwm Dyffryn High School sixth form, year 13

Name	Post-16 pathway	Main friends/ friendship group	Mother's job as described by young men	Father's job as described by young men	Ethnicity
Alan	3 A levels + Key Skills	The Geeks	Secretary at local council	Stepfather Unemployed	White
Birdy	3 A levels + Key Skills	The Valley Boiz	Post Office owner	Post Office owner	White
Bob	2 A levels + Key Skills	Freddy, Shaggy	?	?	White
Brad	1 A level + Key Skills 2 BTECs	The Valley Boiz	Course assessor at local college	Self employed wall and floor tiler	White
Bruce	2 A levels + Key Skills 1 AS level	The Emos	Part-time cleaner	Unknown (did not see father)	White
Bunk	3 A levels + Key Skills	The Valley Boiz	Admin assistant at local council	Plumber for local authority	White
Carr	1 A level + Key Skills 1 BTEC	Boys in younger school year groups (Year 11 or 12)	Factory worker	?	White
Clive	2 BTECs + Key Skills	The Valley Boiz	Office administrator	Electrical fitter	White
Cresco	2 BTECs + Key Skills (1 at local college)	The Valley Boiz	Cleaner	Retired bus driver	White
Dai	2 BTECs + Key Skills	The Valley Boiz	?	?	White
Davies	2 A levels + Key Skills Dropped out before end of course	The Valley Boiz	Housewife	Builder	White
Ed	3 A levels + Key Skills	Tended to sit alone, very quiet, no close friends at school.	Unemployed	Unknown (did not see father)	White

Table A.2 (Continued)

Name	Post-16 pathway	Main friends/ friendship group	Mother's job as described by young men	Father's job as described by young men	Ethnicity
Freddy	1 BTEC + Key Skills (at local college)	Bob, Shaggy	?	'Works in ASDA'	White
Gavin	2 A levels +Key Skills 1 AS level	The Geeks	Housewife	Manager in a hospital	White
Hughesy	2 A levels + Key Skills 1 BTEC	The Valley Boiz	Part-time work in a supermarket	Bus driver	White
Ieuan	3 A levels + Key Skills	The Geeks	Housewife	Mineral surveyor	White
Jimmy	3 A levels + Key Skills	Leon, Frankie, Ian, Bakers	Ticket sales assistant in train station	Train driver	White
Jonesy	3 A levels + Key Skills Dropped out before end of course	The Valley Boiz	Absent, lives in France with new partner	'Works in big office somewhere in Cardiff'	White
Leon	3 A levels + Key Skills	The Geeks, Jimmy	Secretary	Teacher	White
Nibbles	3 A levels + Key Skills	The Geeks	Dead	Absent Stepfather incapacity benefits	White
Nixon	3 A levels +Key Skills	The Geeks	Primary school teacher	Driving instructor	White
Rhys	1 BTEC + Key Skills	Cresco, but mainly boys in year group below (Year 12)	Psychiatric nurse	?	White
Ruben	3 A levels	The Geeks	Midwife	Supply teacher	White
Sam	3 A levels + Key Skills	The Geeks	Manager in a supermarket	Caretaker	White
Scooter	2 A levels	Bob	?	Mechanic	White
Scott	4 A levels + Key Skills	The Geeks	Housewife	Retired mechanic	White
Scud	3 A levels + Key Skills	Stig, tended to only socialize with friends from his church	'Stays at home'	?	White

Sean	3 A levels + Key Skills	The Geeks	Secretary	Self-employed mechanic	White	
Shaggy	2 BTECs	The Valley Boiz	Housewife	Unknown (did not see father) Stepfather scaffolder	White	
Sin	3 A levels + Key Skills	The Geeks	Takeaway owner	Takeaway owner	Chinese	
Stig	1 A level 1 BTEC (at local college)	Scud, William	Caretaker in old peoples' home	Carer at old peoples' home	White	
Tomo	3 A levels	The Valley Boiz, Trevor	Small factory owner	Housewife	White	
Trevor	3 A levels Dropped out before end of course	Tomo, others outside school	?	Factory worker	White	
Wayne	1 A level	Limited time at school, so friends outside it	'Don't work'	?	White	
William	1 BTEC (at local college)	Stig, boys in younger year groups (Year 11, 12)	Cleaner	Unknown	White	

Notes

1 Introduction

1. Although I've maintained the original names of the major cities and towns in South Wales through this book, a pseudonym has been chosen to replace the main research community. I have done this in order to go some way to protect the identity of the young men that participated in the study and in keeping with ethical guidelines on anonymity.
2. The Times, *Men in Crisis*. 27 November 2010.
3. See Beynon (2002) and Roberts (2014) for an excellent summary of these issues.
4. Also see Halberstam (1998) for a debate on female masculinities.
5. See Swain (2006) and Pascoe (2007) for an overview of its application in a range of studies.
6. Of course, as Connell and Messerschmidt (2005) have pointed out in their reappraisal of the definition of hegemonic masculinity, it is always confined to context and to power relations in a specific moment and time. So, in some contexts, like a university classroom, it could be that 'inclusive masculinities' might occupy the hegemonic position. Hegemonic masculinity is also about relations with women – not just about men with men – and can operate on an individual, micro-social and socio-structural level.

2 The Valleys: History, Modernity and Masculinities

1. For an excellent map of the area, see *The Valleys Guide* http://www.thevalleys.co.uk/explore/explore-the-valleys.aspx [Date accessed: 26 March 2015].
2. See, for example, recent media representations of these communities and its inhabitants in the television series *Stella*, and the MTV reality show *The Valleys*.
3. Even though the singular term is often used, the Rhondda Valley is in fact split into two valleys Rhondda Fach (little) and Rhondda Fawr (large). See Cameron (2002) and Skelton (2000) for particular discussions about the Rhondda.
4. Tower Colliery had been in operation since the mid-19 century and was nationalized in 1947. In 1994, British Coal decided that the mine was no longer economic and opted to close it. In early 1995, the miners opted to use money from their redundancy pay to buy back the colliery against stiff Conservative government resistance and the mine reopened as a workers' cooperative. The coal seams continued to be worked until 2008, 14 years after it was deemed uneconomic.
5. RCT is the 13 largest principle area of Wales in terms of geographical size and measures around 424 square kilometres (RCT 2007). It has a total population of 234,100 (ONS 2012). Due to issues of anonymity and shifting regional

boundaries, statistics are drawn from the wider local authority area as I found them to be more reliable and up to date.
6. See http://hansard.millbanksystems.com/lords/1909/nov/09/mines-eight-hours-act [Date accessed: 26 February 2015].
7. See http://www.legislation.gov.uk/ukpga/Geo5/9-10/48/enacted [Date accessed: 21 March 2015].
8. See Kenway et al. (2006) on similar areas in Australia.

3 The Valley Boiz: Re-traditionalizing Masculinity

1. Although the coalition government announced the end to the EMA in 2010 with no new claims eligible after January 2011, EMA continues in Wales, Scotland and Northern Ireland (see http://www.studentfinancewales.co.uk [Date accessed: 18 March 2015]).
2. Nicknames or slightly modified surnames e.g. Hughes to Hughesy, or first names such as David to Dai were used by members of the group when referring to each other, continuing a very long tradition amongst Welsh Men.
3. Despite being situated in highly deprived community, Cwm Dyffryn High School ran an extensive programme of school trips with skiing and foreign language excursions to Europe every year.
4. According to The Coalmining Resource History Centre website, the Overman was in constant charge of everything underground, including the work, people and the ventilation and was similar is status to that of a foreman in a factory (see http://www.cmhrc.co.uk/site/literature/glossary/index.html#o [Date accessed: 18 March 2015]).
5. JD Wetherspoon is one of the biggest high street pub chains in Britain with over 800 pubs. It also owns the Lloyds No. 1 pub chain and Wetherspoon Hotels (see http://www.jdwetherspoon.co.uk/home/about-us [Date accessed: 17 February 2015]).
6. The name of the pub has been changed.
7. 'Bros before hoes' is an expression used between men to indicate that male friends should always come before females.
8. 'Pulling' refers to the practice of attracting a person for a range of sexual purposes ranging from French kissing to sexual intercourse.
9. There were also differences in the percentages of males and females taking certain other subjects. At AS and A2 level, boys were approximately three times more likely than girls to take physics and twice as likely to take maths and ICT. Apart from English language and literature, girls were also approximately twice as likely as boys to take psychology, sociology and art & design.
10. See Jackson (2003) and Jackson and Dempster (2009) which have centred on academic 'denial' and issues around 'effortless' achievement.
11. After a merger with some other higher education institutions, the university has since been rebranded as the University of South Wales.
12. For further details of the Engineering Education Scheme Wales (EESW), see http://www.stemcymru.org.uk/ [Date accessed: 27 March 2015].

180 Notes

5 The Emos: Alternative Masculinities?

1. Participants chose their own pseudonyms, many of which reflect their musical tastes. Bruce chose his because it was the lead singer's name of one of his favourite bands Iron Maiden and Jack chose his after the musician Jack White.

6 Working-Class Masculinities in Vocational Education and Training Courses

1. For discussion of their shortcomings see Mizen 1995.
2. The three separate colleges allowed me access to follow Bakers, Ian and Frankie during their lessons, after they themselves had agreed to me shadowing them. The young men actually suggested this to me on a night out in Cwm Dyffryn and it became a key part of the study. Without their encouragement and interest, the colleges might not have allowed access. Information leaflets about the wider study were provided to other students and teachers on these courses and as they were not formally interviewed, consent forms were not required.
3. Scholarships, exhibitions and bursaries held by a person receiving full time instruction as university, technical college or similar educational establishments are exempt from income tax by Section 776 ITTOIA.
4. In should be noted that in South Wales and the UK more generally, when applied to cars and car culture, cruising does not refer to sexual activities between men, but as form of driving with a purpose to be seen.
5. When the lecturer mentioned this during a conversation with me in the workshop, I actually laughed and assumed he was joking. On further discussion it appeared he was deadly serious, and I immediately wrote this quote down in my notebook so as not to forget it.
6. The British Racing School is based at Newmarket in Suffolk in the South-East of England. It is the principal centre for training in the horse racing industry, providing a large range of courses and training opportunities ranging from jockey apprenticeships, to equine management programmes (see http://www.brs.org.uk [Date accessed: 16 January 2015]).
7. See for example http://www.dailymail.co.uk/news/article-2141818/A-case-special-branch-Boy-racers-car-tree-neighbours-fed-bad-driving.html or http://www.telegraph.co.uk/news/uknews/crime/8619849/Boy-racer-reverses-down-dual-carriageway-to-escape-police.html [Date accessed: 19 March 2015].
8. A 'doughnut' is created when the driver of a car rotates the rear of the vehicle around the front wheels continuously, thereby creating circular skid marks and tyre smoke. See http://www.modernracer.com/tips/rwddoughnuts.html [Date accessed: 19 March 2015].

7 Jimmy the Chameleon: Multiple Performances of Self

1. See http://www.bbc.co.uk/nature/life/Chameleon and http://phenomena.nationalgeographic.com/2013/12/10/chameleons-convey-different-info-with-different-body-parts/ [Date accessed: 21 December 2014].

2. Zach Effron is an American actor who started in the Disney franchise High School Musical (see http://www.zefron.com/ [Date accessed: 10 October 2014]).
3. Sonisphere is a large heavy metal festival which tours Europe during the summer months (see http://sonisphere.co.uk/ [Date accessed: 23 October 2014]).
4. Now renamed as Cardiff Metropolitan University.
5. Now renamed as the University of South Wales.

Appendix 1: 'Doing' Ethnography: Understanding, Researching and Representing Young Working-Class Masculinities

1. For the impact of Facebook on friendships see Robards and Bennett, 2011.
2. The boys who participated in the Year 11 focus group interviews also had to return signed parental consent forms before taking part.

References

Adamson, D. and Jones, S. (1996) *The South Wales Valleys: Continuity and Change*. Treforest: University of Glamorgan.

Adkins, L. (1999) Community and economy: A retraditionalization of gender? *Theory, Culture and Society*. 16(1), pp. 119–139.

Adkins, L. (2002) *Revisions: Gender and Sexuality in Late Modernity*. Buckingham: Open University Press.

Anderson, B. (1983) *Imagined Communities*. London: Verso.

Anderson, Elijah. (1999) *Code of the Street: Decency, Violence and the Moral Life of the Inner City*. New York: WW Norton and Company.

Anderson, Eric. (2009) *Inclusive Masculinity: The Changing Nature of Masculinities*. London: Routledge.

Archer, L., Halsall, A. and Hollingworth, S. (2007) Class, gender, (hetero) sexuality and schooling: Paradoxes within working-class girls' engagement with education and post16 aspirations. *British Journal of Sociology of Education*. 28(2), pp. 165–180.

Arnot, M. (2004) Male working-class identities and social justice: A reconsideration of Paul Willis's learning to labor in light of contemporary research in: Dolby, N. Dimitriadis, G. and Willis, P. eds. *Learning to Labor in New Times*. New York: Routledge Falmer, pp. 17–40.

Arnot, M., David, M. and Weiner, G. (1999) *Closing the Gender Gap: Post-war Education and Social Change*. Cambridge: Polity Press.

Arnot, R. P. (1975) *South Wales Miners, Glowyr De Cymru. A History of the South Wales Miners' Federation (1914–1926)* Cardiff: Cymric Federation Press.

Atkinson, P. and Housley, W. (2003) *Interactionism an Essay in Sociological Amnesia*. London: Sage.

Atkinson, P., Coffey, A., Delamont, S., Loftland, J. and Loftland, L. eds. (2007) *Handbook of Ethnography Second Edition*. London: Sage.

Baker, J. (2010) Great expectations and post-feminist accountability: Young women living up to the 'successful girls' discourse. *Gender and Education*. 22(1), pp. 1–15.

Baldwin, B. (1986) *Mountain Ash and Penrhiwceiber Remembered in Pictures*. Cowbridge: D. Brown & Sons Ltd.

Baldwin, B. and Rogers, H. (1994) *Mountain Ash, Penrhiwceiber and Abercynon, The Archive Photographs Collection*. Basingstoke: NPI Media Group.

Ball, S. (1981) *Beachside Comprehensive: A Case-Study of Secondary Schooling*. Cambridge: Cambridge University Press.

Ball, S., Maguire, M. and Macrae, S. (2000) *Choice, Pathways and Transitions Post-16*. London: RoutledgeFalmer.

Bates, I. (1990) No roughs and no really brainy ones: The interaction between family background, gender and vocational training on a BTEC national fashion design course. *Journal of Education and Work*. 4(1), pp. 79–90.

Bates, I. (1991) Closely observed training: An exploration of links between social structures, training and identity. *International Studies in the Sociology of Education*. (1&2), pp. 225–243.
Bates, I. and Riseborough, G. eds. (1993) *Youth and Inequality*. Milton Keynes: Open University Press.
Bauman, Z. (1998) *Globalization: The Human Consequences*. New York: Columbia University Press.
BBC. (2005) *Mining Job Losses 'not replaced'* [Online]. Available at: http://news.bbc.co.uk/1/hi/wales/4317517.stm [Date accessed: 26 March 2015].
BBC. (2008) *Coal Mine Closes with Celebration* [Online]. Available at: http://news.bbc.co.uk/1/hi/wales/7200432.stm [Date accessed: 26 March 2015].
Beasley, C. (2012) Problematising Contemporary Men/Masculinities Theorising, the Contribution of Raewyn Connell and Conceptual-Terminology Tensions Today. *British Journal of Sociology*, 63(4), pp. 747–765.
Beck, U. (1999) *World Risk Society*. Cambridge: Polity Press.
Beck, U. and Beck-Gernsheim, E. (2002) *Individualization: Institutionalized Individualism and Its Social and Political Consequences*. London: Sage.
Bell, D. (2000) Farm boys and wild men: Rurality, masculinity, and homosexuality. *Rural Sociology*. 65(4), pp. 547–561.
Bengry-Howell, A. (2005) *Performative Motorcar Display*. Unpublished PhD Thesis: University of Birmingham, UK.
Bengry-Howell, A. and Griffin, C. (2007) Self-made motormen: The material construction of working-class masculine identities through car modification. *Journal of Youth Studies*. 10(4), pp. 439–458.
Berg, L. D. and Longhurst, R. (2003) Placing masculinities and geography. *Gender, Place and Culture*. 10(4), pp. 351–360.
Beynon, H. (1973) *Working for Ford*. Wakefield: EP Publishing.
Beynon, J. (2002) *Masculinities and Culture*. Buckingham: Open University Press.
Birke, Lynda. (2007) 'Learning to speak horse': The culture of 'natural' horsemanship. *Society and Animals*. 15, pp. 217–240.
Birke, L. and Brandt, K. (2009) Mutual corporeality: Gender and human/horse relationship. *Women's Studies International Forum*. 32, pp. 189–197.
Blackshaw, T. (2003) *Leisure Life, Myth, Masculinity and Modernity*. London: Routledge.
Bradley, H. and Ingram N. (2012) Banking on the Future: Choices, aspirations and economic hardship in working-class student experience in: Atkinson, W. Roberts, S. and Savage, M. eds. *Class Inequalities in Austerity Britain*. Basingstoke: Palgrave Macmillan, pp. 51–69.
Brandth, B. and Haugen, M. (2000) From lumber jack to business manager. *Journal of Rural Studies*. 57(3), pp. 145–153.
Breen, R. and Jonsson, J. (2005) Inequality of opportunity in comparative perspective: Recent research on educational attainment and social mobility. *Annual Review of Sociology*. 31, pp. 223–243.
Brickell, C. (2005) Masculinities, performativity and subversion. *Men and Masculinities*. 8(1), pp. 24–43.
Brittan, A. (1989) *Masculinity and Power*. Oxford: Blackwell.
Brown, P. (1987) *Schooling Ordinary Kids, Inequality, Unemployment and the New Vocationalism*. London: Tavistock.

Brown, S. and Macdonald, D. (2008) Masculinities in physical recreation: The (re)production of masculinist discourses in vocational education. *Sport, Education and Society.* 13(1), pp. 19–37.

Bullivant, B. M. (1978) *The Way of Tradition.* Melbourne: Australian Council for Educational Research.

Burrows, R. and Gane, N. (2006) Geodemographics, software and class. *Sociology.* 40(5), pp. 793–812.

Butler, D. and Charles, N. (2011) Exaggerated femininity and tortured masculinity. *British Sociological Association Annual Conference.* London: London School of Economics, April 5–7.

Butler, J. (1990) *Gender Trouble.* New York: Routledge.

Cahill, S., Distler, E. W., Lachowertz, C., Meaney, A., Tarallo, R. and Willard, T. (1985) Meanwhile backstage: Public bathrooms and the interaction order. *Journal of Contemporary Ethnography.* 14, pp. 33–58.

Canaan, J. (1996) 'One thing leads to another': Drinking, fighting and working-class masculinities in: Mac an Ghaill, M. ed. *Understanding Masculinities.* Buckingham: Open University Press, pp. 114–125.

Comeau, C. D. and Kemp, C. (2007) Intersections of age and masculinities in the information technology industry. *Ageing and Society.* 27(2), pp. 215–232.

Cameron, S. (2002) *Rhondda Voices.* London: Tempus Pub Limited.

Carrabine, E. and Longhurst, B. (2002) Consuming the car: Anticipation, use and meaning in contemporary youth culture. *The Sociological Review.* 50(2), pp. 181–196.

Carrigan, T., Connell, R. W. and Lee. J. (1985) Towards a new sociology of masculinity. *Theory and Society.* 14(5), pp. 551–604.

Cassidy, R. (2002) *The Sport of Kings: Kinship, Class and Thoroughbred Breeding in Newmarket.* Cambridge: Cambridge University Press.

Childers, M. (2002) 'The parrot or the pit bull'? Trying to explain working-class life. *Signs: Journal of Women in Culture and Society.* 28(1), pp. 201–220.

Chodorow, N. (1978) *The Reproduction of Mothering: Psychoanalysis and the Sociology of Gender.* Berkeley: University of California Press.

Clatterbaugh, K. (1997) *Contemporary Perspectives on Masculinity: Men, Women, and Politics in Modern Society.* Colorado: Westview Press.

Clare, A. (2000) *On Men: Masculinity in Crisis.* London: Chatto and Windus.

Coalfield Web Materials (CWM) project. (2002) *South Wales Coalfield Timelines* [Online]. University of Wales Swansea. Available at: http://www.agor.org.uk/cwm/timeline.asp [Date accessed: 27 March 2015].

Cockburn, C. (1983) *Brothers: Male Dominance and Technological Change.* London: Pluto Press.

Cockburn, C. (1985) *Machinery of Dominance: Women, Men and Technical Know-How.* London: Pluto.

Coffey, A. (1999) *The Ethnographic Self: Fieldwork and the Representation of Identity.* London: Sage.

Cohen, S. (1972) *Folk Devils and Moral Panics: The Creation of the Mods and Rockers.* London: MacGibbon and Lee.

Cohen, M. (1998) 'A habit of healthy idleness': Boys' underachievement in historical perspective in: Epstein, D. Elwood, J. Hey, V. and Maw, J. eds. *Failing Boys?: Issues in Gender and Achievement.* Buckingham: Open University Press, pp. 19–34.

Collinson, D. (1988) Engineering humour: Masculinity, joking and conflict in shop floor relations. *Organization Studies*. 1(3), pp. 58–76.
Collinson, D. (1992) *Managing the Shop Floor: Subjectivity, Masculinity and Workplace Culture*. Berlin: Walter De Gruyter.
Collinson, D. L. and Hearn, J. (1996) *Men as Managers, Managers as Men: Critical Perspectives on Men, Masculinities and Managements*. London: Sage.
Connell, R. W. (1987) *Gender and Power: Society, the Person, and Sexual Politics*. Stanford: Stanford University Press.
Connell, R. W. (1989) Cool guys, swots and wimps: The interplay of masculinity and education. *Oxford Review of Education*. 15, pp. 291–303.
Connell, R. W. (1990) An iron man: The body and some contradictions of hegemonic masculinity in: Messner, M. and Sabo, D. eds. *Sport, Men and the Gender Order*. Champaign: Human Kinetics Books, pp. 83–99.
Connell, R. W. (1995) *Masculinities*. Cambridge: Polity.
Connell, R. W. (2000) *The Men and the Boys*. Cambridge: Polity Press.
Connell, R. W. (2001) Introduction and overview. *Feminism & Psychology*. 11, pp. 5–9.
Connell, R. W. (2007) *Southern Theory*. Cambridge: Polity.
Connell, R. W. (2008) Masculinity construction and sports in boys' education: A framework for thinking about the issue. *Sport, Education and Society*. 13(2), pp. 131–145.
Connell, R. W. (2009) *Gender, Second Edition*. Cambridge: Polity Press.
Connell, R. W. and Messerschmidt, J. W. (2005) Hegemonic masculinity rethinking the concept. *Gender and Society*. 19(6), pp. 829–859.
Cornwall, A. and Lindisfarne, N. eds. (1994) *Dislocating Masculinity, Comparative Ethnography*. Oxon: Routledge.
Corrigan, P. (1979) *Schooling the Smash Street Kids*. London: Macmillan Press.
Cuffley Industrial Heritage Society (CIHS). (1997) *South Wales Coalfield* [Online]. http://www.cihs.org.uk/index.php?option= com_content&view= article& id= 31:driving-south-wales-coal-mining&catid= 10:driving-tours&Itemid= 20 [Date accessed: 27 March 2015].
Cusick, P. (1973) *Inside High School: The Students' World*. New York: Holt, Rinehart and Winston.
Cynon Valley History Society. (2001) *Cynon Coal: History of a Mining Valley*. Llandysul: Gomer Press.
Daily Mail. (2012) Stoned to death for being an emo: Ninety Iraqi students killed for having 'strange hair and tight clothes' [Online]. http://www.dailymail.co.uk/news/article-2112960/90-students-Iraq-stoned-death-having-Emo-hair-tight-clothes.html#ixzz2vf50y7a5 [Date accessed: 11 March 2014].
Dalley-Trim, L. (2007) The boys' present: Hegemonic masculinity: A performance of multiple acts. *Gender and Education*. 19(2), pp. 199–217.
Dashper, K (2012) 'Dressage is Full of Queens!' Masculinity, Sexuality and Equestrian Sport, Sociology, 46(6), pp. 1109–1124.
Davies, B. (1994) *Poststructuralist Theory and Classroom Practice*. Geelong: Deakin University Press.
Davies, J. and Jenkins, N. (2008) *The Welsh Academy Encyclopaedia of Wales*. Cardiff: University of Wales Press.
Day, G. (2002) *Making sense of Wales*. Cardiff: University of Wales Press.

De Boise, S. (2014) I'm not homophobic, 'I've got gay friends': Evaluating the validity of inclusive masculinity. *Men and Masculinities*, Ifirst article. 16 October, 1097184X14554951.

Delamont, S. (2000) The anomalous beasts: Hooligans and the sociology of education. *Sociology*. 34(1), pp. 95–111.

Delamont, S. (2002) *Fieldwork in Educational Settings, Methods, Pitfalls and Perspectives, 2nd Edition*. London: Routledge.

Delamont, S. and Atkinson, P. (1995) *Fighting Familiarity*. Cresskill, NJ: Hampton Press.

Delphy, C. (1977) *The Main Enemy*. London: Women's Research and Resources Centre.

Demetriou, D. (2001) Connell's concept of hegemonic masculinity: A critique. *Theory and Society*. 30(3), pp. 337–361.

Denzin, N. and Lincoln, Y. (1994) *Handbook of Qualitative Research*. Newbury Park, CA: Sage.

Denzin, N. and Lincoln, Y. eds. (2005) *The SAGE Handbook of Qualitative Research, Third Edition*. London: Sage.

Dews, C. L. and Law, C. L. eds. (1995) *This Fine Place So Far from Home, Voices of Academics from the Working Class*. Philadelphia: Temple University Press.

Dicks, B. (2004) *Culture on Display: The Production of Contemporary Visitability*. Buckinghamshire: Open University Press.

Dinnerstein, D. (1976) *Mermaid and the Minotaur: Sexual Arrangements and Human Malaise*. New York: Harper and Row.

Ditton, J. (1977) *Part-Time Crime: An Ethnography of Fiddling and Pilferage*. London: MacMillan.

Dolby, N. Dimitriadis, G. and Willis, P. eds. (2004) *Learning to Labor in New Times*. New York: Routledge Falmer.

Donaldson, M. (1993) What is hegemonic masculinity? *Theory and Society*. 22(5), pp. 643–657.

Edley, N. and Wetherell, M. (1996) Masculinity, power and identity in: Mac an Ghaill, M. ed. *Understanding Masculinity*. Buckingham: Open University Press, pp. 97–113.

Edley, N. Wetherell, M. (1997) Jockeying for position: The construction of masculine identities. *Discourse & Society*. 8(2), pp. 203–217.

Egan, D. (1987) *A History of the South Wales Mining Valleys, 1840–1980*. Cardiff: Gomer Press.

Emerson, R. M. Fretz, R. I. and Shaw, L. L. (1995) *Writing Ethnographic Fieldnotes*. London: The University of Chicago Press.

Epstein, D. (1998) Are you a girl or are you a teacher? The least adult role in research about gender and sexuality in a primary school in: Walford, G. ed. *Doing Research about Education*. London: Falmer Press, pp. 27–41.

Epstein, D. Elwood, J. Hey, V. and Maw, J. eds. (1998) *Failing Boys?: Issues in Gender and Achievement*. Buckingham: Open University Press.

Epstein, D. and Johnson, R. (1998) *Schooling Sexualities*. Buckingham: Open University Press.

Everhart, R. (1977) Between stranger and friend: Some consequences of 'long term' fieldwork in schools. *American Educational Research Journal*. 14(1), pp. 1–15.

Fevre, R. (1999) The Welsh economy in: Dunkerley, D. and Thompson, A. eds. *Wales Today*. Cardiff: University of Wales, pp. 61–74.
Fevre, R. and Thompson, A. (1999) Social theory and Welsh identities in: Fevre, R. and Thompson, A. eds. *Nation, Identity and Social Theory, Perspectives from Wales*. Cardiff: University of Wales Press, pp. 3–24.
Fisher, M. J. (2009) 'Being a chameleon': Labour processes of male nurses performing bodywork. *Journal of Advanced Nursing*. 65(12), pp. 2668–2677.
Flood, M. (2008) *The Men's Bibliography; A Comprehensive Bibliography on Men, Masculinities, Gender and Sexualities*, 18 Edition. http://mensbiblio.xyonline.net/.
Flood, M. Gardiner, J. K. Pease, B. and Pringle, K. eds. (2007) *International Encyclopaedia of Men and Masculinities*. London: Routledge.
Foucault, M. (1978) *The History of Sexuality, Volume 1*. New York: Vintage.
Foucault, M. (1980) *Power/Knowledge: Selected Interviews and Other Writings 1972–1977*. London, Harvester Press.
Francis, B. (2000) *Boys, Girls and Achievement: Addressing the Classroom Issues*. Oxon: Routledge Falmer.
Francis, B. and Skelton, C. (2005) *Reassessing Gender and Achievement, Questioning Contemporary Key Debates*. Abingdon: Routledge.
Francis, B. Hutchings, M. and Archer, L. (2003) Subject choice and occupational aspirations among pupils at girls' schools. *Pedagogy, Culture & Society*. 11(3), pp. 423–440.
Francis, B. Read, B. and Skelton, C. and (2012) *The Identities and Practices of High Achieving Pupils: Negotiating Achievement and Peer Cultures*. London: Continuum International.
Francis, B. Skelton, C. and Read, B. (2010) The simultaneous production of educational achievement and popularity: How do some pupils accomplish it? *British Educational Research Journal*. 36(2), pp. 317–334
Francis, H. and Smith, D. (1998) *The Fed: A History of the South Wales Miners in the 20th Century*. Cardiff: University of Wales Press.
Frosh, S. Phoenix, A. and Pattman, R. (2002) *Young Masculinities*. Basingstoke: Palgrave.
Fuller, A. and Unwin, L. (2003) Creating a 'modern apprenticeship': A critique of the UK's multisector, social inclusion approach. *Journal of Education and Work*. 16(1), pp. 5–21.
Fuller, A. Beck, V. and Unwin, L. (2005) The gendered nature of apprenticeship: Employers' and young people's perspectives. *Education and Training*. 47(4/5), pp. 298–311.
Gagnon, J. and Simon, W. (1973) *Sexual Conduct*. London: Hutchinson.
Gard, M and Meyenn, R. (2000) Boys, bodies, pleasure and pain: Interrogating contact sports in schools. *Sport, Education and Society*. 5(1), pp. 19–34.
Geertz, C. (1973) *The Interpretation of Cultures: Selected Essays*. New York: Basic Books.
Giddens, A. (1991) *Modernity and Self-Identity: Self and Society in the Late Modern Age*. Cambridge: Polity.
Gibson, C. (2014) Cowboy masculinities: Relationality and rural identity in: Gorman-Murray, A. and Nobel, P. eds. *Masculinities and Place*. Farnham: Ashgate, pp. 125–139.

Gillborn, D. (2009) Education: The numbers game and the construction of white racial victimhood in: Sveinsson, K. ed. *Who Cares about the White Working Class?* London: Runnymede, pp. 15–22.

Gillborn, D. and Mirza, H. (2000) *Educational Inequality – Mapping Race, Class and Gender: A Synthesis of Research Evidence.* London: Ofsted.

Goffman, E. [1956] (1959) *The Presentation of Self in Everyday Life.* New York: Doubleday, Anchor Books.

Goffman, E. (1963) *Stigma: Notes on the Management of Spoiled Identity.* Englewood Cliffs: Prentice-Hall (Pelican Books Edition).

Goffman, E. (1974) *Frame Analysis: An Essay on the Organization of Experience.* New York: Harper and Row.

Goffman, E. (1976) Gender display. *Studies in the Anthropology of Visible Communication.* 3, pp. 69–77.

Goffman, E. (1977) The arrangement between the sexes. *Theory and Society.* 4, pp. 301–331.

Goffman, E. (1981) *Forms of Talk.* Philadelphia: University of Philadelphia Press.

Goffman, E. (1983) The interaction order. *American Sociological Review.* 48, pp. 1–17.

Goffman, E. (1989) On fieldwork. *Journal of Contemporary Ethnography.* 18(2), pp. 123–132.

Gorard, S. Lewis, J. and Smith, E. (2004) Disengagement in Wales: Educational, social and economic issues. *Welsh Journal of Education.* 13(1), pp. 118–147.

Gorely, T. Holroy, R. and Kirk, D. (2003) Masculinity, the habitus and the construct of gender: Towards a gender-relevant physical education. *British Journal of the Sociology of Education.* 24(4), pp. 429–448.

Gospel, H. (1995) The decline of apprenticeship in Britain. *Industrial Relations Journal.* 26(1), pp. 32–44.

Granié, M.-A. and Papafava, E. (2011) Gender stereotypes associated with vehicle driving among French preadolescents and adolescents. *Transportation Research Part F.* 14, pp. 341–353.

Gramsci, A. (1971) *Selections from the Prison Notebooks.* London: International Publishers.

Grant, R. (1991) *Cynon Valley in the Age of Iron.* Stroud: Alan Sutton Publishing.

Grazian, D. (2007) The girl hunt: Urban nightlife and the performance of masculinity as collective activity. *Symbolic Interaction.* 30(2), pp. 221–243.

Green, A. and White, R. (2007) *Attachment to Place.* York: Joseph Rowntree Foundation.

Halberstam, J. M. (1998) *Female Masculinity.* Durham, NC: Duke University Press.

Hall, T. Coffey, A. and Lashua, B. (2009) Steps and stages: Rethinking transitions in youth and place. *Journal of Youth Studies.* 12(5), pp. 547–561.

Halsey, A. H. (1996) *No Discouragement: An Autobiography.* Basingstoke: Macmillan Press.

Hammersley, M. and Atkinson, P. (1995) *Ethnography: Principles in Practice, Second Edition.* New York: Routledge.

Hargreaves, D. H. (1967) *Social Relations in a Secondary School.* London: Routledge and Kegan Paul.

Harris, J. (2007) Cool Cymru, Rugby union and an imagined community. *International Journal of Sociology.* 27(3/4), pp. 151–162.
Harris, K. (2000) Roots? The relationship between the global and the local within the extreme metal scene, *Popular Music.* 19(1), pp. 3–30.
Hartig, K. (2000) Claiming the freeway: Young male drivers in pursuit of independence, space and masculinity. *Journal of Interdisciplinary Gender Studies.* 5(1), pp. 36–50.
Hartman, H. (1976) Economic dimensions of occupational segregation – economists approaches to sex segregation in labor market appraisal. *Signs.* 1, pp. 181–199.
Haywood, C. and Mac an Ghaill, M. (1996) Schooling masculinities in: Mac an Ghaill, M. ed. *Understanding Masculinities.* Buckingham: Open University Press, pp. 50–60.
Haywood, C. and Mac an Ghaill, M. (1997) 'A man in the making': Sexual masculinities within changing training cultures. *The Sociological Review.* pp. 576–590.
Heward, C. (1988) *Making a Man of Him: Parents and Their Son's Education at an English Public School 1929–1950.* London: Routledge.
Heward, C. (1996) Masculinities and families in: Mac an Ghaill, M. ed. *Understanding Masculinities.* Buckingham: Open University Press, pp. 35–49.
Hey, V. (2003) Joining the club? Academic and working-class femininities. *Gender and Education.* 15(3), pp. 319–335.
Hobbs, D. (1988) *Doing the Business: Entrepreneurship, the Working Class, and Detectives in the East End of London.* Oxford: Clarendon Press.
Hobbs, D. (1993) Peers, careers, and academic fears: Writing as field-work in: Hobbs, D. and May, T. eds. *Interpreting the Field.* Oxford: Oxford University Press, pp. 45–66.
Hodkinson, P. (2002) *Goth. Identity, Style Subculture.* Oxford: Berg.
Hodkinson, P. and Hodkinson, H. (1995) Markets, outcomes and the quality of vocational education and training: Some lessons from a youth credits pilot scheme. *The Vocational Aspect of Education.* 47(3), pp. 209–255.
Hoff-Sommers, C. (2000) *The War against Boys: How Misguided Feminism Is Harming Our Young Men.* New York: Simon & Schuster.
Hoff Summers, C. (2013) *The War against Boys: How Misguided Policies are Harming Our Young Men (Second Edition).* New York: Simon & Schuster.
Holland, S. and Scourfield, J. (1998) Ei gwrol ryfelwyr. Reflections on body, gender, class and nation in Welsh rugby in: Richardson, J. and Shaw, A. eds. *The Body and Qualitative Research.* Farnham: Ashgate, pp. 56–71.
Hollingworth, S. and Williams, K. (2009) Constructions of the working-class 'other' among urban, white, middle-class youth: 'Chavs', subcultures and the valuing of education. *Journal of Youth Studies.* 12(5), pp. 467–482.
Hopkins, P. and Noble, G. (2009) Masculinities in place: Situated identities, relations and intersectionality. *Social and Cultural Geography.* 10(8), pp. 811–819.
House of Emo. (2010) [Online]. Available at: http://houseofemo.com
Howe, P. D. (2001) Women's rugby and the nexus between embodiment, professionalism and sexuality: An ethnographic account. *Football Studies.* 4(2), pp. 77–91.

Howe, P. D. (2003) An ethnographic account of women's rugby in: Bolin, A. and Granskeg, J. eds. *Athletic Intruders, Ethnographic Research on Women, Culture and Exercise.* New York: State University of New York Press, pp. 227–246.

Hughey, M. (2011) Backstage discourse and the reproduction of white masculinities. *The Sociological Quarterly.* 52(1), pp. 132–153.

Humphries, J. (1981) Protective, legislation, the capitalism state and working-class men: The case of the 1842 mines regulation act. *Feminist Review.* 7, pp. 1–31.

Hurn, S. (2008) What's love got to do with it? The interplay of sex and gender in the commercial breeding of welsh cobs. *Society and Animals.* 16, pp. 23–44.

Ingram, N. (2009) Working-class boys, educational success and the misrecognition of working class culture. *British Journal of Sociology of Education.* 30(4), pp. 421–434.

Ingram, N. (2011) Within school and beyond the gate: The complexities of being educationally successful and working class. *Sociology.* 45(2), pp. 287–302.

Jackson, B. and Marsden, D. (1962) *Education and the Working Class.* London: Routledge & Kegan Paul.

Jackson, C. (2003) Motives for laddishness at school: Fear of failure and fear of the feminine. *British Educational Research Journal.* 29(4), pp. 583–598.

Jackson, C. and Dempster, S. (2009) I sat back on my computer ... with a bottle of whisky next to me: Constructing cool masculinity through effortless achievement in secondary and higher education. *Journal of Gender Studies.* 18(4), pp. 341–356.

Jackson, P. (1991) The cultural politics of masculinity: Towards social geography. *Transactions, Institute of British Geography.* 16(1), pp. 199–213.

Jackson, P (1994) Black male: Advertising and the cultural politics of masculinity. *Gender, Place and Culture: A Journal of Feminist Geography.* 1(1), pp. 49–59.

Jackson, S. and Scott, S. (2010) Rehabilitating interactionism for a feminist sociology of sexuality. *Sociology.* 44(5), pp. 811–826.

Jagose, A. (1996) *Queer Theory: An Introduction.* New York: New York University Press.

Janssen, D. (2008) *International Guide to Literature on Masculinity.* Harrison: Men's Studies Press.

Jephcote, M. Salisbury, J. and Rees, G. (2009) The learning journey, students experiences of further education in Wales. *Contemporary Wales.* 22(1), 141–157.

John, A. and Williams, G. eds. (1980) *Glamorgan County History. Vol V, Industrial Glamorgan from 1700–1970.* Cardiff: Cardiff University of Wales Press for the Glamorgan County History Trust.

Jones, M. R. (1999) Social change in Wales since 1945 in: Dunkerley, D. and Thompson, A. eds. *Wales Today.* Cardiff: University of Wales Press, pp. 11–23.

Junker, B. H. (1960) *Field Work: An Introduction to the Social Sciences.* Chicago: University of Chicago Press.

Kamoche, K. and Maguire, K. (2011) Pit sense: Appropriation of practice-based knowledge in a UK coalmine. *Human Relations.* 64(5), pp. 725–744.

Keddie, A. (2007) Games of subversion and sabotage: issues of power masculinity, class, rurality and schooling. *British Journal of Sociology of Education* 28(2), pp. 181–194.

Kehily, M. J. and Pattman R. (2006) Middle class struggle? Identity work and leisure among sixth formers in the UK, British. *Journal of Sociology of Education.* 27(1), pp. 37–52.
Kendall, L. (1999) Nerd nation: Images of nerds in US popular culture. *International Journal of Cultural Studies.* 2(2), pp. 260–283.
Kendall, L. (2000) 'Oh no! I'm a nerd!' Hegemonic masculinity on an online forum. *Gender and Society.* 14(2), pp. 256–274.
Kenway, J. and Hickey-Moody, A. (2009) Spatialized leisure-pleasures, global flows and masculine distinctions. *Social, Cultural Geography.* 10(8), pp. 837–852.
Kenway, J. and Kraack, A. (2004) Reordering work and destabilizing masculinity in: Dolby, N. et al. eds. *Learning to Labor in New Times.* New York: RoutledgeFalmer, pp. 95–109.
Kenway, J., Kraak, A. and Hickey-Moody, A. (2006) *Masculinity beyond the Metropolis.* Basingstoke: Palgrave.
Kessler, S. and McKenna, W. (1978) *Gender: An Ethnomethodological Approach.* Chicago: University of Chicago Press.
Kessler, S. Ashenden, D. J. Connell, R. W. and Dowsett, G. W. (1985) Gender relations in secondary schooling. *Sociology of Education.* 58, pp. 34–48.
Kimmel, M. (1996) *Manhood in America.* New York: Free Press.
Kimmel, M. (2006) *Manhood in America, Second Edition.* New York: Oxford University Press.
Kimmel, M. ed. (1987) *Changing Men: New Directions in Research on Men and Masculinities.* London: Sage.
Kimmel, M. Hearn, I. and Connell R. W. eds. (2005) *Handbook of Studies on Men and Masculinities.* London: Sage.
Kruse, H. (1993) Subcultural identity in alternative music culture. *Popular Music.* 12(1), pp. 31–43.
Lacey, C. (1970) *High Town Grammar, The School as a Social System.* Manchester: Manchester University Press.
Latimer, J. and Birke, L. (2009) Natural relations: Horses, knowledge and technology. *Sociological Review.* 57, pp. 1–27.
Latour, B. (1987) *Science in Action: How to Follow Scientists and Engineers through Society.* Harvard: Harvard University Press.
Larkin, R. W. (1979) *Suburban Youth in Cultural Crisis.* New York: Oxford University Press.
Larsen, E. A. (2006) A vicious oval: Why women seldom reach the top in American harness racing. *Journal of Contemporary Ethnography.* 35, pp. 119–147.
Le Berre, F. (2009) *The Chameleon Handbook.* New York: Barron's Educational Series.
Lefebvre, H. [1974] (2001) *The Production of Space.* Oxford: Blackwell.
Lewis, D. G. (1980) *The University and the Colleges of Education in Wales, 1925–1978.* Cardiff: University of Wales.
Lingard, B. Martino, W. and Mills, M. (2009) *Boys and Schooling: Beyond Structural Reform.* Basingstoke: Palgrave Macmillan.
Lucey, H. Melody, J. and Walkerdine, V. (2003) Uneasy hybrids: Psychosocial aspects of becoming educationally successful for working-class young women. *Gender and Education.* 15(3), pp. 285–299.

Lumsden, K. (2009) Do we look like boy racers? The role of the folk devil in contemporary moral panics. *Sociological Research Online*. 14(1) http://www.socresonline.org.uk/14/1/2.html

Lush, A. J. (1941) *The Young Adult in South Wales*. Cardiff: University of Wales Press Board.

Mac an Ghaill, M. (1994) *The Making of Men*. Buckingham: Open University Press.

Mac an Ghaill, M. ed. (1996) *Understanding Masculinities*. Buckingham: Open University Press.

MacInnes, J. (1998) *The End of Masculinity*. Buckingham: Open University Press.

MacInnes, J. and Perez-Diaz, J. (2009) The reproductive revolution. *The Sociological Review*. 57(2), pp. 262–284.

Macleod, J. (1995) *Ain't No Making It, Aspirations and Attainment in a Low-Income Neighbourhood*. Oxford: Westview Press.

Madden, A. (2005) Gendered subject choices in: Claire, H. ed. *Gender in Education 3–19 – A Fresh Approach*. London: Association of Teachers and Lecturers, pp. 94–107.

Maines. D. (2001) *The Faultline of Consciousness: A View of Interactionism in Sociology*. New York: Aldine de Gruyer.

Mannay, D. (2014) Who should do the dishes now? Exploring gender and housework in contemporary urban South Wales. *Contemporary Wales*. 27(1), pp. 21–39.

Martin, P. (1998) Why can't a man be more like a woman? Reflections on Connell's masculinities. *Gender and Society*. 12(4), pp. 472–474.

Martino, W. (1999) 'Cool boys', 'Party animals', 'Squids' and 'Poofters': Interrogating the dynamics and politics if adolescent masculinities in school. *British Journal of Sociology of Education*. 20(2), pp. 239–263.

Martino, W. and Meyenn, B. eds. (2001) *What about the Boys?: Issues of Masculinity in Schools*. Buckingham: Open University Press.

Massey, D. (1984) Introduction, Geography matters in: Massey, D. and Allen, J. eds. *Geography Matters*. Cambridge: Cambridge University Press, pp. 1–11.

Massey, D. (1994) *Space, Place and Gender*. Cambridge: Polity Press.

Massey, D. (1995) *Spatial Divisions of Labour: Social Structures and the Geography of Production, Second Edition*. Basingstoke: MacMillan.

McCormack, M. (2012) *The Declining Significance if Homophobia, How Teenage Boys Are Redefining Masculinity and Heterosexuality*. New York: Oxford University Press.

McCormack, M. (2014) The intersection of youth masculinities, decreasing homophobia and class: An ethnography. *The British Journal of the Sociology of Education*. 65 (1), pp. 130–149.

McDowell, L. (1997) *Capital Culture: Gender at work in the City*. Oxford: Blackwell.

McDowell, L. (2000) Learning to serve? Employment aspirations and attitudes of young working-class men in an era of labour market restructuring. *Gender, Place and Culture*. 7(4), pp. 389–416.

McDowell, L. (2002) Masculine discourse and dissonances: Strutting 'lads', protest masculinity and domestic respectability. *Environment and Planning D: Society and Space*. 20, pp. 97–119.

McDowell, L. (2003) *Redundant Masculinities*. Oxford: Blackwell.

McDowell, L. (2007) Respect, deference, respectability and place: What is the problem with/for working class boys? *Geoforum*. 38, pp. 276–286.

McDowell, L. (2012) Post-crisis, post-ford and post-gender? Youth identities in an era of austerity. *Journal of Youth Studies*. 15(5), pp. 573–590.

Mellstrom, U. (2004) Machines and masculine subjectivity: Technology as an integral part of men's life experiences. *Men and Masculinities*. 6(4), pp. 368–382.

Mendick, H. and Francis, B. (2012) Boffin and geek identities: Abject or privileged? *Gender and Education*. 24(1), pp. 15–24.

Messner, M. and Sabo, D. eds. (1990) *Sport, Men and the Gender Order*. Champaign: Human Kinetics Books.

Messner, M. (2001) Friendship, intimacy and sexuality in: Whitehead, S. M. and Barrett, F. J. eds. *The Masculine Reader*. Cambridge: Polity Press, pp. 253–265.

Miller, J. (1995) Trick or treat? The autobiography of the question. *English Quarterly*. 27(3), pp. 22–26.

Miller, L. and Budd, J. (1999) The development of occupational sex-role stereotypes, occupational preferences and academic subject preferences of children ages 8, 12 and 16. *Educational Psychology*. 19(1), pp. 17–35.

Mills, C. W. (1959) *The Sociological Imagination*. New York: Oxford University Press.

Mizen, P. A. J. (1995) *The State, Young People and Youth Training: In and against the Training State*. London: Mansell.

Moore, R. (2005) Alternative to what? Subcultural capital and the commercialization of a Music scene. *Deviant Behaviour*. 26, pp. 229–252.

Moore, R. (2010) *Smells Like Teen Spirit, Music Youth Culture and Social Crisis*. New York: New York University Press.

Morgan, D. (1992) *Discovering Men*. London: Routledge.

Morgan, K. O. (1981) *Rebirth of a Nation: Wales, 1880–1980*. Oxford: Oxford University Press.

Morgan, D. (2006) The crisis in masculinity in: David, K. Evans, M. and Lorber, J. eds. *The Handbook of Gender and Women's Studies*. London: Sage, pp. 109–124.

Morris, E. (2012) *Learning the Hard Way: Masculinity, Place, and the Gender Gap in Education*. New Brunswick, NJ: Rutgers University Press.

Mullins, C. W. and Cherbonneau, M. G. (2011) Establishing connections: Gender, motor vehicle theft, and disposal networks. *Justice Quarterly*. 28(2), pp. 278–302.

Marusza, J. (1997) Skill school boys: Masculine identity formation among white boys in an urban high school vocational Autoshop program. *The Urban Review*. 29(3), pp. 175–187.

Nayak, A. (2003a) *Race, Place and Globalization, Youth Cultures in a Changing World*. Oxford: Berg.

Nayak, A. (2003b) Last of the 'real geordies'? White masculinities and the subcultural response to deindustrialisation. *Environment and Planning D: Society and Space*. 21, pp. 7–25.

Nayak, A. (2003c) 'Boyz to men': Masculinities, schooling and labour transitions in de-industrial times. *Educational Review*. 55(2), pp. 147–159.

Nayak, A. (2006) Displaced masculinities: Chavs, youth and class in the post-industrial City. *Sociology*. 40(5), pp. 813–831.

Nayak, A. (2009) Beyond the pale: Chavs, youth and social class in: Sveinsson, K. ed. *Who Cares about the White Working Class?* London: Runnymede, pp. 28–35.

Nespor, J. (2000) Topologies of masculinity, Gendered spatialities of preadolescent boys in: Lesko, N. ed. *Masculinities at School*. London: Sage, pp. 27–48.

O'Connor, C. and Kelly, K. (2006) Auto theft and youth culture: A nexus of masculinities, femininities and car culture. *Journal of Youth Studies*. 9(3), pp. 247–267.

O'Neill, R. (2015) Whither critical masculinties studies? Notes on inclusive masculinity theory, postfeminism and sexual politics. *Men and Masculinties*. 18(1), pp. 100–120.

Office for National Statistics (ONS). (2012) *Local authority profile, Rhondda, Cynon, Taff, local authority* [Online]. Available at: www.nomisweb.co.uk [Date accessed: 15 March 2015].

Ortiz, S. (2003) Muted masculinity as an outsider strategy: Gender sharing in ethnographic work with wives of professional athletes. *Symbolic Interaction*. 26(4), pp. 601–611.

Osgood, J. (2005) Who cares? The classed nature of childcare. *Gender and Education*. 17(3), pp. 289–304.

Osgood, J. Francis, B. and Archer, L. (2006) Gendered identities and work placement: Why don't boys care? *Journal of Education Policy*. 21(3), pp. 305–321.

Parker, A. (1996a) Sporting masculinities: Gender relations and the body in: Mac an Ghaill, M. ed. *Understanding Masculinities*. Buckingham: Open University Press. pp.126–138.

Parker, A. (1996b) The construction of masculinity within boys' physical education. *Gender and Education*. 8(2), pp. 141–157.

Parker, A. (2006) Lifelong learning to labour: Apprenticeship, masculinity and communities of practice. *British Educational Research Journal*. 32(5), pp. 687–701.

Parsons, T. (1954) *Essays in Sociological Theory*. New York: Free Press.

Pascoe, C. J. (2007) *Dude You're a Fag: Masculinity and Sexuality in High School*. Berkeley: University of California Press.

Pawluch, D. Shaffir, W. and Miall, C. (2005) *Doing Ethnography: Studying Everyday life*. Toronto: Canadian Scholars' Press Inc.

Pearson, G. (1993) Foreword, Talking a good fight, Authenticity and distance in the ethnographer's craft in: Hobbs, D. and May, T. eds. *Interpreting the Field*. Oxford: Oxford University Press, pp. vi–xx.

Penlington, N. (2010) Masculinity and domesticity in 1930s South Wales: Did unemployment change the domestic division of labour? *Twentieth Century British History*. 21(3), pp. 281–299.

Peters, B. M. (2010) Emo gay boys and subculture: Post punk, Queer youth and (Re) thinking images of masculinity. *Journal of LGBT Youth*. 7(2), pp. 129–146.

Platt, L. (2007) Making education count: The effects of ethnicity and qualifications on intergenerational social class mobility. *The Sociological Review*. 55(3), pp. 485–508.

Pleck, J. (1987) The theory of male sex-role identity: Its rise and fall, 1936 to the present in: Brod, H. ed. *The Making of Masculinities: The New Men's Studies*. Boston: Allen and Unwin, pp. 21–38.

Plummer, K. (2007) Queers, bodies and post-modern sexualities: A note on revisiting the 'sexual' in symbolic interactionism in: Kimmell, M. ed. *The Sexual Self, the Construction of Sexual Scripts*. Nashville: Vanderbilt University Press, pp. 16–30.

Reay, D. (2002) Shaun's Story: Troubling discourses of white working-class masculinities. *Gender and Education.* 14(3), pp. 221–234.
Reay, D. David, M. and Ball, S. (2005) *Degrees of Choice, Social Class, Race and Gender in Higher Education.* Stoke on Trent: Trentham Books Limited.
Reay, D. Crozier, G. and Clayton, J. (2009) Strangers in paradise: Working class students in elite universities. *Sociology.* 43(6), pp. 1103–1121
Redman, P. and Mac an Ghaill, M. (1997) Educating Peter, The making of a history man in: Steinberg, D. et al. eds. *Border Patrols: Policing the Boundaries of Heterosexuality.* London: Cassell, pp. 162–182.
Rees, G. and Delamont, S. (1999) Education in Wales in: Dunkerley, D. and Thompson, A. eds. *Wales Today.* Cardiff: University of Wales Press, pp. 233–249.
Rees, G. and Stroud, D. (2004) *Regenerating the Coalfields, the South Wales Experience.* Tredegar: The Bevan Foundation.
Renold, E. (2001) Learning the 'Hard' way: Boys, hegemonic masculinity and the negotiation of learner identities in the primary school. *British Journal of Sociology of Education.* 22(3), pp. 369–384.
Renold, E. (2004) 'Other' boys: Negotiating non-hegemonic masculinities in the primary school. *Gender and Education.* 16(2), pp. 249–266.
Rhondda Cynon Taf (RCT). (2006) *Review of the Rhondda Cynon Taf Economic Regeneration Strategy.* Llantwit Fardre: Robert Higgins Associates.
Rhondda Cynon Taf (RCT). (2007) *Pride of Place Heritage Strategy 2007–10* [Online]. Available at: http://www.rhondda-cynon-taf.gov.uk/stellent/groups/ Public/documents/Publications/019806.pdf [Date accessed: 26 March 2015].
Rhondda Cynon Taf (RCT). (2012) *Economic Regeneration Strategy* [Online]. Available at: http://www.rctcbc.gov.uk/en/relateddocuments/publications/ developmentandregeneration/economicregenerationstrategy2012-2015.pdf [Date accessed: 27 January 2015].
Rhondda Cynon Taf (RCT). (2014) Cabinet Meeting, Report of the Group Director, Corporate Service. Available at: http://www.rctcbc.gov.uk/en/council democracy/democracyelections/councillorscommittees/meetings/cabinet/ 2014/03/19/reports/agendaitem7draftoutcomeagreementwiththewelshgovern ment.pdf [Date accessed: 20 March 2015].
Richardson, D. (2010) Youth masculinities: Compelling male heterosexuality. *British Journal of Sociology.* 61(4), pp. 737–756.
Riches, G. (2014) Brothers of metal! Metal masculinities, Moshpit practices and homosociality in: Roberts, S. ed. *Change and Continuities in Contemporary Masculinities.* Basingstoke: Palgrave MacMillan, pp. 88–105.
Riseborough, G. (1992) The cream team: An ethnography of BTEC national diploma (catering and hotel management) students in a tertiary college. *British Journal of Sociology of Education.* 13(2), pp. 215–245.
Robards, B and Bennett, A. (2011) MyTribe: Post-subcultural manifestations of belonging on social network sites. *Sociology.* 45(2), pp. 303–317.
Roberts, S. (2013) Boys will be boys...won't they? Change and continuities in contemporary young working-class masculinities, *Sociology.* 47(4), pp. 671–686.
Roberts, K. and Atherton, G. (2011) Career development among young people in Britain today: Poverty of aspiration or poverty of opportunity? *International Journal of Education Administration and Policy Studies.* 3(5), pp. 59–67.

Roberts, S. ed. (2014) *Change and Continuities in Contemporary Masculinities*. Basingstoke: Palgrave MacMillan.
Rutherford, J. (1988) Who's that man? in: Chapman, R. and Rutherford, J. eds. *Male Order: Unwrapping Masculinity*. London: Lawrence and Wishart, pp. 21–67.
Ryan, P. and Unwin, L. (2001) Apprenticeship in the British 'training market'. *National Institute Economic Review*. 178, pp. 99–114.
Salisbury, J. and Jephcote, M. (2010) Mucking in and mucking out: Vocational learning in Animal Care. *Teaching and Teacher Education*. 26, pp. 71–81.
Schrock, D. and Schwalbe, M. (2009) Men, masculinity and manhood arts. *Annual Review of Sociology*. 35, pp. 377–395.
Scourfield, J. and Drakeford, M. (1999) Boys from nowhere: Finding Welsh man and putting them in their place. *Contemporary Wales*. 12, pp. 3–17.
Scourfield, J. Dicks, B. Drakeford, M. and Davies, A. (2006) *Children, Place and Identity: Nation and Locality in Middle Childhood*. London, Routledge.
Segal, L. (2007) *Slow Motion. Changing Masculinities, Changing Men*. 3rd edition. Basingstoke: Palgrave Macmillan.
Sennett, R. and Cobb, J. (1972) *The Hidden Injuries of Class*. New York: Alfred A. Knopf.
Sewell, J. (1975) *Colliery Closure and Social Change*. Cardiff: University of Wales Press.
Sewell, T. (1997) *Black Masculinities and Schooling. How Black Boys Survive Modern Schooling*. Stoke on Trent: Trentham.
Simpson, P. (2014) Oppression, acceptance or civil indifference? Middle-aged gay men's accounts of 'heterospace' in: Roberts, S. ed. *Change and Continuities in Contemporary Masculinities*. Basingstoke: Palgrave MacMillan, pp. 70–87.
Skeggs, B. (1986) Gender reproduction and further education: domestic apprenticeships. *British Journal of Sociology of Education*, 9(2), pp. 131–149.
Skeggs, B. (1992) 'Paul Willis, learning to labour', in: Barker, M. and Beezer, A. eds. *Reading into Cultural Studies*. London: Routledge, pp. 181–196
Skeggs, B. (1997) *Formation of Class and Gender, Becoming Respectable*. London: Sage.
Skeggs, B. (2004) *Class, Self, Culture*. London: Routledge.
Skeggs, B. (2009) Haunted by the spectre of judgement: Respectability, Value and affect in class relations in: Sveinsson, K. ed. *Who Cares about the White Working Class?* London: Routledge, pp. 36–44.
Skelton, C. and Francis, B. (2009) *Feminism and 'The Schooling Scandal'*. Abington: Routledge.
Skelton, T. (2000) 'Nothing to do, nowhere to go?': Teenage girls and 'public' space in the Rhondda Valleys South Wales in: Holloway, S. L. and Valentine, G. eds. *Children's Geographies*. Abingdon: Routledge, pp. 80–99.
Smith, D. (1984) *Wales! Wales?* London: George Allen and Unwin.
Smith, D. (1999) *Wales, A Question for History*. Bridgend: Poetry Wales Press Ltd.
Stahl, G. (2015) *Identity, Neoliberalism and Aspiration: Educating White Working-Class Boys*. New York: Routledge.
Stonewall. (2007) *The Experiences of Young Gay People in Britain's Schools*. London: Stonewall.
Swain, J. (2000) The Money's good, the fame's good, the girls are good: The role of playground football in the construction of young boys masculinities in a junior school. *British Journal of Sociology of Education*. 21(1), pp. 95–109.

Swain, J. (2006) Reflections on patterns of masculinity in school settings. *Men and Masculinities*. 8(3), pp. 331–349.

Syal, R. (2013) British male identity crisis 'spurring machismo and Heartlessness'. *The Guardian*, 14 May. Available at: http://www.theguardian.com/politics/2013/may/14/male-identity-crisismachismo-abbott [Date accessed: 4 March 2015].

Tarrant, A. Terry, G. Ward, M. R. M. Ruxton, S. Robb, M. and Featherstone, B. (2015) Are male role models really the solution? Interrogating the 'war on boys' through the lens of the 'male role model' discourse. *Boyhood Studies*. 8(1), pp. 60–83.

Teaching and Learning Research Programme [TLRP]. (2008) *No. 52 – Inside Further Education: The Social Context of Learning*. ESRC.

The Guardian Online. (2006) The web's fourth most dangerous word? Emo. *The Guardian* [Online]. Available at: http://www.guardian.co.uk/technology/blog/2008/aug/06/thewebsfourthmostdangerous [Date accessed: 25 February 2015].

The International Lesbian, Gay, Bisexual, Trans and Intersex Association [ILGA] (2014) *State-Sponsored Homophobia Report: A World Survey of Laws: Criminalisation, Protection and Recognition of Same-Sex Love*. [Online]. Available at: www.ilga.org [Date accessed: 17 January 2015].

The Times. Men in crisis. *The Times*, 27 November 2010.

Thorne, B. (1993) *Gender Play, Girls and Boys in School*. Buckingham: Open University Press.

Thurnell-Read, T. (2012) What happens on tour: The premarital stag tour, homosocial bonding and male friendship. *Men and Masculinities*. 15(3), pp. 249–270.

Tsitsos, W. (1999) Rules of rebellion: Slam dancing, Moshing and the American alternative scene. *Popular Music*. 18(3), pp. 397–414.

Tolson, A. (1977) *The Limits of Masculinity*. Indiana: Tavistock.

Town, S. (1978) *After the Mines: Changing Employment Opportunities in a South Wales Valley*. Cardiff: University of Wales Press.

University College Union [UCU]. (2009) 'LOCATION, LOCATION, LOCATION – The widening education gap in Britain and how where you live determines your chances' [Online] Available at: http://www.ucu.org.uk/media/pdf/k/k/ucu_locationreport_oct09.pdf [Date accessed: 26 March 2015].

Urry, J. (2000) *Sociology Beyond Societies*. London: Routledge.

Van Hoven, B. and Horschelmann, K. (2005) *Spaces of Masculinities*. London: Routledge.

Van Maanen, J. (1988) *Tales from the Field, on writing Ethnography*. Chicago: University of Chicago Press.

Valli, L. (1985) *Becoming Clerical Workers*. Boston: Routledge & Kegan Paul.

Weeks, J. (2007) *The World We Have Won: The Remaking of Intimate and Erotic Life*. London: Routledge.

Welsh Assembly Government [WAG]. (2001) *The Learning Country*. Cardiff: WAG.

Welsh Assembly Government [WAG]. (2002) *Learning Country; Learning Pathways 14–19, A Consultation Document*. Cardiff: WAG.

Welsh Assembly Government [WAG]. (2006a) *The Learning Country 2: Delivering the Promise*. Cardiff: WAG.

Welsh Assembly Government [WAG]. (2006b) *Turning Heads: A Strategy for the Heads of the Valleys 2020*. Cardiff: WAG.
Welsh Government. (2014) *Welsh Index of Multiple Deprivation 2014*. Cardiff: Statistical Publication Unit.
The Valleys Consortium. (2011) *The Valleys Guide 2011*. Pontypridd: Visit Wales Tourism.
Wakeling, P. (2010) Is there such a thing as a working class academic? in: Taylor, Y. ed. *Classed Intersections – Spaces, Selves, Knowledges*. Farnham: Ashgate, pp. 35–52.
Walker, J. (1988) *Louts and Legends*. Sydney: Allen and Unwin.
Walker, B. and Krushner, S. (1997) *'Understanding Boys' Sexual Health Education and Its Implications for Attitude Change*. ESRC: Centre for Applied Research in Education.
Walker, L. Butland, D. Connell, R. W. (2000) Boys on the road: Masculinities, car culture, and road safety education. *The Journal of Men's Studies*. 8(2), pp. 153–169.
Walkerdine, V. (2009) Steel, identity, community: Regenerating identities in a South Wales town in: Wetherell, M. ed. *Identities in the 21st Century*. Basingstoke: Palgrave Macmillan.
Walkerdine, V. (2010) Communal beingness and affect: An exploration of trauma in an ex-industrial community. *Body & Society*. 16(1), pp. 91–116.
Walkerdine, V. and Jimenez, L. (2012) *Gender, Work and Community after De-Industrialisation: A Psychosocial Approach to Affect*. Basingstoke: Palgrave Macmillan.
Walkerdine, V. Lucey, H. and Melody, J. (2001) *Growing Up Girl: Psychosocial Explorations of Gender and Class*. London: Palgrave.
Ward, M. R. M. (2014) 'You get a reputation if you're from the valleys': The stigmatization of place in young working-class men's lives in: Thurnell-Read, T. and Casey, M. eds. *Men, Masculinities, Travel and Tourism*. Basingstoke: Palgrave MacMillan, pp. 89–104.
Warren, C. and Hackney, J. (2000) *Gender Issues in Ethnography*. Thousand Oaks, CA: Sage.
Warren, S. (1997) Who do these boys think they are? An investigation into the construction of masculinities in a primary classroom. *International Journal of Inclusive Education*. 1(2), pp. 207–222.
Weaver-Hightower, M. B. (2008) *The Politics of Policy in Boys' Education: Getting Boys Right*. New York: Palgrave Macmillan.
Weil, K. (2006) Men and Horses, Circus studs, Sporting males and the performance of purity in fin-de-Siècle France. *French Cultural Studies*. 17(1), pp. 87–105.
Weiner, G. Arnot, M. David, M. (1997) Is the future female? Female success, Male disadvantage and changing patterns in education in: Halsey, A. H. Lauder, H. Brown, P. and Wells, A. S. eds. *Education, Culture, Economy, Society*. Oxford: Oxford University Press, pp. 620–630.
Weis, L. (1985) *Between Two Worlds: Black Students in an Urban Community College*. London: Routledge & Kegan.
Weis, L. (1990) *Working Class without Work: High School Students in a De-Industrializing Economy*. New York: Routledge.

Weis, L. (2004) Revisiting a 1980s 'Moment of critique' class, gender and the new economy in: Dolby, N. et al. eds. *Learning to Labor in New Times*. New York: RoutledgeFalmer, pp. 111–132.

Weis, L. (2006) Masculinity, whiteness and the new economy: An exploration of privilege and loss. *Men and Masculinities*. 8(3), pp. 262–272.

Weis, L. (2008) Toward a re-thinking of class as nested in race and gender: Tracking the white working class in the final quarter of the twentieth century in: Weis, L. ed. *The Way Class Works, Readings on School, Family and the Economy*. New York: Routledge, pp. 291–304.

Welsh European Funding Office Objective 1 [WEFO]. (2012) [Online] Available at: http://wefo.wales.gov.uk/programmes/20002006/objective1/?lang=en [Date accessed: 5 January 2015].

West, C. (1996) Goffman in feminist perspective. *Sociological Perspectives*. 39(3), pp. 353–369.

West, C. and Zimmerman, D. (1987) Doing gender. *Gender and Society*. 1(2), pp. 125–151.

Wetherell, M. and Edley, N. (1999) Negotiating hegemonic masculinity: Imaginary positions and psycho-discursive practices. *Feminism and Psychology*. 9(3), pp. 335–356.

Whitehead, S. and Barrett, F. eds. (2001) *The Masculinities Reader*. Cambridge: Polity Press.

Williams, C. Evans, N. and O'Leary, P. eds. (2003) *A Tolerant Nation? Exploring Ethnic Diversity in Wales*. Cardiff: University of Wales.

Williams, G. A. (1985) *When Was Wales?* Harmondsworth: Penguin.

Williams, R. (1960) *Border Country*. London: Chatto and Windus.

Williams, R. (2003) Wales and England in: Williams, D. ed. *Who Speaks for Wales? Nation, Culture, Identity. Raymond Williams*. Cardiff: University of Wales Press, pp. 16–26.

Willis, P. (1977) *Learning to Labour, How Working Class Kids Get Working Class Job*. Farnborough: Saxon House.

Willis, P. (1979) Masculinity and the wage form in: Clark, J. Critcher, C. and Johnson, R. eds. *Working Class Culture*. London: Hutchinson, pp. 185–201

Wilson, T. M. (2005) Drinking cultures: Sites and practices in the production and expression of identity in: Wilson, T. M. ed. *Drinking Cultures, Alcohol and Identity*. pp. 1–24.

Winlow, S. (2001) *Badfellas: Crime, Tradition and New Masculinities*. Oxford: Berg.

Wollstonecraft, M. (1989) *The Complete Works of Mary Wollstonecraft*. Todd, J. and Butler, M. ed. London: William Pickering.

Wood, J. (1984) Grouping towards sexism: Boys sex talk in: McRobbie, A. and Nava, M. eds. *Gender and Generation*. London: Macmillan, pp. 54–84.

Zekany, E. (2011) *The Gendered Geek: Performing Masculinities in Cyberspace*. Unpublished Masters Dissertation, Budapest, Central European University.

# Index

Note: Locators followed by 'n' refer to notes section.

Abbott, Diane, 5
Adamson, D., 22
Adkins, L., 30, 152
alienation, 97–101
'alternative scene' youth culture, 95, 96–7
analytic sets, 18
Anderson, B., 26
Anderson, Elijah, 5, 10–12, 18, 130–1
Anderson, Eric, 11, 35, 37
appearance, 14
Archer, L., 108
Arnot, M., 5, 31, 107
Arnot, R. P., 23, 27
Atherton, G., 27
Atkinson, P., 15, 107, 166, 169–70
autobiography of the question, 16–18

Baker, J., 107
Baldwin, B., 24–5
Ball, S., 18, 31, 35, 159
Barrett, F., 8
Bates, I., 4, 9, 107
Bauman, Z., 4
BBC, 24
Beck, U., 4, 30, 104
Beck-Gernsheim, E., 4
Bell, D., 33
Bengry-Howell, A., 123
Bennett, A., 181n1
Berg, L. D., 33, 36
Beynon, H., 83, 115
Beynon, J., 6, 10, 40, 178n3
Birke, L., 116, 122
Blackshaw, T., 53
boyishness, 87–9
Bradley, H., 4, 159
Brandt, K., 116
Brandth, B., 33
Breen, R., 31, 159
Brickell, C., 13, 109

British Coal, 178n4
British Racing School, 117, 180n6
Brittan, A., 8
Brown, P., 31, 74, 98
Brown, S., 107–8
Budd, J., 108
Bullivant, B. M., 35
bullying, 97–101
   minimizing, 99
   outside school, 99–100
Burrows, R., 80
Butland, D., 60
Butler, D., 116
Butler, J., 15, 109

Cahill, S., 166
Cameron, S., 24–5, 178n3
Canaan, J., 29
car culture, 60–1
   in Australia, 123
   'boy racer' subculture of, 122
   and continuation of front, 60–1
   Cwm Dyffryn's, 124–5
   performing masculinity through, 123–6
Carrabine, E., 123
Carrigan, T., 8–9
Cassidy, R., 116
chameleonisation of masculinity, 151–3
Charles, N., 116
Cherbonneau, M. G., 60
Childers, M., 18
Chodorow, N., 7
Clare, A., 5
class relations, 9
Clatterbaugh, K., 10
coal industry, 23
   employment levels in, 23
   shutting of collieries, 24
   strikes in, 23

200

Coal Miners Regulation Act, 28
Coal Mines Act, 28
The Coalmining Resource History
  Centre, 179n4
Cobb, J., 93
Cockburn, C., 83, 108, 115
Coffey, A., 16, 165
Cohen, M., 12
Cohen, S., 123
Collinson, D., 29
Collinson, D. L., 29
Comeau, C.D., 75
complicit masculinity, 10
Connell, R. W., 2, 6–10, 12, 31, 35–7,
  58, 60, 74–5, 79, 100, 107, 109,
  116, 131, 135, 141, 151, 178n6
Cornwall, A., 8, 22
Corrigan, P., 29, 74
crisis of the gender order, 6
crowd surfing, 96
Cuffley Industrial Heritage Society
  (CIHS), 23
cultural heritage, 24–6
  see also cultural
Cusick, P., 35, 165
Cwm Dyffryn, 17, 21
  drinking heritage, 52
  overview of, xii
  in the post-millennium era, 26–7
  unemployment in, 26
Cwm Dyffryn High School, 175–7
Cynon Valley History Society, 23–4, 28

Daily Mail, 98
Dalley-Trim, L., 31
David, M., 8, 179n2
Davies, B., 15
Davies, J., 25
Day, G., 22, 25, 29–30, 36
De Boise, S., 12
de-industrialization, 3–4
  and working-class men, 4
de-industrialized communities, 129,
  149
Delamont, S., 30, 72, 74, 107, 169
Delphy, C., 7
Demetriou, D., 10
Dempster, S., 179n10
Denzin, N., 16, 166, 170

Dews, C. L., 18
Dicks, B., 26, 36
Dimitriadis, G., 152
Dinnerstein, D., 7
Discovering Men (Morgan), 8
Ditton, J., 166
Dolby, N., 152
Donahue, Steve, 141
Donaldson, M., 10
Drakeford, M., 34
drinking heritage, 51–3
  see also heritage
drug taking, 58–60

economic restructuring, 95, 108
Edley, N., 10, 31, 49, 82, 136
education
  access to, 4–5
  in Cwm Dyffryn, 72
  provision for coal miners, 25
  in the South Wales Valleys, 72
  and Welsh society, 72
  see also school
educational institutions, 155–6
Educational Maintenance Allowance
  (EMA), 41
Effron, Zac, 132, 181n2
Egan, D., 23
Emerson, R. M., 166
The Emos, 19
  alienation, bullying and
    intimidation, 97–101
  'alternative scene' and being an
    'emo', 96–7
  hetero-normativity and
    homophobia, 103–4
  introduction, 95–6
  real 'alternative', 101–3
employment
  and industrial masculinity, 29
  opportunities, access to, 4–5
  status and forms of, 5
Epstein, D., 5, 16, 62, 74, 167
ethnicity, 107
  social construction of masculinities
    and, 35
  VET and, 107
ethnographic moment, 35

ethnography, 35–6
  criticisms of specific elements, 35
  longitudinal, 150
  and masculinity, 35
  multilayered dimensions of, 36
  reality and, 153
Everhart, R., 35, 165

Facebook, 3
feminism
  and sex roles, 7
  and sociology of masculinity, 8
Fevre, R., 25–6
Fields, Gracie, 24
Fisher, M. J., 37
Flood, M., 9
Foucault, M., 15
Frame Analysis (Goffman), 111
Francis, B., 5–6, 32, 74–5, 107, 151
Francis, H., 23, 25, 32
Frosh, S., 38, 133
Fuller, A., 107–8

Gagnon, J., 15
Gane, N., 80
Gard, M., 80
The Geeks, 19
  bullying, 78
  classroom practices, 80–7
  contradictions, 89–91
  educational achievement, 74–80
  escape practices, 92–4
  family biographies, 74–80
  introduction, 74–80
  mature heterosexuality, 87–9
  respect for teachers, 86–7
  social interaction, 80–7
  social pressures, 89–91
  subject-choice, 74–80
Geertz, C., 2
gender
  identities, 107, 112
  order, crisis of the, 6
  sex roles, 7
  and social interaction, 15
  see also women
General Certificate in Secondary Education (GCSE) exams, 44
Gibson, C., 116

Giddens, A., 4
Gillborn, D., 4–5
Goffman, E., 1, 7–8, 13–15, 32, 36–7, 47, 51, 61, 69, 75, 108, 111, 120, 130, 153, 169, 173
  on appearance, 14
  on front performance, 14
  on individuals' interaction situations, 13–15
  on manner, 14
Gorard, S., 27
Gorely, T., 46
Gospel, H., 108
Gramsci, A., 9
Granié, M.-A., 60
Grant, R., 22
Grazian, D., 13–14, 55
Green, A., 31
Griffin, C., 123
Guardian Online, The, 98
guitar-based bands, 96

Hackney, J., 169
Halberstam, J. M., 178n4
Hall, T., 36
Halsey, A. H., 18
Hammersley, M., 170
Handbook of Men and Masculinities, 8
Hargreaves, D. H., 35, 73–4
Harris, J., 39
Hartig, K., 96
Hartman, H., 7
Haywood, C., 35, 107, 115
Heads of the Valleys, 25
health care provision, for coal miners, 25
Hearn, J., 8, 29
hegemonic masculinity, 9–10, 131, 178n6
heritage
  cultural, 24–6
  drinking, 51–3
  industrial, 22–4, 40–4
hetero-normativity, 103–4
heteronormative self, 144
  see also self
heterosexual masculinity, 55–8
Heward, C., 49, 130
Hey, V., 18

Index 203

Hickey-Moody, A., 60, 107, 123
Hobbs, D., 17, 169
Hodkinson, H., 108
Hodkinson, P., 96
Hoff-Sommers, C., 5
Holland, S., 38–9
Hollingworth, S., 31
homophobia, 11, 103–4
Hopkins, P., 34
Horschelmann, K., 33
House of Emo, 33
Housley, W., 15
Howe, P. D., 39, 52, 55
Hughey, M., 14
Humphries, J., 28–9
Hurn, S., 116

Inception, 85
inclusive masculinities, 11, 130
industrial heritage
 South Wales Valleys, 22–4
 The Valley Boiz, 40–4
 see also heritage
industrialization, 155–6
industrial masculinities, 27–30
Ingram, N., 4–5, 31, 74, 159
interactionism, 15–16
International Lesbian, Gay, Bisexual, Trans and Intersex Association (ILGA), 12
interview-based studies, 153
intimidation, 97–101

Jackson, B., 31, 73
Jackson, C., 179n10
Jackson, P., 33
Jackson, S., 15–16, 37
Jagose, A., 15
Janssen, D., 9
JD Wetherspoon, 179n5
Jenkins, N., 25, 97, 100
Jephcote, M., 107, 116
Jimenez, L., 28, 30, 153
Jimmy the Chameleon
 academic achiever, 133–8
 athlete, 139–42

code-shifting and multiple performances of, 129–32
friendships and girlfriends, 142–7
introduction, 129
party boy, 138–9
John, A., 22
Johnson, R., 16
Jones, M. R., 22, 24
Jones, S., 22
Jonsson, J., 31, 159
Junker, B. H., 165

Kamoche, K., 49
Kehily, M.J., 49
Kelly, K., 123
Kemp, C., 75
Kendall, L., 75
Kenway, J., 4–5, 30–1, 33, 35, 60, 70, 74, 107, 123, 179n8
Kessler, S., 7, 31
Kimmel, M., 7–8, 12, 29, 80
knowledge economy, 4
Kraack, A., 30
Kruse, H., 96

Lacey, C., 35, 73
Larkin, R. W., 35
Larsen, E. A., 116
Latimer, J., 116, 122
Latour, B., 33
Law, C. L., 18
The Learning Country, 3
Learning Country, Learning Pathways 14-19, 3
The Learning Country 2: Delivering the Promise, 3–4
Le Berre, F., 132
Lee, J., 8–9
Lefebvre, H., 34
Lewis, D. G., 72
Lincoln, Y., 16, 159, 166, 170
Lindisfarne, N., 8
Lingard, B., 5
Longhurst, B., 123
Longhurst, R., 33, 36
longitudinal ethnography, 150
Lucey, H., 137, 152
Lumsden, K., 123
Lush, A. J., 29

Mac an Ghaill, M., 8, 31, 35, 40, 62, 74, 82, 107, 109, 115, 136
Macdonald, D., 107–8
MacInnes, J., 5, 36
Madden, A., 108
Maguire, K., 49
Maines, D., 15
male camaraderie, 39
male chauvinism, 115
Mannay, D., 34
manners, 14
marginalized masculinity, 10
Marsden, D., 31, 73
Martin, P., 10
Martino, W., 5, 31, 35, 74–5
Marusza, J., 115
Masculinities (Connell), 8
masculinity/ies
 academic and vocational 'frames', 154–5
 beyond educational institutions and legacy of industrialization, 155–6
 chameleonisation of, 151–3
 complicit, 10
 contemporary, 7
 crisis in, 5–6
 dominant or hegemonic form of, 142, 178n6
 and drinking, 55
 feminized form of, 119, 122
 final thoughts, 157–8
 hegemonic, 9–10
 heterosexual, 55–8
 implications for policy and practice, 156–7
 industrial, 27–30
 marginalized, 10
 negotiating, 169
 as network, 33–4
 performing through car culture, 123–6
 sociology of, 6–9
 softer, 11–13
 stoic forms of, 119
 studious, 73–4
 subordinated, 9
 theorization of, 9–11
 tortured, 116–22
 traditional, reaffirming in VET, 110–16
 working-class, 16, 34, 106–28
 see also specific masculinities
Massey, D., 30, 32–4
mature heterosexuality, 87–9
McCormack, M., 11–12, 49
McDowell, L., 3–5, 11, 29–30, 33, 74, 155
McKenna, W., 7
Mellstrom, U., 60
Melody, J., 137
Mendick, H., 75, 151
Messerschmidt, J. W., 10, 31, 131, 135, 151, 178n6
Messner, M., 8, 35, 46, 80
Meyenn, B., 5
Meyenn, R., 80
Miall, C., 15
Miller, J., 16
Miller, L., 108
Mills, C. W., 16
Mine Regulation Act, 27
Mirza, H., 4–5
Mizen, P. A. J., 180
Modern Apprenticeship programme, 108, 111
Moore, R., 96
Morgan, D., 6, 8, 169
Morgan, K. O., 23
Morris, E., 74, 132
moshing, 96
Mullins, C. W., 60
multiple performances of a masculine self
 being Jimmy, 132–47
 chameleonisation of masculinity, 131–2
 code-shifting and, 129–32
 introduction, 129
muscular intellectualness, 82, 136

Nayak, A., 2, 5, 35, 41, 46, 155
Nespor, J., 33
Noble, G., 34
Not in Employment, Education or Training (NEET), 26
NPower, 111

O'Connor, C., 123
Office for National Statistics (ONS), 26–7, 30, 178n5
O'Neill, R., 12
Organisation for Economic Co-Operation and Development (OECD) education system of countries under, 3
Ortiz, S., 169
Osgood, J., 108

Papafava, E., 60
Parker, A., 31, 108
Parsons, T., 7
Pascoe, C. J., 7, 31, 35, 75, 178n5
Pattman, R., 49
Pawluch, D., 15
Pearson, G., 165, 170
Penlington, N., 49
personal front, 47
Peters, B. M., 98
piss take, 83–4
'pits', 96
Platt, L., 31
Pleck, J., 7
Plummer, K., 15
power relations, 47–9
The Presentation of Self in Everyday Life (Goffman), 14

racist humour, 115
Reay, D., 4, 37, 74, 107–8, 131, 159
Redman, P., 62, 82, 136
Rees, G., 22–3, 72, 107
Renold, E., 35, 62, 74
Rhondda Cynon Taf (RCT), 26–7, 178n5
Rhondda Valley, 22, 26
Richardson, D., 155
Riches, G., 96
Riseborough, G., 107
risky behaviours, 51–61
Robards, B, 181n1
Roberts, K., 27
Roberts, S., 5–6, 9, 12, 98, 130, 178n3
Robeson, Paul, 24
Rogers, H., 24–5
Rugby Union, 39

Rutherford, J., 29
Ryan, P., 108

Sabo, D., 8, 46
Salisbury, J., 107, 116
school
 male subcultural identity and ethnography, 35
 transition to work, 3–5
 see also education
Schrock, D., 1, 13, 15, 34, 152
Schwalbe, M., 1, 13, 15, 34, 152
Scott, S., 15–16, 37, 74, 80, 84, 89–90, 94, 110, 159, 165, 169
Scourfield, J., 34, 38–9
Segal, L., 5, 12
self
 code-shifting and multiple performances of a masculine, 129–32
 front presentation of, 152
 heteronornative, 144
 multiple performances of, 129–48
Sennett, R., 93
service sector, 4
Sewell, J., 30
Sewell, T., 31
sexist humour, 115
sex roles, 7
sexuality, 103, 115
Shaffir, W., 15
Simon, W., 15, 160
Simpson, P., 12, 161, 165
The Simpsons, 86
Skeggs, B., 5, 31, 74, 107
Skelton, C., 6, 107
Skelton, T., 178n3
slam dancing, 96
Smith, D., 22–5, 27, 36
social class, 107
 inequality, 6
social interaction, 15, 33, 61, 154
 classroom practices and, 80–9
 The Geeks, 80–7
 and gender, 15
social networking sites, 3
social pressures, 89–91
sociology, 33
softer masculinity, 11–13

Sonisphere, 181n3
SouthWales Miners Federation, 23
South Wales Valleys, 1
  brief history of the, 22–6
  cultural heritage, 24–6
  drinking heritage, 51–3
  industrial heritage, 22–4
  industrial masculinities in the, 27–30
  young masculinities 'at risk' in, 30–5
Spaces of Masculinity, 33
Stahl, G., 62
Stonewall, 12
Stroud, D., 22–3
studious masculinities, 73–4
subordinated masculinity, 9
Swain, J., 32, 35, 151, 178n5
Syal, R., 5

Tarrant, A., 5
teachers
  language used by, 154–5
  respect for, and The Geeks, 86–7
Teaching and Learning Research Programme (TLRP), 107
theoretical amnesia, 15
Thompson, A., 25
Thorne, B., 15
Thurnell-Read, T., 90
The Times, 5
Tolson, A., 8, 83
topologies of masculinity, 33
tortured masculinity, 116–22
  into the arena, 118–20
  stables, 120–2
Tower Colliery, 178n4
Town, S., 30
traditional masculinities, reaffirming in VET, 110–16
Tsitsos, W., 96, 102

United Kingdom
  crisis of masculinity, 5–6
  formal qualifications in, 3
University College Union (UCU), 25, 27
Unwin, L., 108
Urry, 33

The Valley Boiz, 18–19
  archetypal masculinity, 40
  car culture, 60–1
  casual behaviour, 49–51
  continuation of education, 45–6
  drinking habit, 52–5
  drug taking, 58–60
  family biographies, 40–4
  heterosexual masculinity, 55–8
  industrial heritage, 40–4
  power relations, 47–9
  risky behaviours, 51–61
  sexual storytelling, 49–51
  studying English literature, 62–6
  uniform, 46–7
Valli, L., 107
Van Hoven, B., 33
Van Maanen, J., 16
violent inner-city neighbourhoods, 131
vocational education and training (VET)
  gendered and classed nature of, 107–9
  reaffirming traditional masculinities in, 110–16
  working-class masculinities in, 106–28

Wakeling, P., 17–18, 74
Walker, B., 145
Walker, J., 31
Walker, L., 60, 123
Walkerdine, V., 4, 28, 30, 39, 74, 137, 152–3
Ward, M.R.M., 5, 11
Warren, C., 169
Warren, S., 31
Weaver-Hightower, M. B., 5
Weeks, J., 30, 72
Weil, K., 116
Weiner, G., 5
Weis, L., 5, 30, 74, 80, 107–8, 115
Welsh Assembly Government (WAG), 3–4, 25
Welsh European Funding Office Objective 1 (WEFO), 25
Welsh Government, 3–4, 26
  and education system, 3–4

West, C., 1, 13, 15, 34, 154, 169
Wetherell, M., 10, 31, 49, 82, 136
White, R., 31
Whitehead, S., 8
Williams, C., 22
Williams, G. A., 22–3
Williams, K., 31
Williams, R., 72
Willis, P., 3–4, 28–9, 31, 35, 40, 53, 74, 83, 113, 115, 142, 152, 165
Wilson, T. M., 52
Winlow, S., 18, 28, 35
Wollstonecraft, M., 7
women
  as labour force, 30
  Mine Regulation Act and, 27
  objectification of, 87, 91, 152
  patriarchal oppression of, 8
  voting rights in UK for, 7
  see also gender
Wood, J., 145
work
  industrial, 51–3
  interaction at, 29
  physical, 28
  transition from school to, 3–5
working-class masculinities, 16, 34, 106–28, 161–74
  Bakers, Ian and Frankie, 109–10
  balancing act, 169–72
  data analysis, 172–3
  ethical considerations, 173–4
  gendered and classed nature of vocational education and training, 107–9
  individual interviews, 165–6
  interpretation, 172–4
  introduction, 106–7
  managing field relationships, 166–8
  negotiating masculinity, 169
  outside college, performing masculinity through car culture, 123–6
  practical performances, 112–14
  reaffirming traditional masculinities in VET, 110–16
  setting and participants, 161–5
  subject frames, 108–9
  theoretical (re)production, 114–6
  tortured masculinity, 116–22
  understanding, researching and representing, 161–74
  in vocational education and training courses, 106–28
working-class men
  defined, 80
  and de-industrialization, 4
  educational achievement, 73–4
  exhibition of forms of power, 29
  school leaving age in 1970s, 3

Youth Training Schemes, 108

Zekany, E., 75
Zimmerman, D., 1, 13, 15, 34, 154, 169

Printed and bound by CPI Group (UK) Ltd, Croydon, CR0 4YY